CAT TAILS

Traditional tales, fables and sagas that feature our feline friends

Compiled, Adapted & Edited by Clive Gilson

Tales from the World's Firesides

Cat Tails, edited by Clive Gilson, Solitude, Bath, UK

www.clivegilson.com

First print edition © 2024, Clive Gilson

All rights reserved. No portion of this book may be reproduced in any form without permission from the publisher, except as permitted by United Kingdom copyright law.

This is a work of fiction. Names, characters, places, and incidents either are the products of the author's imagination or are used fictitiously. Any resemblance to actual persons, living or dead, businesses, companies, events, or locales is entirely coincidental.

Printed by IngramSpark

ISBN: 978-1-915081-31-5

I have edited Clive Gilson's books for over a decade now – he's prolific and can turn his hand to many genres. poetry, short fiction, contemporary novels, folklore, and science fiction – and the common theme is that none of them ever fails to take my breath away. There's something in each story that is either memorably poignant, hauntingly unnerving, or sidesplittingly funny.

Lorna Howarth, *The Write Factor*

Tales From The World's Firesides is a grand project. I've collected '000's of traditional texts as part of other projects, and while many of the original texts are available through channels like Project Gutenberg, some of the narratives can be hard to read by modern readers, and so the Fireside project was born. Put simply, I collect, collate and adapt traditional tales from around the world and publish them as a modern archive. I'm not laying any claim to insight or specialist knowledge, but these collections are born out of my love of storytelling and I hope that you'll share my affection for traditional tales, myths & legends.

Chapter image by Gordon Johnson from Pixabay
Cover image by Clive Gilson

CONTENTS

Preface
How The First Cat Was Created
The Fox And The Cat
The Cat And The Cradle
The Cat In The Bag
The Cat And The Mouse
Why The Cat Kills Rats
Kisa The Cat
Johnny Reed's Cat
The Vampire Cat Of Nabéshima
The Spectral Cat
A Cat, A Mouse, A Lizard And An Owl
The Grave Prince And The Beneficent Cat
How The Manx Cat Lost Her Tail
The Colony Of Cats
Mikko The Fox And Mirri The Cat
The Crow And Cat Of Hopkins Hill
The Lion And The Cat
Dinah Cat And The Witch
The Cat On The Dovrefell
Why Do Cats And Dogs Fight? #1
Why Do Cats And Dogs Fight? #2
The Bear, The Dog, And The Cat
The Tigers And The Cat
The Greedy Cat

Story Of The Foolish Teacher, The Foolish Pupils, And The Cat

The White Cat Of Ecija

Domingo's Cat

The Cats Who Made Their Master Rich

The Master Cat; Or, Puss In Boots

The Cat Of Norrhult

Why The Cat Always Falls Upon Her Feet

The Pike and the Cat

The White Cat

The Cat's Elopement

The Greedy Palm-Cat

The Cat and the Mouse

The Cottager And His Cat

The Lazy Cat

Pussy Willow

The Troll Turned Cat

The Hypocritical Cat

Belling The Cat

Brother Rabbit and Mr. Wildcat

The Clever Cat

The Heron, The Cat & The Bramble

The Hen And The Cat

The Cat And The Sparrows

The Contessa's Cat

The Cat Who Guarded The Precepts

The King Of The Cats

The Demon Cat

The Cat Who Became Head-Forester

Seanchan The Bard And The King Of The Cats

Why Do Cats Eat Mice?

King Arthur And The Cat

Whittington And His Cat

Why Does A Cat Sit On The Doorstep In The Sun?

The Cat, The Cock, And The Fox

A 'Rastle With A Wildcat

Bobcat And Birch Tree

Cat And Dog

Cat And Mouse In Partnership

Cat-Skin

The Old Woman's Cat

About The Editor

Preface

I've been collecting and telling stories for a couple of decades now, having had several of my own works published in recent years. My particular focus is on short story writing in the realms of magical realities and science fiction fantasies.

I've always drawn heavily on traditional folk and fairy tales, and in so doing have amassed a collection of many thousands of these tales from around the world. It has been one of my long-standing ambitions to gather these stories together and to create a library of tales that tell the stories of places and peoples from the four corners of our world.

One of the main motivations for me in undertaking the project is to collect and tell stories that otherwise might be lost or, at best forgotten. Given that a lot of my sources are from early collectors, particularly covering works produced in the late eighteenth century, throughout the nineteenth century, and in the early years of the twentieth century, I do make every effort to adapt stories for a modern reader. Early collectors had a different world view to many of us today, and often expressed views about race and gender, for example, that we find difficult to reconcile in the early years of the twenty-first century. I try, although with varying degrees of success, to update these stories with sensitivity while trying to stay as true to the original spirit of each story as I can.

I also want to assure readers that I try hard not to comment on or appropriate originating cultures. It is almost certainly true that the early collectors of these tales, with their then prevalent world views, have made assumptions about the originating cultures that have given us these tales. I hope that you'll accept my mission to preserve these tales, however and wherever I find them, as just that. I have, therefore, made sure that every story has a full attribution, covering both the original collector / writer and the collection title that this version has been adapted from, as well as having notes about publishers and other relevant and, I hope, interesting source data. Wherever possible I have added a cultural or indigenous attribution as well, although for some of the tiles, the country-based theme is obvious.

This volume, *Cat Tails*, collects a host of stories from around the world that feature our feline friends. It seems to me that cats hold a special place in folk tales, fairy tales, myths, and legends across various cultures.

Cats are, for example, often depicted as mysterious creatures, with their nocturnal habits and solitary nature adding an air of intrigue. This mystery makes them captivating figures in storytelling.

In many cultures, cats are associated with knowledge, secrets, and the supernatural. They are sometimes depicted as guardians of hidden realms or keepers of ancient wisdom.

Cats are also known for their independence and self-reliance, which can symbolize traits such as cunning, resourcefulness, and freedom. This makes them popular characters in stories where independence and cleverness are valued.

One of the more obvious cat themes is their long association with magic and witchcraft due to their enigmatic behaviour and their historical role in hunting pests like mice and rats, which were seen as carriers of disease and associated with the occult. In many tales, they are depicted as companions to witches or possessing supernatural abilities themselves. In European folklore in particular, cats are often portrayed as familiars, magical animals that assist witches or sorcerers in their spells and rituals. This further strengthens their association with the mystical and the otherworldly.

Cats' ability to adapt to various environments and their prowess as hunters contribute to their symbolic significance in stories as symbols of survival and resilience.

And let's not forget that cats have been revered and even worshipped in certain cultures throughout history, such as ancient Egypt, where they were associated with the goddess Bastet. This cultural significance has definitely contributed to their prominence in mythology and folklore.

Overall, the multifaceted nature of cats, from their mysterious behaviours to their historical roles, makes them rich and versatile characters in folk tales, fairy tales, myths, and legends around the world.

As for the Fireside Tales project, these titles will grow over coming years to tell lost and forgotten tales from every continent, and even then, I'll just be scratching the surface of the world's lore and love. That's the great gift in storytelling. Since the first of our ancestors sat around in a cave, contemplating an ape's place in the world, we have, as a species, told each other stories of magic and cunning and caution and love. When I began to read through tales from the Celts, tales from Indonesia, tales from Africa and the Far East, tales from everywhere, one of the things that struck me clearly was just how similar are our roots. We share characters and characteristics. The nature of these tales is so similar underneath the local camouflage. Human beings clearly share a storytelling heritage so much deeper than the world that we see superficially as always having been just as it is now.

These tales were originally told by firelight as a way of preserving histories and educating both adult and child. These tales form part of our shared heritage, witches, warts, fantastic beasts, and all. They can be dark and violent. They can be sweet and loving. They are we and we are they in so many ways. I've loved reading and re-reading these stories. I hope you do too.

Clive

Bath 2024

Cat Tails – Feline Fairy Tales, Myths And Legends

How The First Cat Was Created

This is an Irish tale

This tale has been adapted from Legends Of Saints And Sinners by Douglas Hyde. The book was published in 1914 by The Gresham Publishing Company Ltd, London, Dublin and Belfast. The legends in the collection cover a wide range of themes, including miracles, martyrdom, penance, temptation, and redemption. They explore the virtues and vices of humanity, as well as the intercession of saints and divine intervention in the lives of ordinary people.

One day, the Virgin Mary and her Son were traveling along the road. They passed a house where a woman was winnowing wheat. The Blessed Virgin went inside and asked for a handful of wheat, but the woman refused.

"Go back to her," said her Son, "and ask in the name of God."

Mary went back, but the woman refused again.

"Go back once more," He said, "and ask if you may put your hand in a pail of water, then into the heap of wheat, and take whatever sticks to your hand."

Mary did as He asked, and the woman allowed her to do so. When she came back out, Jesus said, "Don't lose a single grain of that wheat, for it is very valuable."

As they continued on their way, they looked back and saw a flock of demons heading towards the house. Mary was worried they might harm the woman.

"Don't worry," said Jesus, "because she gave you alms, they cannot harm her."

They travelled until they reached a mill owned by a man named Martin. Jesus said to His mother, "Since the mill is working, go ask if they will grind this little bit of wheat for you."

Mary went inside and asked the boy working there to grind the wheat. "It's not worth my time to grind such a small amount," he said.

Martin overheard and told the boy, "Do it for her; she might need it badly."

The boy ground the wheat and gave Mary all the flour from it. As they continued on their way, the mill suddenly filled with flour as white as snow. Martin realized this was a miracle and understood that it was the Son of God and His Mother who had visited.

He ran after them, crossing fields in such haste that he injured his chest on a hawthorn spike. Despite the pain, he continued until he caught up with them. When Jesus saw Martin's wound, He healed it immediately. He told Martin that he was a worthy man in God's eyes and instructed him to place a fistful of the flour under a dish until morning.

Martin did as he was told, placing the dish upside down over the flour. His servant girl, seeing this, decided to do the same with her own dish.

The next morning, Martin lifted his dish and out came a fine sow with a large litter of piglets. The girl lifted her dish, and out came a big mouse with a bunch of baby mice. Martin, realizing they were bad, threw his mitten at them, and it turned into a cat that began to kill the mice. This, according to the story, was the beginning of cats.

From that day on, Martin was known as a saint, but which Saint Martin he became is not specified.

Cat Tails – Feline Fairy Tales, Myths And Legends

The Fox And The Cat

This is a Russian tale

This tale has been adapted from Cossack Fairy Tales and Folk Tales by R. Nisbet Bain. The book was published in 1916 by George G. Harrap & Company, London. The Cossacks are a group of predominantly East Slavic-speaking people who historically inhabited the Pontic-Caspian steppe, known for their distinctive culture, traditions, and folklore. The book contains a selection of traditional tales and legends passed down orally among the Cossack communities. These stories offer insights into the worldview, values, and cultural practices of the Cossack people, reflecting their historical experiences, beliefs, and imagination.

In a certain forest there once lived a fox, and near to the fox lived a man who had a cat that had been a good mouser in its youth, but was now old and half blind. The man didn't want puss any longer, but not liking to kill it, took it out into the forest and lost it there.

Then the fox came up and said, "Why, Mr Shaggy Matthew! How do you do! What brings you here?"

"Alas!" said Pussy, "my master loved me as long as I could bite, but now that I can bite no longer and have left off catching mice - and I used to catch them finely once - he doesn't want to kill me, but he has left me in the wood where I must perish miserably."

"No, dear Pussy!" said the fox. "You leave it to me, and I'll help you to get your daily bread."

"You are very good, dear little sister foxy!" said the cat, and the fox built him a little shed with a garden round it to walk about in.

Now one day the hare came to steal the man's cabbage. "Kreem-kreem-kreem!" he squeaked. But the cat popped his head out of the window, and when he saw the hare, he put up his back and stuck up his tail and said, "Ft-t-t-t-t-Frrrrrrr!" The hare was frightened and ran away and told the bear, the wolf, and the wild boar all about it.

"Never mind," said the bear, "I tell you what, we'll all four give a banquet, and invite the fox and the cat, and do for the pair of them. Now, look here! I'll steal the man's mead, and you, Mr Wolf, steal his fat-pot, and you, Mr Wildboar, root up his fruit-trees, and you, Mr Bunny, go and invite the fox and the cat to dinner."

So they made everything ready as the bear had said, and the hare ran off to invite the guests. He came beneath the window and said, "We invite your little ladyship Foxey-Woxey, together with Mr Shaggy Matthew, to dinner" Then he ran back again.

"But you should have told them to bring their spoons with them," said the bear.

"Oh, what a head I've got! If I didn't quite forget!" cried the hare, and back he went again, ran beneath the window and cried, "Mind you bring your spoons!"

"Very well," said the fox.

So the cat and the fox went to the banquet, and when the cat saw the bacon, he put up his back and stuck out his tail, and cried, "Mee-oo, mee-oo!" with all his might.

But they thought he said, "Ma-lo, ma-lo!" (which means: 'What a little!)

"What!" said the bear, who was hiding behind the beeches with the other beasts. "We four have been getting together all that we could, and this pig-faced cat calls it too little! What a monstrous cat he must be to have such an appetite!"

They were all very frightened. The bear ran up a tree, and the others hid where they could. When the cat saw the boar's bristles sticking out behind the bushes he thought it was a mouse, and put up his back and cried, "Ft! ft! ft! Frrrrrrr!"

Then they were more frightened than ever. And the boar went into a bush still farther off, and the wolf went behind an oak, and the bear got down from the tree, and climbed up into a bigger one, and the hare ran right away.

But the cat stayed where he was and ate the bacon, and the little fox gobbled up the honey, and they ate and ate till they couldn't eat any more, and then they both went home licking their paws.

The Cat And The Cradle

This is a Dutch tale

This tale has been adapted from Dutch Fairy Tales for Young Folks by William Elliot Griffis. The book was published in 1918 by Thomas Y. Crowell & Co., New York. The book features a selection of fairy tales and folk stories from Dutch culture, including both well-known tales and lesser-known gems. These stories often incorporate elements of magic, adventure, morality, and humour, offering readers a glimpse into the imaginative world of Dutch folklore.

In the early ages, when our far-off ancestors lived in the woods, ate acorns, slept in caves, and dressed in the skins of wild animals, they had no horses, cows or cats. Their only pets and helpers were dogs. The men and the dogs were more like each other than they are now.

However, they knew about bees. So the women gathered honey and from it they made mead. Not having any sugar, the children enjoyed tasting honey more than anything else, and it was the only sweet thing they had.

By and by, cows were brought into the country and the Dutch soil being good for grass, the cows had plenty to eat. When these animals multiplied, the people drank milk and learned to make cheese and butter. So the Dutch boys and girls grew fat and healthy.

The oxen were so strong that they could pull logs of wood or draw a plough. So, little by little, the forests were cut down and grassy meadows, full of bright coloured flowers, took their place. Houses were built and the people were rich and happy.

Yet there were still many cruel men and bad people in the land. Sometimes, too, floods came and drowned the cattle and covered the fields with sand, or salt water. In such times, food was very scarce. Thus it happened that not all the babies born could live, or every little child be fed. The baby girls especially were often left to die, because war was common and only boys, that grew into strong warriors, were wanted.

It grew to be a custom that families would hold a council and decide whether the baby should be raised or not. But if anyone should give the infant even a tiny drop of milk, or food of any kind, it was allowed to live and grow up. If no one gave it milk or honey, it died. No matter how much a mother might love her baby, she was not allowed to put milk to its lips, if the grandmother or elders forbade it. The young bride, coming into her husband's home, always had to obey his mother, for she was now as a daughter and one of the family. All lived together in one house, and the grandmother ruled all the women and girls that were under one roof.

This was the way of the world, when our ancestors were pagans, and not always as kind to little babies as our own mothers and fathers are now. Many times was the old grandmother angry, when her son had taken a wife and a girl was born. If the old woman expected a grandson, who should grow up and be a fighter, with sword and spear, and it turned out to be a girl, she was mad as fire. Often the pretty bride, brought into the house, had a hard time of it, with her husband's mother, if she did not in time have a baby boy. In those days a "Herman," a "War Man" and "German" were one and the same word.

Now when the good missionaries came into Friesland, one of the first of the families to receive the gospel was one named Altfrid. With his bride, who also became a Christian, Altfrid helped the missionary to build a church. By and by, a sweet little baby was born in the family and the parents were very happy. They loved the little thing sent from God, as fathers and mothers love their children now.

But when someone went and told the pagan grandmother that the new baby was a girl instead of a boy, the old woman flew into a rage and would have gone at once to get hold of the baby and put it to death. Her lameness, however, made her move slowly, and she could not find her crutch, for the midwife, who knew the bad temper of the grandmother, had purposely hid it. The old woman was angry, because she did not want any more females in the big house, where she thought there were already too many mouths to fill. Food was hard to get, and there were not enough war men to defend the tribe. She meant to get the new baby and throw it to the wolves. The old grandmother was a pagan and still worshipped the cruel gods that loved fighting. She hated the new religion, because it taught gentleness and peace.

But the midwife, who was a neighbour, feared that the old woman was malicious and she had hidden her crutch. This she did, so that if the baby was a girl, she could save its life. The midwife was a good woman, who had been taught that the Great Creator loves little girls as well as boys.

So when the midwife heard the grandmother storm and rave, while hunting for her crutch, she ran first to the honey jar, dipped her forefinger in it and put some drops of honey on the baby's tongue. Then she passed it out the window to some women friends, who were waiting outside. She knew the law, that if a child tasted food, it must be allowed to live.

The kind women took the baby to their home and fed it carefully. A hole was drilled in the small end of a cow's horn and the warm milk, fresh from the cow, was allowed to fall, drop by drop, into the baby's mouth. In a few days the little one was able to suck its breakfast slowly out of the horn, while one of the girls held it. So the baby grew bigger every day. All the time it was carefully hidden.

The foolish old grandmother was foiled, for she could never find out where the baby girl was, which all the time was growing strong and plump. Her father secretly made her a cradle and he and the babe's mother came often to see their child. Everyone called her Honig-je', or Little Honey.

Now about this time, cats were brought into the country and the children made such pets of them that some of the cows seemed to be jealous of the attentions paid to Pussy and the kittens. These were the days when cows and people all lived under one long roof. The children learned to tell the time of day, whether it was morning, noon or night by looking into the cats' eyes. These seemed to open and shut, very much as if they had doors.

The fat pussy, which was brought into the house where Honig-je' was, seemed to be very fond of the little girl, and the two, the cat and the child, played much together. It was often said that the cat loved the baby even more than her own kittens. Everyone called the affectionate animal by the nickname of Dub-belt-je', which means Little Double; because this puss was twice as loving as most cat mothers are. When her own furry little babies were very young, she carried them from one place to another in her mouth. But this way, of holding kittens, she never tried on the baby. She seemed to know better. Indeed, Dub-belt-je' often wondered why human babies were born so naked and helpless, for at an age when her kittens could feed themselves and run about and play with their tails and with each other, Honig-je' was not yet able to crawl.

But other dangers were in store for the little girl. One day, when the men were out hunting, and the women went to the woods to gather nuts and acorns, a great flood came. The waters washed away the houses, so that everything floated into the great river, and then down towards the sea.

What had, what would, become of our baby? So thought the parents of Honig-je', when they came back to find the houses swept away and no sign of their little daughter. Dub-belt-je' and her kittens, and all the cows, were gone too.

Now it had happened that when the flood came and the house crashed down, baby was sound asleep. The cat, leaving its kittens, that were now pretty well grown up, leaped up and on to the top of the cradle and the two floated off together. Pretty soon they found themselves left alone, with nothing in sight that was familiar, except one funny thing. That was a wooden shoe, in which was a fuzzy little yellow chicken hardly four days old. It had been playing in the shoe, when the floods came and swept it off from under the very beak of the old hen, that, with all her other chicks, was speedily drowned.

On and on, the raging flood bore baby and puss, until dark night came down. For hours more they drifted until, happily, the cradle was swept into an eddy in front of a village. There it spun round and round, and might soon have been borne into the greater flood, which seemed to roar louder as the waters rose.

Now a cat can see sometimes in the night, better even than in the day, for the darker it becomes, the wider open the eyes of puss. In bright sunshine, at noon, the inside doors of the cat's eyes close to a narrow slit, while at night these doors open wide. That is the reason why, in the days before clocks and watches were made, the children could tell the time of day by looking at the cat's eyes. Sometimes they named their pussy Klok'-oog, which means Clock Eye, or Bell Eye, for bell clocks are older than clocks with a dial, and because in Holland the bells ring out the hours and quarter hours.

Puss looked up and saw the church tower looming up in the dark. At once she began to meow and caterwaul with all her might. She hoped that someone in one of the houses near the riverbank might catch the sound. But none seemed to hear or heed. At last, when Puss was nearly dead with howling, a light appeared at one of the windows. This showed that someone was up and moving. It was a boy, who was named Dirck, after the saint Theodoric, who had first, long ago, built a church in the village. Then Puss opened her mouth and lungs again and set up a regular cat-scream. This wakened all her other relatives in the village and every Tom and Kitty made answer, until there was a cat concert of meows and caterwauls.

The boy heard, rushed down-stairs, and, opening the door, listened. The wind blew out his candle, but the brave lad was guided by the sound which Pussy made. Reaching the bank, he threw off his wooden klomps, plunged into the boiling waters, and, seizing the cradle, towed it ashore. Then he woke up his mother and showed her his prize. The way that baby laughed and crowed, and patted the horn of milk, and kicked up its toes in delight over the warm milk, which was brought, was a joy to see. Near the hearth, in the middle of the floor, Dub-belt-je', the puss, was given some straw for a bed and, after purring joyfully, was soon, like the baby, sound asleep.

Thus the cat warned the boy, and the boy saved the baby, that was very welcome in a family where there were no girls, but only a boy. When Honig-je' grew up to be a young woman, she looked as lovely as a princess and in the church was married to Dirck! It was the month of April and all the world was waking to flowers, when the wedding procession came out of the church and the air was sweet with the opening of the buds.

Before the next New Year's day arrived, there lay in the same cradle, and put to sleep over the same rockers, a baby boy.

Cat Tails – Feline Fairy Tales, Myths And Legends

When they brought him to the font, the good grandmother named him Luid-i-ger. He grew up to be the great missionary, whose name in Friesland is, even today, after a thousand years, a household word. He it was who drove out bad fairies, vile enchanters, wicked spirits and terrible diseases. Best of all, he banished "eye-bite," which was the name the people gave to witchcraft. Luid-i-ger, also, made it hard for the naughty elves and sprites that delude men.

After this, it was easy for all the good spirits, that live in kind hearts and noble lives, to multiply and prosper. The wolves were driven away or killed off and became very few, while the cattle and sheep multiplied, until everybody could have a woollen coat, and there was a cow to every person in the land.

But the people still suffered from the floods, that from time to time drowned the cattle and human beings, and the ebb tides, that carried everything out to sea. Then the good missionary taught the men how to build dykes, that kept out the ocean and made the water of the rivers stay between the banks. The floods became fewer and fewer and at last rarely happened. Then Santa Klaus arrived, to keep alive in the hearts of the people the spirit of love and kindness and good cheer forever.

At last, when nearly a hundred years had passed away, Honig-je', once the girl baby, and then the dear old lady, who was kind to everybody and prepared the way for Santa Klaus, died. Then, also, Dub-belt-je' the cat, that had nine lives in one, died with her. They buried the old lady under the church floor and stuffed the pussy that everybody, kittens, boys, girls and people loved. By and by, when the cat's tail and fur fell to pieces, and ears tumbled off, and its glass eyes dropped out, a skilful artist chiselled a statue of Dub-belt-je', which still stands over the tomb in the church. Every year, on Santa Klaus day, December sixth, the children put a new collar around its neck and talk about the cat that saved a baby's life.

The Cat In The Bag

This is an Irish tale

This tale has been adapted from Ancient Legends, Mystic Charms and Superstitions of Ireland by Jane Francesca Wilde. The book was published in 1919 by Chatto and Windus, London. This tale appears, unnamed, in her introduction to work featuring cats. The book delves into various aspects of Irish folklore, including myths, legends, folk tales, superstitions, and beliefs surrounding magic and the supernatural. It covers a wide range of topics, from ancient gods and heroes to fairies, witches, and ghostly apparitions.

A farmer's daughter, a pretty coquette, attracted the attention of the young squire of the place. But though he was willing to carry on a flirtation, the young gentleman had no idea of debasing his proud lineage by an alliance. Yet a marriage was exactly what the girl desired, and which she was determined to accomplish. So she and a friend, an accomplice, searched the village till they found a black cat, black as night, with only three white hairs on the breast. Him they seized, and having tied up the animal in a bag, they proceeded to throw him from one to the other over a low wall, till the poor beast was quite dead. Then at midnight they began their unholy work. The liver and heart were extracted in the name of the Evil One, and then boiled down until they became so dry that they could easily be reduced to a powder, which was kept for use when opportunity offered.

This soon came; the young squire arrived one evening as usual, to pay a visit to the pretty Nora, and began to make love to the girl with the ordinary amount of audacity and hypocrisy. But Nora had other views, so she made the tea by her little fire in a black teapot, for this was indispensable, and induced her lover to stay and partake of it with her, along with a fresh griddle cake. Then cunningly she infused the powder into his cup and watched him as he drank the tea with feverish anxiety.

The result was even beyond her hopes. A violent and ardent passion seemed suddenly to have seized the young man, and he not only made earnest love to the pretty Nora, but offered her his hand in marriage, vowing that he would kill himself if she refused to become his lawful bride. To avoid such a catastrophe, Nora gently yielded to his request, and from that evening they were engaged. Daily visits followed from the young squire, and each time that he came Nora took care to repeat the charm of the love powder, so that the love was kept at fever heat, and finally the wedding day was fixed.

The family of the young squire were, however, not quite contented, especially as rumours of witchcraft and devil's dealings were bruited about the neighbourhood. And on the very eve of the marriage, just as the young man was pouring forth his vows of eternal love to the bride expectant, the door was burst open, and a body of men entered, headed by the nearest relations of the squire, who proceeded at once to belabour the young bridegroom with hazel sticks in the most vigorous manner. In vain the bride tried to interpose. She only drew the blows on herself, and finally the young man was carried away half stunned, lifted into the carriage and driven straight home, where he was locked up in his own room, and not allowed to hold any communication with the bride elect.

The daily doses of the powder having thus ceased, he began to recover from the love madness, and finally the fever passed away. And he looked back with wonder and horror on the fatal step he had so nearly taken. Now he saw there was really witchcraft in it, which the power of the hazel twigs had completely broken. And the accomplice having confessed the sorcery practised on him by Nora and herself, he hated the girl henceforth as much as he had once loved her.

And after a little he went away on foreign travel, and remained abroad for three years. When he returned, he found that Nora had degenerated into a withered little witch-faced creature, who was shunned by everyone, and jeered at for the failure of her wicked spells, which had all come to nothing, though she had the Evil One himself to aid her, for such is the fate of all who deal in sorcery and devil's magic, especially with the help of Satan's chief instrument of witchcraft—the black cat.

The Cat And The Mouse

This is an English tale

This tale has been adapted from English Fairy Tales by Joseph Jacobs. The book was published in 1890 by David Nutt, London. The book contains a diverse selection of fairy tales and folk stories that originate from various regions of England. Jacobs gathered these tales from oral tradition, folklore sources, and literary sources, aiming to preserve and showcase the rich heritage of English storytelling.

The cat and the mouse
Play'd in the malt-house:

The cat bit the mouse's tail off.

"Pray, puss, give me my tail."

"No," says the cat, "I'll not give you your tail, till you go to the cow, and fetch me some milk."

First she leapt and then she ran,
Till she came to the cow, and thus began:

"Pray, Cow, give me milk, that I may give cat milk, that cat may give me my own tail again."

"No," said the cow, "I will give you no milk, till you go to the farmer, and get me some hay."

First she leapt, and then she ran,
Till she came to the farmer and thus began:

"Pray, Farmer, give me hay, that I may give cow hay, that cow may give me milk, that I may give cat milk, that cat may give me my own tail again."

"No," says the farmer, "I'll give you no hay, till you go to the butcher and fetch me some meat."

First she leapt, and then she ran,
Till she came to the butcher, and thus began:

"Pray, Butcher, give me meat, that I may give farmer meat, that farmer may give me hay, that I may give cow hay, that cow may give me milk, that I may give cat milk, that cat may give me my own tail again."

"No," says the butcher, "I'll give you no meat, till you go to the baker and fetch me some bread."

First she leapt and then she ran,

Till she came to the baker, and thus began:

"Pray, Baker, give me bread, that I may give butcher bread, that butcher may give me meat, that I may give farmer meat, that farmer may give me hay, that I may give cow hay, that cow may give me milk, that I may give cat milk, that cat may give me my own tail again."

"Yes," says the baker, "I'll give you some bread,

But if you eat my meal, I'll cut off your head."

Then the baker gave mouse bread, and mouse gave butcher bread, and butcher gave mouse meat, and mouse gave farmer meat, and farmer gave mouse hay, and mouse gave cow hay, and cow gave mouse milk, and mouse gave cat milk, and cat gave mouse her own tail again!

Cat Tails – Feline Fairy Tales, Myths And Legends

Why The Cat Kills Rats

This is a West African tale

This tale has been adapted Folk Stories From Southern Nigeria by Elphinstone Dayrell. The book was published in 1910 by Longmans, Green And Co., London And New York. Folk Stories From Southern Nigeria contains a rich assortment of folk tales, myths, legends, and fables drawn from the oral traditions of different Nigerian ethnic groups, including the Efik, Ibibio, and Igbo peoples.

Ansa was King of Calabar for fifty years. He had a very faithful cat as a housekeeper, and a rat was his house-boy. The king was an obstinate, headstrong man, but was very fond of the cat, who had been in his store for many years.

The rat, who was very poor, fell in love with one of the king's servant girls, but was unable to give her any presents, as he had no money.

At last he thought of the king's store, so in the night-time, being quite small, he had little difficulty, having made a hole in the roof, in getting into the store. He then stole corn and native pears, and presented them to his sweetheart.

At the end of the month, when the cat had to render her account of the things in the store to the king, it was found that a lot of corn and native pears were missing. The king was very angry at this, and asked the cat for an explanation. But the cat could not account for the loss, until one of her friends told her that the rat had been stealing the corn and giving it to the girl.

When the cat told the king, he called the girl before him and had her flogged. The rat he handed over to the cat to deal with, and dismissed them both from his service. The cat was so angry at this that she killed and ate the rat, and ever since that time whenever a cat sees a rat she kills and eats it.

Kisa The Cat

This is an Icelandic tale

This tale has been adapted from The Brown Fairy Book by Andrew Lang. The book was published in 1904 by Longman, Green And Company, London. Lang was a Scottish poet, novelist, literary critic, and contributor to the field of anthropology. Lang is perhaps best known for his "Fairy Books" series, which includes collections of fairy tales from around the world.

Once upon a time there lived a queen who had a beautiful cat, the colour of smoke, with china-blue eyes, which she was very fond of. The cat was constantly with her, and ran after her wherever she went, and even sat up proudly by her side when she drove out in her fine glass coach.

"Oh, pussy," said the queen one day, "you are happier than I am! For you have a dear kitten just like yourself, and I have nobody to play with but you."

"Don't cry," answered the cat, laying her paw on her mistress's arm. "Crying never does any good. I will see what can be done."

The cat was as good as her word. As soon as she returned from her drive she trotted off to the forest to consult a fairy who dwelt there, and very soon after the queen had a little girl, who seemed made out of snow and sunbeams. The queen was delighted, and soon the baby began to take notice of the kitten as she jumped about the room, and would not go to sleep at all unless the kitten lay curled up beside her.

Two or three months went by, and though the baby was still a baby, the kitten was fast becoming a cat, and one evening when, as usual, the nurse came to look for her, to put her in the baby's cot, she was nowhere to be found. What a hunt there was for that kitten, to be sure! The servants, each anxious to find her, as the queen was certain to reward the lucky man, searched in the most impossible places. Boxes were opened that would hardly have held the kitten's paw; books were taken from bookshelves, lest the kitten should have got behind them, drawers were pulled out, for perhaps the kitten might have got shut in. But it was all no use. The kitten had plainly run away, and nobody could tell if it would ever choose to come back.

Years passed away, and one day, when the princess was playing ball in the garden, she happened to throw her ball farther than usual, and it fell into a clump of rose-bushes. The princess of course ran after it at once, and she was stooping down to feel if it was hidden in the long grass, when she heard a voice calling her. "Ingibjorg! Ingibjorg!" it said, "have you forgotten me? I am Kisa, your sister!"

"But I never had a sister," answered Ingibjorg, very much puzzled, for she knew nothing of what had taken place so long ago.

"Don't you remember how I always slept in your cot beside you, and how you cried till I came? But girls have no memories at all! Why, I could find my way straight up to that cot this moment, if I was once inside the palace."

"Why did you go away then?" asked the princess. But before Kisa could answer, Ingeborg's attendants arrived breathless on the scene, and were so horrified at the sight of a strange cat, that Kisa plunged into the bushes and went back to the forest.

The princess was very much vexed with her ladies-in-waiting for frightening away her old playfellow, and told the queen who came to her room every evening to bid her good-night.

"Yes, it is quite true what Kisa said," answered the queen, "I should have liked to see her again. Perhaps, some day, she will return, and then you must bring her to me."

Next morning it was very hot, and the princess declared that she must go and play in the forest, where it was always cool, under the big shady trees. As usual, her attendants let her do anything she pleased, and sitting down on a mossy bank where a little stream tinkled by, they soon fell sound asleep. The princess saw with delight that they would pay no heed to her, and she wandered on and on, expecting every moment to see some fairies dancing round a ring, or some little brown elves peeping at her from behind a tree. But, alas, she met none of these. Instead, a horrible giant came out of his cave and ordered her to follow him. The princess felt much afraid, as he was so big and ugly, and began to be sorry that she had not stayed within reach of help, but as there was no use in disobeying the giant, she walked meekly behind.

They went a long way, and Ingibjorg grew very tired, and at length began to cry.

"I don't like girls who make horrid noises," said the giant, turning round. "But if you want to cry, I will give you something to cry for." And drawing an axe from his belt, he cut off both her feet, which he picked up and put in his pocket. Then he went away.

Poor Ingibjorg lay on the grass in terrible pain, and wondering if she should stay there till she died, as no one would know where to look for her. How long it was since she had set out in the morning she could not tell—it seemed years to her, of course, but the sun was still high in the heavens when she heard the sound of wheels, and then, with a great effort, for her throat was parched with fright and pain, she gave a shout.

"I am coming!" was the answer, and in another moment a cart made its way through the trees, driven by Kisa, who used her tail as a whip to urge the horse to go faster. Directly Kisa saw Ingibjorg lying there, she jumped quickly down, and lifting the girl carefully in her two front paws, laid her upon some soft hay, and drove back to her own little hut.

In the corner of the room was a pile of cushions, and these Kisa arranged as a bed. Ingibjorg, who by this time was nearly fainting from all she had gone through, drank greedily some milk, and then sank back on the cushions while Kisa fetched some dried herbs from a cupboard, soaked them in warm water and tied them on the bleeding legs. The pain vanished at once, and Ingibjorg looked up and smiled at Kisa.

"You will go to sleep now," said the cat, "and you will not mind if I leave you for a little while. I will lock the door, and no one can hurt you." But before she had finished the princess was asleep. Then Kisa got into the cart, which was standing at the door, and catching up the reins, drove straight to the giant's cave.

Leaving her cart behind some trees, Kisa crept gently up to the open door, and, crouching down, listened to what the giant was telling his wife, who was at supper with him.

"The first day that I can spare I shall just go back and kill her," he said. "It would never do for people in the forest to know that a mere girl can defy me!" And he and his wife were so busy calling Ingibjorg all sorts of names for her bad behaviour, that they never noticed Kisa stealing into a dark corner, and upsetting a whole bag of salt into the great pot before the fire.

"Dear me, how thirsty I am!" cried the giant by-and-by.

"So am I," answered the wife. "I do wish I had not taken that last spoonful of broth. I am sure something was wrong with it."

"If I don't get some water I shall die," went on the giant. And rushing out of the cave, followed by his wife, he ran down the path which led to the river.

Then Kisa entered the hut, and lost no time in searching every hole till she came upon some grass, under which Ingeborg's feet were hidden, and putting them in her cart, drove back again to her own hut.

Ingibjorg was thankful to see her, for she had lain, too frightened to sleep, trembling at every noise.

"Oh, is it you?" she cried joyfully, as Kisa turned the key. And the cat came in, holding up the two neat little feet in their silver slippers.

"In two minutes they shall be as tight as they ever were!" said Kisa. And taking some strings of the magic grass which the giant had carelessly heaped on them, she bound the feet on to the legs above.

"Of course you won't be able to walk for some time. You must not expect that", she continued. "But if you are very good, perhaps, in about a week, I may carry you home again."

And so she did, and when the cat drove the cart up to the palace gate, lashing the horse furiously with her tail, and the king and queen saw their lost daughter sitting beside her, they declared that no reward could be too great for the person who had brought her out of the giant's hands.

"We will talk about that by-and-by," said the cat, as she made her best bow, and turned her horse's head.

The princess was very unhappy when Kisa left her without even bidding her farewell. She would neither eat nor drink, nor take any notice of all the beautiful dresses her parents bought for her.

"She will die, unless we can make her laugh," one whispered to the other. "Is there anything in the world that we have left untried?"

"Nothing except marriage," answered the king. And he invited all the handsomest young men he could think of to the palace, and bade the princess choose a husband from among them.

It took her some time to decide which she admired the most, but at last she fixed upon a young prince, whose eyes were like the pools in the forest, and his hair of bright gold. The king and the queen were greatly pleased, as the young man was the son of a neighbouring king, and they gave orders that a splendid feast should be got ready.

When the marriage was over, Kisa suddenly stood before them, and Ingibjorg rushed forward and clasped her in her arms.

"I have come to claim my reward," said the cat. "Let me sleep for this night at the foot of your bed."

"Is that all?" asked Ingibjorg, much disappointed.

"It is enough," answered the cat. And when morning dawned, no cat that lay upon the bed, but instead a beautiful princess.

"My mother and I were both enchanted by a spiteful fairy," she said. "We could not free ourselves till we had done some kindly deed that had never been done before. My mother died without ever finding a chance of doing anything new, but I took advantage of the evil act of the giant to make you as whole as ever."

Then they were all more delighted than before, and the princess lived in the court until she, too, married, and went away to govern one of her own.

Johnny Reed's Cat

This is an English tale

This tale is my version of an original that appeared in Folk-Lore and Legends of the English by Charles John Tibbitts. The book was published in 1890 by W. W. Gibbings, London.

"Yes, cats are definitely quirky, and they often know more than your average animal. That cat you've been staring at, for instance, will stand on its hind legs at a door with its front paws on the handle, trying to open it like a person, meowing almost like it's talking. That cat is a London cat, brought to me by a cousin who lives there, and its name is Gilpin, after a mayor who was named the same. He's a clever cat, no doubt, but it's not just the London cats that are smarter than the country ones. Who knows, he might even be related to Johnny Reed's own tom-cat."

"And who was Johnny Reed? And what was so special about his cat?"

"Have you never heard of Johnny Reed's cat? It's an old story from the north, and it's true enough, even if some people today might not believe it. My father used to tell the story all the time, and he was from Newcastle, where Johnny Reed lived, working as a parish sexton in a nearby village.

"Johnny Reed was the sexton, as I said, and he and his wife had a cat. It was a well-behaved creature, with no real faults, except for the usual tricks all cats play, which seem to be in their nature. It was all black except for one white paw, and seemed as honest and decent as a cat could be. Tom would have as soon suspected it of being anything more than it seemed as he would one of his own children, like many folks who have cats and don't think twice about them.

"Well, the cat had been with them for years when something strange happened. One night, Johnny was coming home late from the churchyard, where he had been digging a grave for someone who had died suddenly, leaving Johnny with the unexpected task of finishing it by lantern light for the next day's burial. Once he finished his work, he put his tools in the shed, and locked them up, and then he began walking home, hoping his wife would have a fire ready, as the night was cold with a sharp wind blowing over the fields.

"He hadn't gone far when he came to a gate on the roadside. There seemed to be a strange shadow around it, and Johnny saw what looked like little gleaming fires dancing about, some standing still, like flashes of light from windows in buildings on fire. Johnny, who wasn't easily scared, because of his work, said to himself, 'Hullo! What's this? Something I've never seen before,' and he walked straight up to the gate.

The shadow got darker, and the lights brighter the closer he got.

"When he got right up to the gate, he found that the shadow was just nine black cats, some sitting, some dancing around, and the lights were from their eyes. Thinking to scare them off, he called out, 'Sh—sh—sh,' but not a cat moved.

"'I'll soon scatter you, you ugly creatures,' said Johnny, looking for a stone, but there wasn't one to be found in the dark night. Then he heard a voice calling, 'Johnny Reed!'

"'Hullo!' he said, 'who's calling me?'

"'Johnny Reed,' the voice said again.

"'Well,' said Johnny, 'I'm here,' looking around and seeing no one. 'Was it one of you,' he said, joking, to the cats, 'who was calling me?'

"'Yes, of course,' said one of them clearly, 'It's me who has called you three times.'

"Johnny started to feel curious, since it was the first time a cat had ever spoken to him, and he didn't know what it might lead to. He took off his hat to the cat, thinking it might be best to show it respect and hoping a little civility would help.

"'Well, sir,' he said, 'what can I do for you?'

"'It's not much I want from you,' said the cat, 'but it'll be better for you if you do what I tell you. Tell Dan Ratcliffe that Peggy Poyson is dead.'

"'I will, sir,' said Johnny, wondering how he was going to do it, since he didn't know who Dan Ratcliffe was. Then all the cats vanished, and Johnny ran the rest of the way home, shaking from fear and the distance he had to cover.

"'Nan,' he said to his wife as soon as he got in, 'who's Dan Ratcliffe?'

"'Dan Ratcliffe?' she said. 'I never heard of him, and I don't think there's anyone by that name around here.'

"'Nor do I,' he said, 'but I have to find him wherever he is.'

"He told her everything about the cats' message. Their cat, sitting in front of the fire, looked as snug as could be. But when Johnny mentioned the message from the cats, it jumped up and looked at him, saying, 'What! Is Peggy Poyson dead? Then it's time for me to go,' and it sprang through the door and vanished, never to be seen again.

"And did the sexton ever find Dan Ratcliffe? Never. He searched everywhere, but no one knew of such a person. Johnny looked long enough, thinking it might be worse for him if he didn't do his best to please the cats."

"It's hard to say what the cat's really meant, but many people thought, and I tend to agree, that Dan Ratcliffe was Johnny's own cat, based on how it acted, with no one else by that name known. Who Peggy Poyson was, no one could say, but likely, it was some relative of the cat or someone it cared about. We know so little about these creatures and their ways, and with whom and what they're connected."

The Vampire Cat Of Nabéshima

This is a Japanese tale

This tale has been adapted from Algernon Bertram Freeman-Mitford's book, Tales of Old Japan, published by Macmillan And Co., Limited, London & Toronto, in 1871. "The Vampire Cat of Nabéshima" is a well-known Japanese folktale that originates from the Saga Prefecture in Japan. The story is part of Japan's rich folklore, which often includes supernatural elements, such as ghosts, demons, and in this case, a vampire cat known as a "nekomata" or "bakeneko," both of which are mythical, supernatural cats believed to have the power to shapeshift, curse, and possess humans.

There is a tradition in the Nabéshima family that, many years ago, the Prince of Hizen was bewitched and cursed by a cat that had been kept by one of his retainers. This prince had in his house a lady of rare beauty, called O Toyo, and amongst all his ladies she was the favourite, and there was none who could rival her charms and accomplishments. One day the

Prince went out into the garden with O Toyo, and remained enjoying the fragrance of the flowers until sunset, when they returned to the palace, never noticing that they were being followed by a large cat. Having parted with her lord, O Toyo retired to her own room and went to bed.

At midnight she awoke with a start, and became aware of a huge cat that crouched watching her, and when she cried out, the beast sprang on her, and, fixing its cruel teeth in her delicate throat, throttled her to death. What a piteous end for so fair a dame, the darling of her prince's heart, to die suddenly, bitten to death by a cat! Then the cat, having scratched out a grave under the veranda, buried the corpse of O Toyo, and assuming her form, began to bewitch the Prince.

But my lord the Prince knew nothing of all this, and little thought that the beautiful creature who caressed and fondled him was an impish and foul beast that had slain his mistress and assumed her shape in order to drain out his life's blood. Day by day, as time went on, the Prince's strength dwindled away. The colour of his face was changed, and became pale and livid; and he looked like a man suffering from a deadly sickness. Seeing this, his councillors and his wife became greatly alarmed, so they summoned the physicians, who prescribed various remedies for him, but the more medicine he took, the more serious did his illness appear, and no treatment was of any help.

But most of all he suffered in the night-time, when his sleep would be troubled and disturbed by hideous dreams. In consequence of this, his councillors nightly appointed a hundred of his retainers to sit up and watch over him; but, strange to say, towards ten o'clock on the very first night that the watch was set, the guard were seized with a sudden and unaccountable drowsiness, which they could not resist, until one by one every man had fallen asleep. Then the false O Toyo came in and harassed the Prince until morning. The following night the same thing occurred, and the Prince was subjected to the imp's tyranny, while his guards slept helplessly around him. Night after night this was repeated, until three of the Prince's councillors determined themselves to sit up on guard, and see whether they could overcome this mysterious drowsiness. They fared no better than the others, and by ten o'clock were fast asleep. The next day the three councillors held a solemn conclave, and their chief, one Isahaya Buzen, said, "This is a marvellous thing, that a guard of a hundred men should thus be overcome by sleep. Of a surety, the spell that is upon my lord and upon his guard must be the work of witchcraft. Now, as all our efforts are of no avail, let us seek out Ruiten, the chief priest of the temple called Miyô In, and beseech him to put up prayers for the recovery of my lord."

And the other councillors approving what Isahaya Buzen had said, went to the priest Ruiten and engaged him to recite litanies that the Prince might be restored to health.

So it came to pass that Ruiten, the chief priest of Miyô In, offered up prayers nightly for the Prince. One night, at the ninth hour (midnight), when he had finished his religious exercises and was preparing to lie down to sleep, he fancied that he heard a noise outside in the garden, as if someone were washing himself at the well. Deeming this passing strange, he looked down from the window, and there in the moonlight he saw a handsome young soldier, some twenty-four years of age, washing himself, who, when he had finished cleaning himself and had put on his clothes, stood before the figure of Buddha and prayed fervently for the recovery of my lord the Prince. Ruiten looked on with admiration, and the young man, when he had made an end of his prayer, was going away; but the priest stopped him, calling out to him, "Sir, I pray you to tarry a little: I have something to say to you."

"At your reverence's service. What may please you?"

"Pray be so good as to step up here, and have a little talk."

"By your reverence's leave," and with this he went upstairs.

Then Ruiten said, "Sir, I cannot conceal my admiration that you, being so young a man, should have so loyal a spirit. I am Ruiten, the chief priest of this temple, and I am engaged in praying for the recovery of my lord. Pray what is your name?"

"My name, sir, is Itô Sôda, and I am serving in the infantry of Nabéshima. Since my lord has been sick, my one desire has been to assist in nursing him, but, being only a simple soldier, I am not of sufficient rank to come into his presence, so I have no resource but to pray to the gods of the country and to Buddha that my lord may regain his health."

When Ruiten heard this, he shed tears in admiration of the fidelity of Itô Sôda, and said, "Your purpose is, indeed, a good one, but what a strange sickness this is that my lord is afflicted with! Every night he suffers from horrible dreams, and the retainers who sit up with him are all seized with a mysterious sleep, so that no one can keep awake. It is very wonderful."

"Yes," replied Sôda, after a moment's reflection, "this certainly must be witchcraft. If I could but obtain leave to sit up one night with the Prince, I would see whether I could not resist this drowsiness and detect the goblin."

At last the priest said, "I am a friend of Isahaya Buzen, the chief councillor of the Prince. I will speak to him of you and of your loyalty, and will intercede with him that you may attain your wish."

"Indeed, sir, I am most thankful. I am not prompted by any vain thought of self-advancement, should I succeed. All I wish for is the recovery of my lord. I commend myself to your kind favour."

"Well, then, tomorrow night I will take you with me to the councillor's house."

"Thank you, sir, and farewell."

And so they parted.

On the following evening Itô Sôda returned to the temple Miyô In, and having found Ruiten, accompanied him to the house of Isahaya Buzen. Then the priest, leaving Sôda outside, went in to converse with the councillor, and inquire after the Prince's health.

"And pray, sir, how is my lord? Is he in any better condition since I have been offering up prayers for him?"

"Indeed, no. His illness is very severe. We are certain that he must be the victim of some foul sorcery, but as there are no means of keeping a guard awake after ten o'clock, we cannot catch a sight of the goblin, so we are in the greatest trouble."

"I feel deeply for you. It must be most distressing. However, I have something to tell you. I think that I have found a man who will detect the goblin, and I have brought him with me."

"Indeed! who is the man?"

"Well, he is one of my lord's foot-soldiers, named Itô Sôda, a faithful fellow, and I trust that you will grant his request to be permitted to sit up with my lord."

"Certainly, it is wonderful to find so much loyalty and zeal in a common soldier," replied Isahaya Buzen, after a moment's reflection. "Still it is impossible to allow a man of such low rank to perform the office of watching over my lord."

"It is true that he is but a common soldier," urged the priest, "but why not raise his rank in consideration of his fidelity, and then let him mount guard?"

"It would be time enough to promote him after my lord's recovery. But come, let me see this Itô Sôda, that I may know what manner of man he is. If he pleases me, I will consult with the other councillors, and perhaps we may grant his request."

"I will bring him in forthwith," replied Ruiten, who thereupon went out to fetch the young man.

When he returned, the priest presented Itô Sôda to the councillor, who looked at him attentively, and, being pleased with his comely and gentle appearance, said, "So I hear that you are anxious to be permitted to mount guard in my lord's room at night. Well, I must consult with the other councillors, and we will see what can be done for you."

When the young soldier heard this he was greatly elated, and took his leave, after warmly thanking Ruiten, who had helped him to gain his object. The next day the councillors held a meeting, and sent for Itô Sôda, and told him that he might keep watch with the other retainers that very night. So he went his way in high spirits, and at nightfall, having made all his preparations, took his place among the hundred gentlemen who were on duty in the prince's bed-room.

Now the Prince slept in the centre of the room, and the hundred guards around him sat keeping themselves awake with entertaining conversation and pleasant conceits. But, as ten o'clock approached, they began to doze off as they sat; and in spite of all their endeavours to keep one another awake, by degrees they all fell asleep. Itô Sôda all this while felt an irresistible desire to sleep creeping over him, and, though he tried by all sorts of ways to rouse himself, he saw that there was no help for it, but by resorting to an extreme measure, for which he had already made his preparations. Drawing out a piece of oil paper which he had brought with him, and spreading it over the mats, he sat down upon it; then he took the small knife which he carried in the sheath of his dirk, and stuck it into his own thigh. For a while the pain of the wound kept him awake, but as the slumber by which he was assailed was the work of sorcery, little by little he became drowsy again. Then he twisted the knife round and round in his thigh, so that the pain becoming very violent, he was proof against the feeling of sleepiness, and so he kept a faithful watch. Now the oil paper which he had spread under his legs was in order to prevent the blood, which might spurt from his wound, from defiling the mats.

So Itô Sôda remained awake, but the rest of the guard slept, and as he watched, suddenly the sliding-doors of the Prince's room were drawn open, and he saw a figure coming in stealthily, and, as it drew nearer, the form was that of a marvellously beautiful woman some twenty-three years of age. Cautiously she looked around her, and when she saw that all the guard were asleep, she smiled an ominous smile, and was going up to the Prince's bedside, when she perceived that in one corner of the room there was a man yet awake. This seemed to startle her, but she went up to Sôda and said, "I am not used to seeing you here. Who are you?"

"My name is Itô Sôda, and this is the first night that I have been on guard."

"A troublesome office, truly! Why, here are all the rest of the guard asleep. How is it that you alone are awake? You are a trusty watchman."

"There is nothing to boast about. I'm asleep myself, fast and sound."

"What is that wound on your knee? It is all red with blood."

"Oh! I felt very sleepy, so I stuck my knife into my thigh, and the pain of it has kept me awake."

"What wondrous loyalty!" said the lady.

"Is it not the duty of a retainer to lay down his life for his master? Is such a scratch as this worth thinking about?"

Then the lady went up to the sleeping prince and said, "How fares it with my lord tonight?"

But the Prince, worn out with sickness, made no reply. But Sôda was watching her eagerly, and guessed that it was O

Toyo, and made up his mind that if she attempted to harass the Prince he would kill her on the spot. The goblin, however, which in the form of O Toyo had been tormenting the Prince every night, and had come again that night for no other purpose, was defeated by the watchfulness of Itô Sôda; for whenever she drew near to the sick man, thinking to put her spells upon him, she would turn and look behind her, and there she saw Itô Sôda glaring at her, so she had no help for it but to go away again, and leave the Prince undisturbed.

At last the day broke, and the other officers, when they awoke and opened their eyes, saw that Itô Sôda had kept awake by stabbing himself in the thigh; and they were greatly ashamed, and went home crestfallen.

That morning Itô Sôda went to the house of Isahaya Buzen, and told him all that had occurred the previous night. The councillors were all loud in their praises of Itô Sôda's behaviour, and ordered him to keep watch again that night. At the same hour, the false O Toyo came and looked around the room, and all the guard were asleep, excepting Itô Sôda, who was wide awake, and so, being again frustrated, she returned to her own apartments.

Now since Sôda had been on guard the Prince had passed quiet nights, and his sickness began to get better, and there was great joy in the palace, and Sôda was promoted and rewarded with an estate. In the meanwhile O Toyo, seeing that her nightly visits bore no fruits, kept away, and from that time forth the night-guard were no longer subject to fits of drowsiness. This coincidence struck Sôda as very strange, so he went to Isahaya Buzen and told him that of a certainty this O Toyo was no other than a goblin. Isahaya Buzen reflected for a while, and said, "Well, then, how shall we kill the foul thing?"

"I will go to the creature's room, as if nothing were the matter, and try to kill her, but in case she should try to escape, I will beg you to order eight men to stop outside and lie in wait for her."

Having agreed upon this plan, Sôda went at nightfall to O Toyo's apartment, pretending to have been sent with a message from the Prince. When she saw him arrive, she said, "What message have you brought me from my lord?"

"Oh, nothing in particular. Be so kind as to look at this letter," and as he spoke, he drew near to her, and suddenly drawing his dirk cut at her, but the goblin, springing back, seized a halberd, and glaring fiercely at Sôda, said, "How dare you behave like this to one of your lord's ladies? I will have you dismissed." She tried to strike Sôda with the halberd. But Sôda fought desperately with his dirk, and the goblin, seeing that she was no match for him, threw away the halberd, and from a beautiful woman became suddenly transformed into a cat, which, springing up the sides of the room, jumped on to the roof. Isahaya Buzen and his eight men who were watching outside shot at the cat, but missed it, and the beast made good its escape.

So the cat fled to the mountains, and did much mischief among the surrounding people, until the Prince of Hizen ordered a great hunt, and the beast was killed. But the Prince recovered from his sickness; and Itô Sôda was richly rewarded.

Cat Tails – Feline Fairy Tales, Myths And Legends

The Spectral Cat

This is an English tale

This tale has been adapted from Goblin Tales of Lancashire by James Bowker. The book was published in 1878 by W. Swan Sonnenschein & Co. The stories in Goblin Tales of Lancashire explore a variety of themes common in folklore, such as the interplay between humans and supernatural beings, the consequences of greed and mischief, and the importance of kindness and humility.

Long ago, so long, in fact, that the date has been lost in obscurity, the piously-inclined inhabitants of the then thickly wooded and wild country stretching from the sea-coast to Rivington Pike and Hoghton determined to erect a church at Whittle-le-Woods, and a site having been selected, the first stone was laid with all the ceremony due to so important and solemn a proceeding. Assisted by the labours as well as by the contributions of the faithful, the good priest was in high spirits, and as the close of the first day had seen the foundations set out and good piles of materials brought upon the ground ready for the future, he fell asleep congratulating himself upon having lived long enough to see the wish of his heart gratified. Imagine his surprise, however, when, after arising at the break of day, and immediately rushing to his window to gaze upon the work, he could not perceive either foundation or pile of stone. The field in which he expected to observe the promising outline of a church was as green and showing as few marks of disturbance as the neighbouring ones.

"Surely I must have been dreaming," said the good man, as he stood with rueful eyes at the little casement, "for there are not any signs either of the gifts or the labours of the pious sons of the church."

In this puzzled frame of mind, and with a heavy sigh, he once more courted sleep. He had not slumbered long, however, when loud knocks at the door of his dwelling and lusty cries for Father Ambrose disturbed him. Hastily attiring himself, he descended, to find a concourse of people assembled in front of the house, and no sooner had he opened the door than a mason cried out, "Father Ambrose, where are the foundations we laid yesterday, and where is the stone from the quarry?"

"Then I did not simply dream that I had blessed the site?" asked the old man.

Upon which there was a shout of laughter, and a sturdy young fellow asked, "And I did not dream that I carted six loads from the quarry?"

"'h' Owd Lad's had a hand int'," said a labourer, "for t' field's as if foot had never stepped int'".

The priest and his people at once set off to inspect the site, and sure enough it was in the state described by the mason. Cowslips and buttercups decked the expanse of green, which took different shades as the zephyr swept over it.

"Well, I'm fair capped," said a grey-headed old farmer. "I've had things stollen before today, but they've generally been things wi' feathers on and good to eat and not the foundations of a church. The world's getting terrible wicked. We have' to be looking out for another Noah's flood, I warrant."

A peal of laughter followed this sally, but Father Ambrose, who was in no mood for mirth, sternly remarked. "'There is something here which savours of the doings of Beelzebub", and then he sadly turned away, leaving the small crowd of gossips speculating upon the events of the night. Before the father reached his dwelling, however, he heard his name called by a rustic who was running along the road.

"Father Ambrose," cried the panting messenger, "here's the strangest thing happened at Leyland. The foundations of a church and all sorts of building materials have been laid in a field during the night, and Adam the miller is vowing vengeance against you for having trespassed on his land.:

The priest at once returned to the little crowd of people, who were still gaping at the field from which all signs of labour had been so wonderfully removed, and bade the messenger repeat the strange story, which he did at somewhat greater length, becoming loquacious in the presence of his equals, for he enjoyed their looks of astonishment. When the astounding narrative had been told, the crowd at once started for Leyland, their pastor promising to follow after he had fortified himself with breakfast.

When the good man reached the village he had no need to inquire which was Adam the miller's field, for he saw the crowd gathered in a rich-looking meadow. As he opened the gate Adam met him, and without ceremony at once accused him of having taken possession of his field.

"Peace, Adam," said the priest. "The field has been taken not by me, but by a higher power, either good or evil, and I fear the latter,' and he made his way to the people.

True enough, the foundations were laid as at Whittle, and even the mortar was ready for the masons. "I am loth to think that this is a sorry jest of the Evil One," said Father Ambrose. "You must help me to outwit him, and to give him his labour for his pains. Let each one carry what he can, and, doubtless, Adam will be glad to cart the remainder."

This was a proposition the burly miller agreed to at once. Accordingly each of the people walked off with a piece of wood, and Adam started for his team. Before long the field was cleared, and before sunset the foundations were again laid in the original place, and a good piece of wall had been built.

Grown wise by experience, the priest selected two men to watch the place during the night. Naturally enough, these worthies, who by no means liked the task, but were afraid to decline it, determined to make themselves as comfortable as they could under the circumstances.

They therefore carried to the place a quantity of food and drink, and a number of empty sacks, with which they constructed an impromptu couch near the blazing wood fire. Notwithstanding the seductive influence of the liquor, they were not troubled with much company, for the few people who resided in the vicinity did not care to remain out of doors late after what Father Ambrose had said as to the proceeding having been a joke of Satan's. The priest, however, came to see the men, and after giving them his blessing, and a few words of advice, he left them to whatever the night might bring forth.

No sooner had he gone than the watchers put up some boards to shield them from the wind, and, drawing near to the cheerful fire, they began to partake of a homely but plentiful supper. Considering how requisite it was that they should be in possession of all their wits, perhaps it would have been better had not a large bottle been in such frequent use, for, soon after the meal was ended, what with the effects of the by-no-means weak potion, the warmth and odour sent forth by the crackling logs, and the musical moaning of the wind in the branches overhead, they began to feel drowsy, to mutter complaints against the hardship of their lot, and to look longingly upon the heap of sacks.

"If owt comes," said the oldest of the two, "one can see it as well as two, and can awaken the other. Therefore I'm in for a nod." And he at once flung himself upon the rude bed.

"Well," said the younger one, who was perched upon a log close to the fire, "have your own way, and you'll live longer, but I'll wake you soon, ang have a doze myself. That's fair, isn't it?"

To this question there was no response, for the old man was already asleep. The younger one immediately reached for the huge bottle, and after drinking a hearty draught from it placed it within reach, saying, as he did so, 'I'm not afraid o' you, as it is what it is! You are not Belsybub, are you?'

Before long he bowed his head upon his hands, and gazing into the fire gave way to a pleasant train of reflections, in which the miller's daughter played a by-no-means unimportant part. In a little while he, too, began to doze and nod, and the ideas and thronging fancies soon gave way to equally delightful dreams.

Day was breaking when the pair awoke. The fire was out, and the noisy birds were chirping their welcome to the sun. For a while the watchers stared at each other with well-acted surprise.

"I'm afraid you've overslept yourself," said the young fellow, "and really I do think as I've been noddin' a bit myself.' And then, as he turned round he said in shock, "Why, it's gone again! Jacob, old lad! The foundation, and the wall, and all of the lots o' stones are off to Leyland again!'

The field was again clear, grass and meadow flowers covering its expanse, and after a long conference the pair determined that the best course for them to pursue would be that of immediately confessing to Father Ambrose that they had been asleep. Accordingly they wended their way to his house, and having succeeded in arousing him, and getting him to the door, the young man informed him that once more the foundations were missing.

"What took them?" asked the priest. To which awkward query the old man replied that they did not see anything.

"Then you slept, did you?" asked the Father.

"Well," said the young man, "we did nod a minute or two, but we were tired with watching so closely, and, you see, that as can carry the foundations of a church away cannot have much trouble sending ignorant chaps like Jacob and me to sleep again against our will.'

This ended the colloquy, for Father Ambrose laughed heartily at the ready answer. Shortly afterwards, as on the preceding day, the messenger from Leyland arrived with tidings that the walls had again appeared in Adam's field. Again they were carted back, and placed in their original position, and once more a watch was set, the priest taking the precaution of remaining with the men until near upon midnight. Almost directly after he had left the field one of the watchers suddenly started from his seat, and cried, "See yonder, there's something wicked!'

Both men gazed intently, and saw a huge cat, with great unearthly-looking eyes, and a tail with a barbed end. Without any seeming difficulty this terrible animal took up a large stone, and hopped off with it, returning almost immediately for another. This strange performance went on for some time, the two observers being nearly petrified by terror, but at length the younger one said, "'I'm like to put a stop to that work, or he'll say we've been asleep again."

He seized a large piece of wood and crept down the field, the old man following closely behind. When he reached the cat, which took no notice of his approach, he lifted his cudgel, and struck the animal a heavy blow on its head. Before he had time to repeat it, however, the cat, with a piercing scream, sprang upon him, flung him to the ground, and fixed its teeth in his throat. The old man at once fled for the priest. When he returned with him, cat, foundations, and materials were gone, but the dead body of the poor watcher was there, with glazed eyes, gazing at the pitiless stars.

After this terrible example of the power of the fiendish labourer it was not considered advisable to attempt a third removal, and the building was proceeded with upon the site at Leyland chosen by the spectre.

The present parish church covers the place long occupied by the original building, and although all the actors in this story passed away centuries ago, a correct likeness of the cat has been preserved, and may be seen by the sceptical.

A Cat, A Mouse, A Lizard And An Owl

This is an Indian tale

This story has been adapted from a tale originally told by Siddha Mohana Mitra and Nancy Bell in Hindu Tales from the Sanskrit, published in 1919 by MacMillan and Company, London & Canada. The book features a selection of stories drawn from classical Sanskrit literature, including the Panchatantra, Hitopadesha, and other traditional sources. The Panchatantra and Hitopadesha are two of the most famous collections of Indian fables and moral stories. They are believed to have originated over two millennia ago and have been passed down through generations. These tales are often characterized by their use of animal characters to convey moral lessons and practical wisdom.

CHAPTER I

This is the story of four creatures, none of whom loved each other, who lived in the same banyan tree in a forest in India.

Banyan trees are very beautiful and very useful, and get their name from the fact that "banians," as merchants are called in India, often gather together in their shade to sell their goods. Banyan trees grow to a very great height, spreading their branches out so widely that many people can stand beneath them. From those branches roots spring forth, which, when they reach the ground, pierce it, and look like, columns holding up a roof. If you have never seen a banyan tree, you can easily find a picture of one in some dictionary, and when you have done so, you will understand that a great many creatures can live in one without seeing much of each other.

In an especially fine banyan tree, outside the walls of a town called Vidisa, a cat, an owl, a lizard and a mouse, had all taken up their abode. The cat lived in a big hole in the trunk some little distance from the ground, where she could sleep very cosily, curled up out of sight with her head resting on her forepaws, feeling perfectly safe from harm, for no other creature, she thought, could possibly discover her hiding-place.

The owl roosted in a mass of foliage at the top of the tree, near the nest in which his wife had brought up their children, before those children flew away to seek mates for themselves. He too felt pretty secure as long as he remained up there, but he had seen the cat prowling about below him more than once, and was very sure that, if she should happen to catch sight of him when he was off his guard seeking his prey and obliged to give all his attention to what he was doing, she might spring out upon him and kill him. Cats do not generally attack such big birds as owls, but they will sometimes kill a mother sitting in her nest, as well as the little ones, if the father is too far off to protect them.

The lizard loved to lie and bask in the sunshine, catching the flies on which he lived, lying so still that they did not notice him, and darting out his long tongue suddenly to suck them into his mouth. Yet he hid from the owl and the cat, because he knew full well that, tough though he was, they would gobble him up if they happened to be hungry. He made his home amongst the roots on the south side of the tree where it was hottest, but the mouse had his hole on the other side amongst damp moss and dead leaves. The mouse was in constant fear of the cat and the owl. He knew that both of them could see in the dark, and he would have no chance of escape if they once caught sight of him.

CHAPTER II

The lizard and the mouse could only get food in daylight, but the lizard did not have to go far for the flies on which he lived, whilst the mouse had a very dangerous journey to take to his favourite feeding place. This was a barley field a short distance from the banyan tree, where he loved to nibble the full ears, running up the stalks to get at them. The mouse was the only one of the four creatures in the banyan tree who did not feed on others, for, like the rest of his family, he was a vegetarian, that is to say, he ate nothing but vegetables and fruit.

Now the cat knew full well how fond the mouse was of the barley-field, and she used to keep watch amongst the tall stems, creeping stealthily about with her tail in the air and her green eyes glistening, expecting any moment to see the poor little mouse darting hastily along. The cat never dreamt that any danger could come to her, and she trod down the barley, making quite a clear path through it. She was quite wrong in thinking herself so safe, for that path got her into very serious trouble.

It so happened that a hunter, whose great delight was to kill wild creatures, and who was very clever in finding them, noticing every little thing which could show him where they had passed by, came one day into the barley-field. He spied the path directly and cried, "Ha, ha! Some wild animal has been here. Not a very big one. Let's have a look for the footprints!"

So he stooped down to the ground, and very soon saw the marks of pussy's feet. "A cat, I do believe," he said to himself, "spoiling the barley she doesn't want to eat herself. I'll soon pay her out."

The hunter waited until the evening lest the creature should see what he was going to do, and then in the twilight he set snares all over the barley-field. A snare, you know, is a string with a slip-knot at the end of it, and if an animal puts his head or one of his paws into this slip-knot and goes on without noticing it, the string is pulled tight and the poor creature cannot get free.

CHAPTER III

Exactly what the hunter expected happened. The cat came as usual to watch for the mouse, and caught sight of him running across the end of the path. Puss dashed after him, and just as she thought she really had got him this time, she found herself caught by the neck, for she had put her head into one of the snares. She was nearly strangled and could scarcely even mew. The mouse was so close that he heard the feeble mew, and in a terrible fright, thinking the cat was after him, he peeped through the stems of the barley to make sure which way to run to get away from her. What was his delight when he saw his enemy in such trouble and quite unable to do him any harm!

Now it so happened that the owl and the lizard were also in the barley-field, not very far away from the cat, and they too saw the distress their hated enemy was in. They also caught sight of the little mouse peeping through the barley, and the owl thought to himself, "I'll have you, my little friend, now puss cannot do me any harm," whilst the lizard darted away into the sunshine, feeling glad that the cat and the owl were neither of them now likely to trouble their heads about him. The owl flew quietly to a tree hard by to watch what would happen, feeling so sure of having the mouse for his dinner that he was in no hurry to catch him.

CHAPTER IV

The mouse, small and helpless though he was, was a wise little creature. He saw the owl fly up into the tree, and knew quite well that if he did not take care he would serve as dinner to that great strong bird. He knew too that, if he went within reach of the claws of the cat, he would suffer for it.

"How I do wish," he thought to himself, "I could make friends with the cat, now she is in distress, and get her to promise not to hurt me if ever she gets free. As long as I am near the cat, the owl will not dare to come after me."

As he thought and thought, his eyes got brighter and brighter, and at last he decided what he would do. He had, you see, kept his presence of mind, that is to say, he did not let his fear of the cat or the owl prevent him from thinking clearly. He now ventured forth from amongst the barley, and coming near enough to the cat for her to see him quite clearly, but not near enough for her to reach him with her claws, or far enough away for the owl to get him without danger from those terrible claws, he said to the cat in a queer little squeaky voice, "Dear Puss, I do not like to see you in such a fix. It is true we have never been exactly friends, but I have always looked up to you as a strong and noble enemy. If you will promise never to do me any harm, I will do my best to help you. I have very sharp teeth, and I might perhaps be able to nibble through the string round your beautiful neck and set you free. What do you think about it?"

CHAPTER V

When the cat heard what the mouse said, she could hardly believe her ears. She was of course ready to promise anything to anyone who would help her, so she said at once, "You dear little mouse, to wish to help me. If only you will nibble through that string which is killing me, I promise that I will always love you, always be your friend, and however hungry I may be, I will starve rather than hurt your tender little body."

On hearing this, the mouse, without hesitating a moment, climbed up on to the cat's back, and cuddled down in the soft fur near her neck, feeling very safe and warm there. The owl would certainly not attack him there, he thought, and the cat could not possibly hurt him. It was one thing to pounce down on a defenceless little creature running on the ground amongst the barley, quite another to try and snatch him from the very neck of a cat.

The cat of course expected the mouse to begin to nibble through the string at once, and became very uneasy when she felt the little creature nestle down as if to go to sleep, instead of helping her. Poor Pussy could not turn her head so as to see the mouse without drawing the string tighter, and she did not dare to speak angrily lest she should offend him. "My dear little friend," she said, "do you not think it is high time to keep your promise and set me free?"

Hearing this, the mouse pretended to bite the string, but took care not to do so really, and the cat waited and waited, getting more miserable every minute. All through the long night the same thing went on, the mouse taking a little nap now and then, the cat getting weaker and weaker.

"Oh," she thought to herself, "if only I could get free, the first thing I would do would be to gobble up that horrid little mouse."

The moon rose, the stars came out, the wind murmured amongst the branches of the banyan tree, making the unfortunate cat long to be safe in her cosy home in the trunk. The cries of the wild animals which prowl about at night seeking their food were heard, and the cat feared one of them might find her and kill her. A mother tiger perhaps would snatch her, and take her to her hungry cubs, hidden away in the deep forest, or a bird of prey might swoop down on her and grip her in his terrible claws. Again and again she entreated the mouse to be quick, promising that, if only he would set her at liberty, she would never, never, never forget it or do any harm to her beloved friend.

CHAPTER VI

It was not until the moon had set and the light of the dawn had put out that of the stars that the mouse, made any real effort to help the cat. By this time the hunter who had set the snare came to see if he had caught the cat, and the poor cat, seeing him in the distance, became so wild with terror that she nearly killed herself in the struggle to get away.

"Keep still, keep still," cried the mouse, "and I will really save you." Then with a few quick bites with his sharp teeth he cut through the string, and the next moment the cat was hidden amongst the barley, and the mouse was running off in the opposite direction, determined to keep well out of sight of the creature he had kept in such misery for so many hours. Full well he knew that all the cat's promises would be forgotten, and that she would eat him up if she could catch him.

The owl too flew away, and the lizard went off to hunt flies in the sunshine, and there was not a sign of any of the four inhabitants of the banyan tree when the hunter reached the snare. He was very much surprised and puzzled to find the string hanging loose in two pieces, and no sign of there having been anything caught in it, except two white hairs lying on the ground close to the trap. He had a good look round, and then went home without having found out anything.

When the hunter was quite out of sight, the cat came forth from the barley, and hastened back to her beloved home in the banyan tree. On her way there she spied the mouse also hurrying along in the same direction, and at first she felt inclined to hunt him and eat him then and there. On second thoughts however she decided to try and keep friends with him, because he might help her again if she got caught a second time. So she took no notice of the mouse until the next day, when she climbed down the tree and went to the roots in which she knew the mouse was hidden. There she began to purr as loud as she could, to show the mouse she was in a good humour, and called out, "Dear good little mouse, come out of your hole and let me tell you how very, very grateful I am to you for saving my life. There is nothing in the world I will not do for you, if you will only be friends with me."

The mouse only squeaked in answer to this speech, and took very good care not to show himself, till he was quite sure the cat was gone beyond reach of him. He stayed quietly in his hole, and only ventured forth after he had heard the cat climb up into the tree again. "It is all very well," thought the mouse, "to pretend to make friends with an enemy when that enemy is helpless, but I should indeed be a silly mouse to trust a cat when she is free to kill me."

The cat made a good many other efforts to be friends with the mouse, but they were all unsuccessful. In the end the owl caught the mouse, and the cat killed the lizard. The owl and the cat both lived for the rest of their lives in the banyan tree, and died in the end at a good old age.

The Grave Prince And The Beneficent Cat

This is an Austrian tale

This tale has been adapted from Household Stories from the Land of Hofer by Rachel Harriette Busk. The book was published in 1871 by Griffith and Farran, London. Household Stories from the Land of Hofer is a collection of folk tales from the Tyrol region of Austria, which is known for its stunning Alpine landscapes and rich cultural heritage.

There once was a king in Tirol who had three sons. The eldest was grave and thoughtful beyond his years, and he seldom spoke to anyone, took no pleasure in pastimes, and lived apart from those of his age. The other two were clever and merry, always forward at any game, or at any piece of fun, and passed all their time in merry-making and enjoyment.

Now though the eldest son was, by his character, more adapted to make a wise and prudent sovereign, yet the two younger brothers, by their lively, engaging manner, had made themselves much more popular in the country. They were also the favourites of their father, but the eldest was the darling of his mother.

The king was old and stricken in years, and would gladly have given up the cares of government, and passed his declining years in peace, but he could not make up his mind to which of the brothers he should delegate his authority. The queen was persuaded of the excellent capacity of her eldest son, but the two younger were always saying he was half mad, and not fit to govern, and as they had the people on their side, he greatly feared lest the kingdom should be involved in civil war, so he always put off making any arrangement.

One day, however, an ancient counsellor observed to him, that if he really feared that there would be a dispute about the succession, it was much better to have it decided now while he was alive to act as umpire, than that it should happen when they would be left to wrangle with no one to make peace between them.

The king found the counsel good, and decided to retire from the government, and to proclaim his eldest son king in his stead. When the two younger sons, however, heard what he intended to do, they came to him and urged their old charge, that their elder brother was not fit to govern, and entreated the king to halve the kingdom between them. But the king, anxious as he was to gratify them, yet feared to displease the queen by committing so great an injustice against her eldest son, and thus they were no further advanced than before.

Then the old counsellor who had offered his advice before spoke again, and suggested that some task should be set for the three, and that whoever succeeded in that task should then be king beyond dispute.

The three sons all swore to abide by this decision, and the king found the counsel good. But now the difficulty arose, what should he set them to do? They had insisted so much on the weak intellect of the eldest, that the queen feared lest, after all, he should fail in the trial, and her care for him be defeated. She knew he had never practised himself in feats of strength, or in the pursuit of arms, so it was useless proposing such as these for the test, so she persuaded the king to set them something much simpler.

So, having called an assembly of all the people, he proclaimed aloud that the three brothers should travel for a year and a day, and whichever of them should bring him back the finest drinking-horn, he should be the king, and the three sons swore to abide by his award.

The two younger brothers set out with a great retinue, and, as they did not apprehend much difficulty in surpassing their brother in whatever they might undertake, they spent the greater part of the year in amusing themselves, secure in bringing back the best, whatever they might bring.

The eldest set out alone through the forest. In his lonely wanderings he had often observed a strangely beautiful castle on a far-off mountain, concerning which he could find no record in any of his books, nor could he learn that anyone living knew anything about it. He now resolved to make his way there, persuaded that if he was to find something surpassing the work of human hands, it was likely to be in this enchanted castle.

Though it was so high-placed, the way was much easier than he thought, and he was not more than five months getting there, so that he had ample time for exploring its precincts, and yet get back within the appointed date. He had, indeed, to traverse dark forests and steep rocky paths, but when he got near the castle all these difficulties ceased. Here there were only easy slopes of greensward, diapered by sparkling flowers, broad-leaved trees throwing delicious shade, and rills that meandered with a pleasant music. Delicious bowers and arcades of foliage of sweet-scented plants invited to repose, and everywhere luscious fruits hung temptingly within reach. Birds sang on every branch with a soft, dreamy melody which soothed, and disturbed not the lightest slumber.

The prince thought it would have been delightful to pass the remainder of his days there, but he remembered that it was an important mission with which he was entrusted, and he passed on.

A broad flight of marble steps led from these amenities up to the palace, and every now and then a thousand little jets were turned on, to pour their tiny floods over them, and cool them for the tread of those who entered.

And yet no one was near, no one to enjoy all this magnificence! The prince entered the hall, but no one came to meet him. He passed through the long corridors, but all were deserted. He entered one apartment after another, but still no one came. At last he came to one charming boudoir all hung with pink satin, and lace, and beautiful flowers. On a pink satin sofa covered with lace sat a large Cat with soft grey fur, and soft grey eyes, the first living thing he had met!

As he entered, the Cat rose to meet him, walking on her hind-paws, and, holding out her right front-paw in the most gracious manner. The Cat asked him, in a sweet, clear voice, if there was anything she could do for him. Then, as if the effort was too great, she let herself down on all fours, and rubbed her soft grey head against his boots.

Finding her so friendly, he was going to take her up in his arms, but this she would not allow, and she sprang with an agile bound on to a ledge above his head. "And now tell me," said she, "what is it you want me to do for you?"

"Really, Lady Purrer, you are so kind, you confuse me! But, to tell you the truth, I fear…"

"You fear that a poor puss can't be of any use," interposed the Cat, smartly, "and that your requirements are much above her feeble comprehension. But never mind, tell me all the same, there is little doubt that I can help you, and if I can't, the telling me will do you no harm."

"Quite the contrary," replied the prince, "it will be a great pleasure to have your sympathy, for I am in great distress." Her voice was so sweet and kind, that he quite forgot it was only a Cat he was talking to.

"Poor prince!" said the Cat, soothingly. "Tell me all about it, then. But stop, I'll tell you first what I think. I'm sure you are not appreciated at home. I saw it in your look when you first came in. You don't look bright and enterprising, as you ought to look. You look as if you lived too much alone. Oh, you would be twice as handsome if you only looked a little livelier and more energetic..." and then she stopped short, and sneezed a great many times, as if she feared she had said what was not quite proper, and some other sound would efface that of her words.

"There is a great deal of truth in what you say," replied the prince. "They don't care much about me at home, at least my mother does, but my father and brothers don't. And I do live too much alone, but it's not my fault. It's a bad way of mine, and I don't know how to get out of it."

"You want someone to pet you, and spoil you, and make you very happy, and then you would be pleased to go into the society of others, because then you could say to yourself, I'll show them that there's someone who understands me and makes a fuss about me..." and she stopped short, as before.

"But who should care to spoil and pet me?" cried the prince, despondingly, and too much interested in her words to see any reason why she should be confused at what she had said.

"Why, a nice little wife, to be sure!" replied the Cat.

"A wife!" exclaimed the prince. "Oh yes, my father's grey-bearded counsellors will find me some damsel whom it is necessary I should marry for the peace of the kingdom, and to her I shall be tied, and, be she an idiot or a shrew, I shall have no voice in the matter."

"But do you mean to say," retorted the Cat, in a more excited voice, "that if you found a nice little princess, and I don't mean anyone they could with justice object to, but a real princess, who cared very much for you, and made you very happy, very happy indeed, so that you determined to marry her, that you wouldn't be man enough to say to your father and all his counsellors, 'Here is the princess I mean to make my wife. I feel Heaven intended her for me. I am sure she will be the joy of my people, as she is mine, and no other shall share my throne'?"

"Wouldn't I," exclaimed the prince, with energy, starting to his feet, and placing his hand instinctively on his sword, his eye flashing and the colour mounting in his cheek.

"Ah! If you always looked like that! Now, you are handsome indeed!" exclaimed the Cat, enthusiastically, and purred away. "But," she added, immediately after, "all this time you haven't told me what it was you came for."

"Ah!" said the prince, despondingly, at finding himself thus recalled to the prosaic realities of his melancholy life from that brief dream of happiness. "No, because you have been talking to me of more interesting things" (the Cat purred audibly), and then he told her what it was had really brought him there.

"You see, your mother understands your character better than all the rest," said the Cat. "She knew you could be trusted to prove your superiority over your brothers, though the others hope you may fail. However, fail you won't this time, for I can give you a drinking-horn which neither your brothers nor anyone else on earth can match!"

With that she sprang lightly on to the soft carpet, and ran out of the room, beckoning to him to follow her. She led him through a long suite of rooms till they came to a large dining-hall all panelled with oak and filled with dark carved-oak furniture. In the centre of one end of this hall, high up in the panelling, was an inlaid safe or tabernacle curiously wrought. Puss gave one of her agile springs on to the top of this cabinet, and, having opened its folding-doors gently with her paw, disclosed to view a drinking-horn such as the prince had never seen. It was a white semi-transparent horn, but close-grained, like ivory, and all finely carved with designs of curious invention. The dresses of the figures were all made of precious stones cunningly let in, and they sparkled with a vivid lustre, like so many lamps. Then it had a rim, stand, and handle of massive gold exquisitely chased, and adorned with rows of pearls and diamonds.

"Kind Lady Purrer," exclaimed the prince, "you are right, there is no doubt of my success! But how can I ever sufficiently thank you for what you have done for me? For I owe all to you."

"And a little to your own discernment too," said the Cat, archly. "And now, always look as much alive and as bright as you do now, and you will see people will think better of you."

"But when shall I see you again, most sweet counsellor? May I come back and see you again?" pleaded the prince, and he tried to stroke her sleek fur as she rubbed her soft grey head, purring, against his boots. The stroking, however, she would by no means allow, but springing again on to the top of the cabinet, she said, "Oh, yes, it will not be long before you will have to come back to me, I know. But go, now. You have spent more time here than you think, and you have only just enough left to get back within the year."

The prince turned to obey her, and the Cat jumped down, and ran by his side, purring. When he got out into the grounds again, she followed him, climbing from tree to tree, and when he came to the boundary-wall she ran all along on the coping. But here at last they had to part, to her great regret, and for many a lonely mile he still heard her low and plaintive mew.

It was true, he must have spent more time in her pleasant company than he had thought, for when he reached home he found the day of trial had arrived. The streets were deserted, and all the people gathered in the palace to see the drinking-horns his brothers had brought, and talking loudly of their magnificence. He passed through their midst without being recognized, for the people knew him so little, and thus he heard them speak of his younger brothers, "What bright faces they have, and what a merry laugh! It does the heart good to hear them," said one.

"I wonder how the kingdom will be divided, and which half will be to which of them," said another.

"For my part, I don't care to the lot of which I fall, for both are excellent good fellows," replied a third.

And thus they had clearly settled in their own mind that his brothers had carried the day, and they didn't even trouble themselves to think what he would bring, or whether he would come back at all. It was the same thing all the way along. The words were varied, but the same idea prevailed everywhere, and that the younger brothers had made good their claim there was no question at all. The prince's face was growing moody again, but just then one good woman, wiping the soap-suds from her hands as she turned from her washing at the river to join the throng, exclaimed, as she heard some neighbours talking thus, "Hoity toity! it's all very well with you and your laughing princes. A grave one for me, say I! Laughing may lead a man to throw away his money, but it won't teach him to feed the poor, or govern a kingdom. Wait till the Grave Prince comes back! I'll warrant he'll bring the bravest drinking-horn!"

A chorus of mocking laughter greeted her defence of him.

"He bring the bravest drinking-horn!" said one.

"Don't believe he knows what a drinking-horn is for, or drink either!" said another.

"No, his brothers understand that best, at all events. I like a man who can drink his glass."

"And I like one who doesn't drink it, whether he can or not, but keeps his head clear for his business," said the good wife who had defended him before.

And as there were a good many who were too fond of the bottle in the crowd, the laugh raised at him was turned against them.

He had one defender, then, in all that mass of people, but all the rest judged him incapable, and without trial! He was too disheartened, to make his way into the great hall where the success of his brothers was being proclaimed, but instead trod sadly and secretly up to his mother's chamber.

The queen was too distressed at the absence of her favourite son to take part in the jocular scene below, and was seated, full of anxiety, at her window, watching.

"What are you doing here, my son?" she exclaimed, when he entered, "you have but one short half-hour more, and the time will be expired. The sun is already gone down, and the time once past, whatever you have brought, it will avail you not! Haste, my son, to the council-hall!"

"It is useless, mother. Everyone is against me!" cried the prince, and he laid the beautiful flagon on the table, and sank upon a chair.

In the meantime it had grown dark, but the queen, impelled by her curiosity to know what success her son had had, pulled off the wrapper that enclosed the drinking-horn, and instantly the apartment was brilliantly lighted by the light of the precious stones with which it was studded!

"My son, this is a priceless work! This is worth a kingdom! Nothing your brothers can have brought can compare with this. Haste, then, my son!" and she led him along.

It was dark in the council-hall too, but when the queen had dragged her son up to the throne where the king sat, she uncovered the flagon, and the sparkling stones sent their radiance into every part.

Then there was one shout loud of praise. The drinking-horns of the younger brothers, which had anon been so highly extolled, were no more thought of, and everyone admitted that the Grave Prince had won the trial.

The king declared it was too late for any more business that night, the proclamation of the new sovereign would be made the next morning, and in the meantime they all retired to rest, the Grave Prince with some new sensations of satisfaction and hope, and the queen assured of the triumph of her son.

But in the silent night, when all were wrapt in slumber, and the king could not sleep for the anxiety and perplexity which beset him as to his successor, the two young brothers came to him and complained that they had been circumvented. The Grave Prince had always shown himself so gloomy and unenergetic, it was impossible they could conceive he was going to distinguish himself, so they had taken no trouble to beat him, but if their father would but allow another trial, they would undertake he should not have the advantage of them again.

So the next day, instead of proclaiming the new sovereign, the king announced that he had determined there should be a fresh trial of skill, and whichever of the princes should bring him the best hunting-whip, that day year, should have the crown.

The princes set off next day on their travels once more, the eldest son of course directing his towards the castle of the Beneficent Cat.

This time he did not have to traverse a file of deserted halls before meeting her, for she sat looking out for him on the coping of the wall where he had left her mewing so piteously when he last parted from her.

"I told you it would not be long before you would have to come back to me," she said, as he approached. "What can I do for you this time?"

"My brothers are discontented at being beaten with your beautiful beaker," replied the prince, gallantly, "and they have demanded another trial. This time my father sends us in quest of a hunting-whip."

"A hunting-whip?" echoed the Cat. "That is lucky, for I can suit you with one neither they nor anyone else on this earth can surpass!" and she frisked merrily along the path before him till they came to the stables, then she took him into a room where all manner of saddles, and horse-gear, and hunting-horns were stored. But on a high ledge, at the very top of the room, was a dusty hunting-whip of the most unpretending appearance. With one of her bold springs she reached the ledge, and jumped down again with this whip in her mouth.

"It is not much to look at, I admit," she said, as she observed the perplexed look with which the prince surveyed the present, "but its excellent qualities are its recommendation. You have but to crack this whip, and your horse will take anything you put him at, be it a river half a mile wide, or a tree fifty feet high. There are plenty of horses in the stable, saddle any of them you like, and make experience of it for yourself."

The prince did as she bid him, and at the sound of the enchanted whip his mount leapt with equal ease over hills and valleys.

"This is a whip indeed!" exclaimed the prince, his face flushed with the unwonted exercise, and his heart beating high at the idea of being the bearer of such a prize.

"Ah, that's how I like to see you!" said the friendly puss, "I like to see you like that. Now you are handsome indeed!" and she scampered away, as if coyly ashamed of what she had said.

It was not long before she returned, and then she invited the prince into the next room, where an elegant dinner was laid out, of which the Cat did the honours very demurely. A high divan was arranged at the top of the table, on which she reclined, and ate and lapped alternately out of the plates ready before her, while invisible attendants served the viands and filled the glasses.

When they had finished their meal, they went out to repose in the flowery bowers, and when the heat of the day was past, the Beneficent Cat reminded her guest that he must be thinking of going home, if he did not want his brothers to supplant him.

"Must I go so soon, sweet Lady Purrer?" replied the prince. "I know not how to part from you. It seems I should be happy if I were always with you. I have never felt so happy anywhere before!"

"You are very gallant, prince," responded the Cat, "and you have no idea how well it becomes you to look as you do now, but the affairs of your kingdom must be your first thought. You must first secure your succession, and then we must look out for the nice little wife we talked of last time."

"Ah," sighed the Grave Prince, "don't talk of that. That is not for me! No one beautiful enough for me to care about will ever care for me!"

"Not if you look desponding and gloomy, like that," replied the Cat. "Do you know, you look quite like another being when you look so gloomy, and yet you can be so handsome when you look bright and hopeful! But now," she proceeded, laying her soft paw on his arm to arrest the futile justification which rose to his lips, "before you go, I have something very important to tell you. You will now go back, and with the hunting-whip I have given you, you are safe to win the trial which is to establish your right to the kingdom. But there will be yet another trial exacted of you, and you will have to come back again to me. What you are to do then, I must tell you now, for it requires great prudence and courage, and one principal thing is, that you don't say a word to me all the time. Can you promise that?"

"Well, that is hard indeed," said the prince, "but still, if you command it, I think I can promise to obey, for the sake of pleasing you."

"Then the next thing is harder. Do you think you can do whatever I command?"

"Oh yes, I am sure I can promise that!" replied the prince, warmly.

"Mind, whatever I command, then, however hard, or however dreadful it may be?"

"Yes, anything, however hard, or however dreadful!"

"But will you swear it?"

"I see you doubt my courage," said the prince, half offended. "You take me for a fool, like the rest. But no wonder; I know I look like a fool!"

"Now don't look gloomy again! You were so handsome just now when you said so firmly you would do anything. Will you gratify me by swearing?"

"You doubt my courage."

"No, I don't doubt your courage. But I know how terrible a thing I have to command you, and I know how many others have failed before you. Now will you not swear, but to please me?"

"Yes, I swear," said the prince, energetically, "to do whatever it may be that you tell me to do."

"Now, remember, you have undertaken it solemnly. This is what you must do. When you come in, you will find me sitting on the kitchen stove. You must then seize me by my two hind-paws, and dash me upon the hearthstone till there is nothing left of me in your hands, but the fur!"

"Oh dear! I can never do that!" exclaimed the prince, in great embarrassment.

"But you have sworn to do whatever I told you!" replied the Cat.

"Well, but I thought you were going to order me to do something rational, something noble and manly, requiring courage and strength, not a horrible act like this."

"If it is the thing that has to be done, it does not matter what it is. Besides, it does require courage, great courage, and that is why I would not tell you first what it was, because others have failed when they knew what it was."

"And you expect me to have less feeling and affection for you than they?"

"No, but I expect more sense and judgment of you. I expect you to understand and believe that if I say it has to be done, it is really for the best, and that you will trust to me that it is right. And I expect that you will respect your promise, which was made without limit or exception. But now, go. You have no time to lose, if you want to reach home with the hunting-whip in time for the trial."

He rose to leave, and she followed him down the path, purring by his side. And after she had taken leave of him at the boundary-wall, he heard her mewing sad adieus as he went on for many a weary mile.

When the prince reached the council-hall, he found, as before, that his brothers were there first, and that everyone seemed to have decided that they had won the day. In fact no one showed any curiosity to know what he would bring. As he had beaten the other princes by his lustrous jewels before, they had fancied he would bring something of the same sort again, so, to conquer him on his own ground, they had sought out and found two handles of hunting-whips mounted with jewels as sparkling as those of his drinking-horn. When they saw him come in with the shabby old whip the Beneficent Cat had given him, they laughed outright in his face, and the king, in a fit of indignation, ordered him to leave the hall for venturing to insult him by bringing such a present. Some laughed him to scorn, and some abused him, but no one would listen to a word he had to say. At last the tumult was so great that it reached the queen's ears, and when she had learnt what was the matter, she insisted that he should have a hearing allowed him.

When silence had been proclaimed the Grave Prince said, "It is true, my whip is not so splendid as that of my brothers, but jewels are out of place on a hunting-whip, it seems to me. The handle needs to be smooth, so that the hand may take a firm grip of it, rather than to be covered with those points and unevennesses. The merit of my whip is not in the handle, it is in the lash, which has such excellent qualities, that you have but to crack it, and your horse will immediately take you over any obstruction there may be in your way, be it a house or a mountain, or what you will. If you allow me, I will give you proof of its powers."

Then they all adjourned to the terrace in front of the council-hall, where there was a fine avenue of lofty cypresses, and the queen ordered a horse to be brought round from the stables. The people had never seen the prince on horseback before, and when they saw him looking so gallant, and noble, and determined, they could not forbear cheering him, till his younger brothers began to fear that his real worth would soon be found out, and their malice exposed.

Then the prince cracked his whip, and away went the horse over the tops of the high trees, seeming to scrape the clouds as he passed. All the people were lost in admiration, for no one had ever seen such a sight before, and while they were wondering whether it was possible he could have reached the ground in safety from such a height, there was a murmur in the air, and they saw him coming back again over the tree-tops. With no more apparent effort than if he had merely taken a hedge, he came softly to the ground, and then, kneeling gracefully before his father on one knee, without a word of boasting or reproach, he laid the clever whip at his feet.

The king raised him up, and said, aloud to the people that none could deny that it was this whip that had won the trial, but that as it was now late, he must leave the ceremony of proclaiming his successor till the morrow.

All went home for the night, and the old king also went to bed, but he could not sleep for anxiety, thinking of the anger and dissatisfaction of his younger sons. And presently, in the silent hour, they came to him, and said that he must allow them another trial, that it was impossible they could conceive he meant them to bring him a fantastical whip of that sort, or of course they would have brought one which could do much better things. They thought it was the beauty of the workmanship they had to look to, and so they had provided for nothing else. They urged their suit so persistently, that the king, who was now very old and weak, agreed to let them have their way.

Accordingly, next morning he had it proclaimed that the three princes were to make one trial more, and that whichever brought back the most beautiful and virtuous princess for his wife should have the crown.

The three princes set out again early the next morning. The two younger ones provided themselves with jewels and riches, and many precious things for presents, while the eldest took nothing, but walked off alone towards the enchanted castle with a heavy heart.

"It is all up with me now," he said to himself, "after all! Why couldn't my father have been satisfied when I had beaten them twice? Now I have to kill the Beneficent Cat, the only being that ever assisted me, and then I shall have no one to help me at all! They will come back with two beautiful princesses, and I shall come back looking like a fool, because no princess will ever come with me, and they will take my kingdom, and laugh at me into the bargain! If it was not for my mother, I would never come back at all, but it would break her heart if I stayed away, and she is the only one of them who understands me and cares for me."

As he got nearer the castle, he grew more and more sad. "Why did she make me swear? If it hadn't been for that, I could still have escaped doing it, but now I cannot break my oath," and he trudged on.

The gardens looked more lovely than ever. The scent of the flowers seemed sweeter, and the melody of the birds more soothing. All was full of harmony, and he who had never harmed a fly must cruelly use the soft and beautiful Cat who had so befriended him!

He passed through the apartments where puss had purred round him so happily, the dining-room where they had had their pleasant repast together. the boudoir where she had given him such wise counsel. At last he came to the kitchen, and there, sure enough, was the Cat cosily curled round, her soft grey head buried in her long grey fur.

An energy and daring he had never known before seemed suddenly to possess him. He took care not to speak, for she had particularly recommended silence, but, approaching her on tiptoe, seized her rapidly by her hind-paws before she had time to wake from her pleasant slumber, and dashed her several times upon the hearth, scarcely knowing what he did in his horror, till he perceived that he had nothing left in his hand but the soft, limp, grey fur.

He sank upon the ground in tears, and commenced laying it out tenderly before him, when he was woken from his reverie by a mellow ringing laugh, which made him look up, and there before him stood the most beautiful, fairy-like princess that ever was seen on this earth!

"Well done, kind prince! You have nobly kept your word. And see what I have gained thereby. Instead of that grey fur, I now have a form which will perhaps make me worthy to fulfil the condition your father has imposed on you for obtaining your throne!"

Her voice, and the glance of her soft eyes, seemed quite familiar to him. It was the voice which had first inspired him with hope and enterprise, and the mild light which had beamed on him when he said he could be happy to be always near her in her bower. How much more now, when she appeared in such matchless guise!

He remained kneeling at her feet, and asked her if it was indeed true that she could love him and be with him always as his wife.

"No," she replied, raising him up, "it is I who ought to be astonished. I have nothing to refuse, for I owe you all, and as, but for you, I should still be nothing but a poor grey Cat, I belong to you, and am absolutely yours. It is I who have to be astonished, and to ask you if it is possible you who have known me as a Cat can really love me and regard me as worthy to be indeed your wife."

"You are mocking me again, I see," he replied, "but you do not really think me so insensible as not to appreciate your beauty, and the prudence and generosity of which you have given me such abundant proof? No, if you will come with me, I have no fear but that I shall win the trial this time beyond all possibility of demanding another." He spoke warmly, and his face beamed with joy. The princess was leaning on his arm, and looked up in his face as he spoke.

"Ah, now you do look... No, I suppose I mustn't say it now I no longer have my cat-disguise to hide my blushes," she said, archly, and they passed on into the reception-hall.

The attendants were no longer invisible. Together with their mistress they had received their forms and original life, and the corridors and apartments were filled with her people bustling to serve her. A banquet was prepared in the dining-hall, and when they had partaken of it, and had regaled themselves in the bower with happy talk, the princess reminded the prince, now no longer grave, that it was time for them to be going back to his father. A great train of carriages and horses were brought round, with mounted guards and running-footmen, and all the retinue which became a noble princess.

The princess was carried in a litter by six men in embroidered liveries, and her ladies with her, and the prince rode on horseback, close by her side.

This time, though it was near the close of the last day, his brothers had not appeared when he reached the council-hall. The king and the queen received the Beneficent Princess with smiles and admiration, and all the people praised her beauty, and the queen said, "There is no fear, my son, that your brothers can demand another trial this time."

Before she had done speaking, a messenger was hastily ushered into the hall, covered with dust and stains of travel. He came from the two younger princes, and had a sorrowful tale to tell.

They had striven to obtain the hands of the princesses of the neighbouring kingdom, but the king was a prudent sovereign, and discerned their envious, selfish character. When they found he repulsed their advances, they had endeavoured to carry off the princesses by force, but the king had surprised them in the midst of their design, and had had them shut up as midnight robbers.

The old king was in great distress when he heard the news, for his sons had manifestly been taken in the midst of wrong-doing, and he could not defend their acts nor avenge their shame. But the eldest son took on himself the mission of pacifying the neighbouring sovereign and delivering his brothers. Having accomplished this task, the princes were fain to acknowledge that he was not only victor in the trials, but their deliverer also, and they swore to maintain peace with him, and obey him as his faithful subjects.

So the old king proclaimed the Grave Prince for his successor, and married him to the Beneficent Princess, amid great rejoicing of all the people, and the queen had the happiness of seeing her eldest son acknowledged as the most prudent prince, and the ruler of the people, and gifted with a beautiful and devoted wife.

Cat Tails – Feline Fairy Tales, Myths And Legends

How The Manx Cat Lost Her Tail

This is a Manx tale

This tale has been adapted from Manx Fairy Tales by Sophia Morrison. The book was published in 1911 by David Nutt, London. Sophia Morrison was a prominent Manx cultural activist, folklorist, and writer. The book contains a selection of fairy tales, folk stories, and legends from the Isle of Man, an island located in the Irish Sea between England and Ireland. The tales encompass a wide range of themes, including mythical creatures, heroic deeds, magical encounters, and moral lessons, offering readers a glimpse into the unique folklore and storytelling traditions of the Manx people.

When Noah was calling the animals into the Ark, there was one cat who was out mousing and took no notice when he was calling to her. She was a good mouser, but this time she had trouble finding a mouse and she took a notion that she wouldn't go into the Ark without one.

So at last, when Noah had all the animals safe inside, and he saw the rain beginning to fall, and no sign of her coming in, he said, "Who's out is out, and who's in is in!"

And with that he was just closing the door when the cat came running up, half drowned—that's why cats hate the water—and just squeezed in, in time. But Noah had slammed the door as she ran in and it cut off her tail, so she got in without it, and that is why Manx cats have no tails to this day.

That cat said:

Bee bo bend it,
My tail's ended,
And I'll go to Mann
And get copper nails,
And mend it.

The Colony Of Cats

This is an Italian tale

This tale has been adapted from The Book Of Heroes by Andrew Lang. The book was published in 1909 by Longman, Green And Company, London. Lang was a Scottish poet, novelist, literary critic, and contributor to the field of anthropology. Lang is perhaps best known for his "Fairy Books" series, which includes collections of fairy tales from around the world.

Long, long ago, as far back as the time when animals spoke, there lived a community of cats in a deserted house they had taken possession of not far from a large town. They had everything they could possibly desire for their comfort, they were well fed and well lodged, and if by any chance an unlucky mouse was stupid enough to venture in their way, they caught it, not to eat it, but for the pure pleasure of catching it.

The old people of the town related how they had heard their parents speak of a time when the whole country was so overrun with rats and mice that there was not so much as a grain of corn nor an ear of maize to be gathered in the fields, and it might be out of gratitude to the cats who had rid the country of these plagues that their descendants were allowed to live in peace. No one knows where they got the money to pay for everything, nor who paid it, for all this happened so very long ago. But one thing is certain, they were rich enough to keep a servant, for though they lived very happily together, and did not scratch nor fight more than human beings would have done, they were not clever enough to do the housework themselves, and preferred at all events to have someone to cook their meat, which they would have scorned to eat raw.

Not only were they very difficult to please about the housework, but most women quickly tired of living alone with only cats for companions, consequently they never kept a servant long, and it had become a saying in the town, when anyone found herself reduced to her last penny: 'I will go and live with the cats,' and so many a poor woman actually did.

Now Lizina was not happy at home, for her mother, who was a widow, was much fonder of her elder daughter; so that often the younger one fared very badly, and had not enough to eat, while the elder could have everything she desired, and if Lizina dared to complain she was certain to have a good beating.

At last the day came when she was at the end of her courage and patience, and exclaimed to her mother and sister, "As you hate me so much you will be glad to be rid of me, so I am going to live with the cats!"

"Be off with you!" cried her mother, seizing an old broom-handle from behind the door. Poor Lizina did not wait to be told twice, but ran off at once and never stopped till she reached the door of the cats' house. Their cook had left them that very morning, with her face all scratched, the result of such a quarrel with the head of the house that he had very nearly scratched out her eyes. Lizina therefore was warmly welcomed, and she set to work at once to prepare the dinner, not without many misgivings as to the tastes of the cats, and whether she would be able to satisfy them.

Going to and fro about her work, she found herself frequently hindered by a constant succession of cats who appeared one after another in the kitchen to inspect the new servant. She had one in front of her feet, another perched on the back of her chair while she peeled the vegetables, a third sat on the table beside her, and five or six others prowled about among the pots and pans on the shelves against the wall. The air resounded with their purring, which meant that they were pleased with their new maid, but Lizina had not yet learned to understand their language, and often she did not know what they wanted her to do. However, as she was a good, kind-hearted girl, she set to work to pick up the little kittens which tumbled about on the floor, she patched up quarrels, and nursed on her lap a big tabby, the oldest of the community, which had a lame paw.

All these kindnesses could hardly fail to make a favourable impression on the cats, and it was even better after a while, when she had had time to grow accustomed to their strange ways. Never had the house been kept so clean, the meats so well served, nor the sick cats so well cared for. After a time they had a visit from an old cat, whom they called their father, who lived by himself in a barn at the top of the hill, and came down from time to time to inspect the little colony. He too was much taken with Lizina, and inquired, on first seeing her, "Are you well served by this nice, black-eyed little person?"

The cats answered with one voice, "Oh, yes, Father Gatto, we have never had so good a servant!"

At each of his visits the answer was always the same, but after a time the old cat, who was very observant, noticed that the little maid had grown to look sadder and sadder. "What is the matter, my child? Has anyone been unkind to you?" he asked one day, when he found her crying in her kitchen.

She burst into tears and answered between her sobs, "Oh, no! They are all very good to me, but I long for news from home, and I pine to see my mother and my sister."

Old Gatto, being a sensible old cat, understood the little servant's feelings. "You shall go home," he said, "and you shall not come back here unless you please. But first you must be rewarded for all your kind services to my children. Follow me down into the inner cellar, where you have never yet been, for I always keep it locked and carry the key away with me."

Lizina looked round her in astonishment as they went down into the great vaulted cellar underneath the kitchen. Before her stood the big earthenware water jars, one of which contained oil, the other a liquid shining like gold.

"In which of these jars shall I dip you?" asked Father Gatto, with a grin that showed all his sharp white teeth, while his moustaches stood out straight on either side of his face.

The little maid looked at the two jars from under her long dark lashes. "In the oil jar," she answered timidly, thinking to herself, 'I could not ask to be bathed in gold.'

But Father Gatto replied, "No, no, you have deserved something better than that." And seizing her in his strong paws he plunged her into the liquid gold.

Wonder of wonders! When Lizina came out of the jar she shone from head to foot like the sun in the heavens on a fine summer's day. Her pretty pink cheeks and long black hair alone kept their natural colour, otherwise she had become like a statue of pure gold. Father Gatto purred loudly with satisfaction. "Go home," he said, "and see your mother and sisters, but take care if you hear the cock crow to turn towards it. If on the contrary the ass brays, you must look the other way."

The little maid, having gratefully kissed the white paw of the old cat, set off for home, but just as she got near her mother's house the cock crowed, and quickly she turned towards it. Immediately a beautiful golden star appeared on her forehead, crowning her glossy black hair. At the same time the ass began to bray, but Lizina took care not to look over the fence into the field where the donkey was feeding. Her mother and sister, who were in front of their house, uttered cries of admiration and astonishment when they saw her, and their cries became still louder when Lizina, taking her handkerchief from her pocket, drew out also a handful of gold.

For some days the mother and her two daughters lived very happily together, for Lizina had given them everything she had brought away except her golden clothing, for that would not come off, in spite of all the efforts of her sister, who was madly jealous of her good fortune. The golden star, too, could not be removed from her forehead. But all the gold pieces she drew from her pockets had found their way to her mother and sister.

"I will go now and see what I can get out of the pussies," said Peppina, the elder girl, one morning, as she took Lizina's basket and fastened her pockets into her own skirt. "I should like some of the cats' gold for myself," she thought, as she left her mother's house before the sun rose.

The cat colony had not yet taken another servant, for they knew they could never get one to replace Lizina, whose loss they had not yet ceased to mourn. When they heard that Peppina was her sister, they all ran to meet her. "She is not the least like her," the kittens whispered among themselves.

"Hush, be quiet!" the older cats said, "all servants cannot be pretty."

No, decidedly she was not at all like Lizina. Even the most reasonable and large-minded of the cats soon acknowledged that.

The very first day she shut the kitchen door in the face of the tom-cats who used to enjoy watching Lizina at her work, and a young and mischievous cat who jumped in by the open kitchen window and alighted on the table got such a blow with the rolling-pin that he squalled for an hour.

With every day that passed the household became more and more aware of its misfortune.

The work was as badly done as the servant was surly and disagreeable. In the corners of the rooms there were collected heaps of dust, and spiders' webs hung from the ceilings and in front of the window-panes. The beds were hardly ever made, and the feather beds, so beloved by the old and feeble cats, had never once been shaken since Lizina left the house. At Father Gatto's next visit he found the whole colony in a state of uproar.

"Caesar has one paw so badly swollen that it looks as if it were broken," said one. "Peppina kicked him with her great wooden shoes on. Hector has an abscess in his back where a wooden chair was flung at him, and Agrippina's three little kittens have died of hunger beside their mother, because Peppina forgot them in their basket up in the attic. There is no putting up with the creature! Do send her away, Father Gatto! Lizina herself would not be angry with us, she must know very well what her sister is like."

"Come here," said Father Gatto, in his most severe tones to Peppina. And he took her down into the cellar and showed her the same two great jars that he had showed Lizina. "In which of these shall I dip you?" he asked.

Peppina made haste to answer, "In the liquid gold," for she was no more modest than she was good and kind.

Father Gatto's yellow eyes darted fire. "You have not deserved it," he uttered, in a voice like thunder, and seizing her he flung her into the jar of oil, where she was nearly suffocated. When she came to the surface screaming and struggling, the vengeful cat seized her again and rolled her in the ash-heap on the floor, then when she rose, dirty, blinded, and disgusting to behold, he thrust her from the door, saying, "Begone, and when you meet a braying ass be careful to turn your head towards it."

Stumbling and raging, Peppina set off for home, thinking herself fortunate to find a stick by the wayside with which to support herself. She was within sight of her mother's house when she heard in the meadow on the right, the voice of a donkey loudly braying. Quickly she turned her head towards it, and at the same time put her hand up to her forehead, where, waving like a plume, was a donkey's tail.

She ran home to her mother at the top of her speed, yelling with rage and despair, and it took Lizina two hours with a big basin of hot water and two cakes of soap to get rid of the layer of ashes with which Father Gatto had adorned her. As for the donkey's tail, it was impossible to get rid of that, for it was as firmly fixed on her forehead as was the golden star on Lizina's. Their mother was furious. She first beat Lizina unmercifully with the broom, then she took her to the mouth of the well and lowered her into it, leaving her at the bottom weeping and crying for help.

Before this happened, however, the king's son in passing the mother's house had seen Lizina sitting sewing in the parlour, and had been dazzled by her beauty. After coming back two or three times, he at last ventured to approach the window and to whisper in the softest voice, "Lovely maiden, will you be my bride?" and she had answered, "I will."

Next morning, when the prince arrived to claim his bride, he found her wrapped in a large white veil. "This is how maidens are received from their parents' hands," said the mother, who hoped to make the king's son marry Peppina in place of her sister, and had fastened the donkey's tail round her head like a lock of hair under the veil. The prince was young and a little timid, so he made no objections, and seated Peppina in the carriage beside him.

Their way led past the old house inhabited by the cats, who were all at the window, for the report had got about that the prince was going to marry the most beautiful maiden in the world, on whose forehead shone a golden star, and they knew that this could only be their adored Lizina.

As the carriage slowly passed in front of the old house, where cats from all parts of world seemed to be gathered a song burst from every throat:

Mew, mew, mew!

Prince, look quick behind you!

In the well is fair Lizina,

And you've got nothing but Peppina.

When he heard this the coachman, who understood the cat's language better than the prince, his master, stopped his horses and asked, "Does your highness know what the grimalkins are saying?" Then the song broke forth again louder than ever.

With a turn of his hand the prince threw back the veil, and discovered the puffed-up, swollen face of Peppina, with the donkey's tail twisted round her head.

"Ah, traitress!" he exclaimed, and ordering the horses to be turned round, he drove the elder daughter, quivering with rage, to the old woman who had sought to deceive him. With his hand on the hilt of his sword he demanded Lizina in so terrific a voice that the mother hastened to the well to draw her prisoner out. Lizina's clothing and her star shone so brilliantly that when the prince led her home to the king, his father, the whole palace was lit up. Next day they were married, and lived happy ever after, and all the cats, headed by old Father Gatto, were present at the wedding.

Cat Tails – Feline Fairy Tales, Myths And Legends

Mikko The Fox And Mirri The Cat

This is a Finnish tale

This tale has been adapted from Mighty Mikko by Parker Fillmore. The book was published in 1922 by Harcourt, Brace And Company, New York. The story of Mighty Mikko is one of the most popular Finnish folk tales, featuring a clever and resourceful protagonist who outwits his adversaries through wit and cunning.

One day while Mikko the fox was out walking in the forest he met a stranger.

"Good day," he said. "Who are you?"

"I am Mirri," the stranger said, "a poor unfortunate cat out of employment. I had service in a decent family but I've had to leave them."

"Did they treat you badly?" the fox asked.

"No, it wasn't that. They were considerate enough but they kept getting poorer and poorer until finally they hadn't food enough to feed us animals. Then I overheard the master say that soon they'd be forced to eat us and that they'd begin with me. At that I decided it was time for me to run away and here I am."

"My poor Cat," Mikko said, "you've had a cruel experience! Why don't you take service with me?"

"Will I be safe with you?" the cat asked. "Will you protect me?"

"Will I?" the fox repeated boastfully. "My dear Mirri, once it becomes known that you are Mikko's servant all the animals will show you a wholesome respect."

"Well then, I'll enter your service," the cat said.

So the bargain was struck and Mikko at once began to train his new servant.

"Now, Mirri, tell me, what would you do if you suddenly met a Bear?"

"There's just one thing I could do, master: I'd run up a tree."

Mikko laughed.

"You must have more ways than one to meet such a situation! Take me now. There are any of a hundred things that I could do if I met a Bear!"

Just then Osmo, the bear, ambled softly up behind the fox. The cat saw him and instantly flew up a tree. Before Mikko could move Osmo clutched him firmly on the shoulder with his teeth.

"Oh, master, master!" the cat called down from the tree. "What's this? I with my one way have escaped and you with your hundred are caught!"

But Mikko paid no heed to the cat. He twisted his head around and looked reproachfully at the bear.

"Why, Osmo, my dear old friend!" he said, "What in the world do you mean taking hold of me so roughly! Ouch! You're nipping my shoulder, really you are! I don't understand why you're acting this way! Here I've always been such a good friend to you, so faithful, so true, so…"

"What!" rumbled Osmo. "Faithful! True! Oh, you…"

Osmo's feelings overcame him to such an extent that he opened his jaws to roar out freely his denial of Mikko's hypocrisy.

That gave Mikko just the chance he wanted. He jerked quickly away and fled and the bear was left standing with his mouth wide open.

Later when Osmo had ambled off Mikko returned and called the Mirri down from the tree.

"You see, Mirri," he remarked casually, "it wasn't anything at all for me to get the best of the bear!"

He could see that he had vastly impressed Mirri, so he let the subject drop. "Come along, Mirri," he said, "it's time for us to go home."

Cat Tails – Feline Fairy Tales, Myths And Legends

The Crow And Cat Of Hopkins Hill

This is an American tale

This tale is my adaptation of an original from Myths & Legends of Our Own Land: Vol 4 by Charles M. Skinner. The book was published in 1896 by J.P. Lippincott Co., Philadelphia. Myths & Legends of Our Own Land: Vol 4 is a collection of folk tales, myths, legends, and supernatural stories from various regions of the United States. It is part of a larger series of books compiled by Charles M. Skinner, an American author and folklorist, and was published in the late 19th and early 20th centuries.

In a forest near Hopkins Hill, Rhode Island, there is a boulder, four feet in diameter, marked with a peculiar groove. This boulder, known as Witch Rock, got its name two centuries ago when an old woman lived in an abandoned cabin nearby, making the forest feared by the locals. Shadowy figures were seen moving through the trees, items left outside in nearby settlements disappeared overnight despite the absence of tramps, cattle were stricken with strange diseases, stones were mysteriously thrown through windows, crops were ruined by hail and frost, and during storms, the old woman was seen emerging from the woods, seemingly pushing the clouds with her broom.

To this day, the ground within a hundred yards of Witch Rock remains cursed, and any attempt to cultivate it fails. Nearly a century ago, a sceptic named Reynolds proclaimed he would plough through this enchanted area. His neighbours watched from a safe distance. Initially, he made progress, but when he reached the cursed boundary, the plough veered off, and the wooden chip on the plough fell off. After reattaching it, he tried again, but the oxen unyoked themselves, and the chip flew off out of sight.

At this point, most of the onlookers retreated home. Suddenly, a crow flew in from the north, perched on a dead tree, and cawed. John Hopkins, the landowner, shouted at the bird, calling it "Pat Jenkins." The crow then dropped the chip at Reynolds's feet and transformed into an old witch wearing a cocked hat, who descended upon the rock. Before the men could reach her, she changed into a black cat and vanished into the ground. Despite their efforts to hunt and dig, the pursuers found nothing, and one of them inadvertently created the groove in the rock with a strike from his shovel.

After this incident, few people dared to go near the area, and it became overgrown with weeds, trees, and bushes.

The Lion And The Cat

This is a First Nations tale from America

This tale has been adapted from The Brown Fairy Book by Andrew Lang. The book was published in 1904 by Longman, Green And Company, London. Lang was a Scottish poet, novelist, literary critic, and contributor to the field of anthropology. Lang is perhaps best known for his "Fairy Books" series, which includes collections of fairy tales from around the world. The original of this tale was first told as a traditional First Nations tale in North America.

Far away on the other side of the world there lived, long ago, a lion and his younger brother, the wild cat, who were so fond of each other that they shared the same hut. The lion was much the bigger and stronger of the two - indeed, he was much bigger and stronger than any of the beasts that dwelt in the forest, and, besides, he could jump farther and run faster than all the rest. If strength and swiftness could gain him a dinner he was sure never to be without one, but when it came to cunning, both the grizzly bear and the serpent could get the better of him, and he was forced to call in the help of the wild cat.

Now the young wild cat had a lovely golden ball, so beautiful that you could hardly look at it except through a piece of smoked glass, and he kept it hidden in the thick fur muff that went round his neck. A very large old animal, since dead, had given it to him when he was hardly more than a baby, and had told him never to part with it, for as long as he kept it no harm could ever come near him.

In general the wild cat did not need to use his ball, for the lion was fond of hunting, and could kill all the food that they needed, but now and then his life would have been in danger had it not been for the golden ball.

*

One day the two brothers started to hunt at daybreak, but as the cat could not run nearly as fast as the lion, he had quite a long start. At least he thought it was a long one, but in a very few bounds and springs the lion reached his side.

"There is a bear sitting on that tree," he whispered softly. "He is only waiting for us to pass, to drop down on my back."

"Ah, you are so big that he does not see I am behind you," answered the wild cat. And, touching the ball, he just said, "Bear, die!" And the bear tumbled dead out of the tree, and rolled over just in front of them.

For some time they trotted on without any adventures, till just as they were about to cross a strip of long grass on the edge of the forest, the lion's quick ears detected a faint rustling noise.

"That is a snake," he cried, stopping short, for he was much more afraid of snakes than of bears.

"Oh, it is all right," answered the cat. "Snake, die!" And the snake died, and the two brothers skinned it. They then folded the skin up into a very small parcel, and the cat tucked it into his mane, for snakes' skins can do all sorts of wonderful things, if you are lucky enough to have one of them.

All this time they had had no dinner, for the snake's flesh was not nice, and the lion did not like eating bear, perhaps because he never felt sure that the bear was really dead, and would not jump up alive when his enemy went near him. Most people are afraid of something, and bears and serpents were the only creatures that caused the lion's heart to tremble. So the two brothers set off again and soon reached the side of a hill where some fine deer were grazing.

"Kill one of those deer for your own dinner," said the boy-brother, "but catch me another alive. I want him."

The lion at once sprang towards them with a loud roar, but the deer bounded away, and they were all three soon lost to sight. The cat waited for a long while, but finding that the lion did not return, went back to the house where they lived.

It was quite dark when the lion came home, where his brother was sitting curled up in one corner.

"Did you catch the deer for me?" asked the boy-brother, springing up.

"Well, no," replied the man-brother. "The fact is, that I did not get up to them till we had run halfway across the world and left the wind far behind us. Think what a trouble it would have been to drag it here! So, I just ate them both."

The cat said nothing, but he did not feel that he loved his big brother. He had thought a great deal about that deer, and had meant to get on his back to ride him as a horse, and go to see all the wonderful places the lion talked to him about when he was in a good temper. The more he thought of it the sulkier he grew, and in the morning, when the lion said that it was time for them to start to hunt, the cat told him that he might kill the bear and snake by himself, as he had a headache, and would rather stay at home. The little fellow knew quite well that the lion would not dare to go out without him and his ball for fear of meeting a bear or a snake.

The quarrel went on, and for many days neither of the brothers spoke to each other, and what made them still more cross was, that they could get very little to eat, and we know that people are often cross when they are hungry. At last it occurred to the lion that if he could only steal the magic ball he could kill bears and snakes for himself, and then the cat might be as sulky as he liked for anything that it would matter. But how was the stealing to be done? The cat had the ball hung round his neck day and night, and he was such a light sleeper that it was useless to think of taking it while he slept. No! The only thing was to get him to lend it of his own accord, and after some days the lion (who was not at all clever) hit upon a plan that he thought would do.

"Dear me, how dull it is here!" said the lion one afternoon, when the rain was pouring down in such torrents that, however sharp your eyes or your nose might be, you could not spy a single bird or beast among the bushes. "Dear me, how dull, how dreadfully dull I am. Couldn't we have a game of catch with that golden ball of yours?"

"I don't care about playing catch, it does not amuse me," answered the cat, who was as cross as ever, for no cat, even to this day, ever forgets an injury done to him.

"Well, then, lend me the ball for a little, and I will play by myself," replied the lion, stretching out a paw as he spoke.

"You can't play in the rain, and if you did, you would only lose it in the bushes," said the cat.

"Oh, no, I won't. I will play in here. Don't be so ill-natured."

And with a very bad grace the cat untied the string and threw the golden ball into the lion's lap, and composed himself to sleep again.

For a long while the lion tossed it up and down gaily, feeling that, however sound asleep the boy-brother might look, he was sure to have one eye open, but gradually he began to edge closer to the opening, and at last gave such a toss that the ball went up high into the air, and he could not see what became of it.

"Oh, how stupid of me!" he cried, as the cat sprang up angrily, "let us go at once and search for it. It can't really have fallen very far." But though they searched that day and the next, and the next after that, they never found it, because it never came down.

After the loss of his ball the cat refused to live with the lion any longer, but wandered away to the north, always hoping he might meet with his ball again. But months passed, and years passed, and though he travelled over hundreds of miles, he never saw any traces of it.

At length, when he was getting quite old, he came to a place unlike any that he had ever seen before, where a big river rolled right to the foot of some high mountains. The ground all about the riverbank was damp and marshy, and as no cat likes to wet its feet, this one climbed a tree that rose high above the water, and thought sadly of his lost ball, which would have helped him out of this horrible place. Suddenly he saw a beautiful ball, for all the world like his own, dangling from a branch of the tree he was on. He longed to get at it, but was the branch strong enough to bear his weight? It was no use, after all he had done, getting drowned in the water. However, it could do no harm, if he was to go a little way. He could always manage to get back somehow.

So he stretched himself at full length upon the branch, and wriggled his body cautiously along. To his delight it seemed thick and stout. Another movement, and, by stretching out his paw, he would be able to draw the string towards him, when the branch gave a loud crack, and the cat made haste to wriggle himself back the way he had come.

But when cats make up their minds to do anything they generally do it, and this cat began to look about to see if there was really no way of getting at his ball. Yes, there was, and it was much surer than the other, though rather more difficult. Above the bough where the ball hung was another bough much thicker, which he knew could not break with his weight, and by holding on tight to this with all his four paws he could just manage to touch the ball with his tail. He would thus be able to whisk the ball to and fro till, by-and-by, the string would become quite loose, and it would fall to the ground. It might take some time, but the lion's little brother was patient, like most cats.

Well, it all happened just as the cat intended it should, and when the ball dropped on the ground the cat ran down the tree like lightning, and, picking it up, tucked it away in the snake's skin round his neck. Then he began jumping along the shore of the Big Water from one place to another, trying to find a boat, or even a log of wood, that would take him across. But there was nothing. Then, on the other side, he saw two girls cooking, and though he shouted to them at the top of his voice, they were too far off to hear what he said. And, what was worse, the ball suddenly fell out of its snake's skin bag right into the river.

Now, it is not at all an uncommon thing for balls to tumble into rivers, but in that case they generally either fall to the bottom and stay there, or else bob about on the top of the water close to where they first touched it. But this ball, instead of doing either of these things, went straight across to the other side, and there one of the girls saw it when she stooped to dip some water into her pail.

"Oh! what a lovely ball!" cried she, and tried to catch it in her pail, but the ball always kept bobbing just out of her reach.

"Come and help me!" she called to her sister, and after a long while they had the ball safe inside the pail. They were delighted with their new toy, and one or the other held it in her hand till bedtime came, and then it was a long time before they could make up their minds where it would be safest for the night. At last they locked it in a cupboard in one corner of their room, and as there was no hole anywhere the ball could not possibly get out. After that they went to sleep.

In the morning the first thing they both did was to run to the cupboard and unlock it, but when the door opened they started back, for, instead of the ball, there stood a handsome young man.

"Ladies," he said, "how can I thank you for what you have done for me? Long, long ago, I was enchanted by a wicked fairy, and condemned to keep the shape of a ball till I should meet with two maidens, who would take me to their own home. But where was I to meet them? For hundreds of years I have lived in the depths of the forest, where nothing but wild beasts ever came, and it was only when the lion threw me into the sky that I was able to fall to earth near this river. Where there is a river, sooner or later people will come; so, hanging myself on a tree, I watched and waited. For a moment I lost heart when I fell once more into the hands of my old master the wild cat, but my hopes rose again as I saw he was making for the riverbank opposite where you were standing. That was my chance, and I took it. And now, ladies, I have only to say that, if ever I can do anything to help you, go to the top of that high mountain and knock three times at the iron door at the north side, and I will come to you."

So, with a low bow, he vanished from before them, leaving the maidens weeping at having lost in one moment both the ball and the prince.

Dinah Cat And The Witch

This is a Manx tale

This tale has been adapted from Abbie Phillips Walker's book, The Sandman's Hour: Stories for Bedtime, published by Harper & Brothers Publishers, London & New York, in 1917. "Dinah Cat and the Witch" is a traditional folk tale from the Isle of Man, a place known for its rich mythological heritage. The tale is a part of the island's collection of stories that often involve magical creatures, supernatural events, and clever animals.

Once upon a time there was a little girl named Betty. She was an orphan, and a bad landlord turned her out of her home. The only friend she had was a black cat named Dinah. Betty was crying as she walked along the road, and Dinah Cat ran beside her, rubbing against her feet. All at once she ran in front of Betty and stood on her hind legs.

"Do not cry, mistress," she said. "I'll take care of you."

Betty was so surprised to hear Dinah Cat speak that she stopped crying at once. "You poor Dinah Cat," she said, "what can you do? We must go to the city, and if I can find work we shall be able to live. If not, you must take care of yourself, for you can catch mice and keep from starving."

"You come with me, mistress," answered Dinah Cat, "and you will not need to work and you will not starve."

And she put out her paw for Betty to take and walked alongside her. When they came to a path leading into the wood Dinah Cat led Betty along this path until they were in front of two very large trees which had grown together, but there was a big opening in the trunk.

"We'll go in here," said Dinah Cat, and as they stepped through they were in a hall. She led Betty up the stairs to a room where there was a snowy-white bed and pretty furnishings. "Dinner will be served as soon as you are dressed, mistress," said Dinah Cat.

After she had gone Betty looked around, and in the closets she found pretty dresses which just fitted her. She put on one of them, and in a few minutes she was ready for dinner. Just then she heard a soft, scratching noise at the door, and when she opened it Dinah Cat walked in.

"How do you like your new home, mistress?" she asked.

"Very much," Betty answered. "But we cannot live in such a nice house. We have no money, and, besides that, this house must belong to someone. And this dress I have on must belong to some little girl. I should not wear it."

"The dress did belong to a little girl," said Dinah Cat, "but she cannot wear it now, and she wants you to have it. And do not fret about the house. It belongs to me. I cannot tell you any more just now, but you need not worry any more about anything, for you are to live here, if you wish, after you have dinner, for then you will meet a boy, and you may not like him."

Dinah Cat led Betty into a room where the table was set for three persons, and when they were seated a boy about Betty's age came in and sat with them. He wore his hat, and a thick veil hung from it.

"I am sorry I cannot remove my hat," he said, in a very sweet voice, "and I will go away if you'd rather I would."

"Oh no," said Betty, feeling very much like an intruder. "I am very grateful to you for letting me stay, and I will help to do the work."

"You do not need to work," said the boy. "If you will stay we will be very glad."

Betty did not once get a glimpse of his face, he lifted the veil so carefully. And there sat Dinah Cat, using her knife and fork like any lady. Betty smiled to herself when she thought of her eating from a saucer.

Suddenly Dinah Cat slid out of her chair and crawled under it, and the little boy trembled so that his chair shook. Betty looked around to find the cause of their strange behaviour, and saw standing in the doorway an old woman with a staff in her hand. She hobbled over to where Dinah Cat sat and raised the staff. Betty thought she was going to strike her.

"Don't you hurt Dinah Cat!" she cried, running toward the old witch, who was so startled that she dropped the staff, and Betty picked it up.

"Don't let her have it again," said the boy. "That is the cause of all our trouble."

Betty threw the staff in a closet and locked the door. All this time the witch was stepping backward toward the door by which she entered, and she grew smaller with each step. By the time she was out of the house she looked like a black speck, and a breeze blowing just then carried her out of sight. "But how shall we ever be ourselves again?" said the boy. "She has gone, and here we are, in this state."

"Perhaps the stick will do it," said Dinah Cat.

Betty wondered what they meant, and the boy told her that Dinah Cat was his sister before the witch changed her into a cat, and made his face so hideous that he had to wear a veil, and they had lived very happily together. "But one day the old witch came and wanted to live with us, and we let her for a while, but she was so cross and made us so unhappy we told her she must go away. Then she brought all this change upon us, and every once in a while she returns and frightens us, for we do not know what she will change us into next."

"Let me get the stick," said Betty. "Perhaps we can change Dinah Cat to your sister again."

Betty opened the door of the closet, and instead of the stick there was a bright streak of light, and walking on it was a little Fairy who held a wand in her hand.

"You will soon be happy again," she told them. "I have destroyed the stick and the old witch will never return."

Then she walked over to Dinah Cat and touched her with her wand and there stood a little girl about Betty's age in place of the black cat.

"Now close your eyes," said the Fairy, "for I want the boy to remove his veil, and his face is not pleasant to look upon."

Betty did as the Fairy told her, but I am sorry to tell you that she peeked a very little. Betty closed her eyes tight after the first glimpse and waited for the Fairy to tell her to open them again, and when she did there stood the boy with a very smiling face. His sister ran to him and put her arms around him.

"Now we shall be happy," she said, "and Betty will live with us. How can we thank you?" she asked the Fairy.

"Oh, I shall be repaid by seeing you all happy," the Fairy replied. "And now I must go."

"Will we see you again?" asked Betty.

"No," answered the Fairy. "I only appear when people are in trouble, and you will never need me again."

Cat Tails – Feline Fairy Tales, Myths And Legends

The Cat On The Dovrefell

This is a Scandinavian tale – very similar to a later tale in this book, The Cat Of Norrhult

This tale has been adapted from Popular Tales From The Norse by George Webbe Dasent. The book was published in 1856 by George Routledge and Sons, London. The book features a selection of traditional folk tales, myths, and legends from Scandinavia, including stories from Norse mythology and popular folklore. These tales include iconic characters such as gods, giants, trolls, elves, and other mythical beings, as well as ordinary heroes and heroines embarking on fantastical adventures.

Once on a time there was a man up in Finnmark who had caught a great white bear, which he was going to take to the king of Denmark. Now, it so fell out, that he came to the Dovrefell just about Christmas Eve, and there he turned into a cottage where a man lived, whose name was Halvor, and asked the man if he could get house-room there, for his bear and himself.

"Heaven never help me, if what I say isn't true!" said the man, "but we can't give any one house-room just now, for every Christmas Eve such a pack of Trolls come down upon us, that we are forced to flit, and haven't so much as a house over our own heads, to say nothing of lending one to anyone else."

"Oh?" said the man, "if that's all, you can very well lend me your house; my bear can lie under the stove yonder, and I can sleep in the side-room."

Well, he begged so hard, that he got leave to stay there; so the people of the house flitted out, and before they went, everything was got ready for the Trolls; the tables were laid, and there was rice porridge, and fish boiled in lye, and sausages, and all else that was good, just as for any other grand feast.

So, when everything was ready, down came the Trolls. Some were great, and some were small. Some had long tails, and some had no tails at all. Some, too, had long, long noses, and they ate and drank, and tasted everything. Just then one of the little Trolls caught sight of the white bear, who lay under the stove, so he took a piece of sausage and stuck it on a fork, and went and poked it up against the bear's nose, screaming out, "Pussy, will you have some sausage?"

Then the white bear rose up and growled, and hunted the whole pack of them out of doors, both great and small.

Next year Halvor was out in the wood, on the afternoon of Christmas Eve, cutting wood before the holidays, for he thought the Trolls would come again, and just as he was hard at work, he heard a voice in the wood calling out, "Halvor! Halvor!"

"Well", said Halvor, "here I am."

"Have you got your big cat with you still?"

"Yes, that I have", said Halvor, "she's lying at home under the stove, and what's more, she has now got seven kittens, far bigger and fiercer than she is herself."

"Oh, then, we'll never come to see you again", bawled out the Troll away in the wood, and he kept his word, for since that time the Trolls have never eaten their Christmas brose with Halvor on the Dovrefell.

Why Do Cats And Dogs Fight? #1

This is a Romanian tale

This tale has been adapted from Rumanian Bird and Beast Stories translated by Moses Gaster. The book was published in 1915 by Sidgwick & Jackson, Ltd., London. The book features a variety of folk tales from Romania that centre around birds and beasts, including both domestic and wild animals. These stories often anthropomorphize animals, imbuing them with human-like qualities, emotions, and behaviours. The tales explore themes such as friendship, loyalty, cunning, and bravery, offering readers insight into Romanian folklore and cultural values.

In the beginning there was no enmity between the cat and dog, and they lived on friendly terms together and served their master (Adam) faithfully, each one doing its own work. But as you know, it is very much better to have a written agreement at the beginning than to have a row afterwards, so they decided to draw up an agreement defining the work which each had to do, and decided that the dog was to do the work outside the house, and the cat the work inside. For greater safety the dog agreed that the cat should take care of the agreement, and the cat put it in the loft.

After a time, the devil, who could not allow peace to last for a long time, must needs set the dog up against the cat, so one day the dog remarked to the cat that he was not fairly treated, he did not see why he should have all the trouble outside the house, to watch for thieves and protect the house and suffer from cold and rain, and only have scraps and bones for food, and sometimes nothing at all, whilst the cat had all the comfort, purring and enjoying herself, and living near the hearth in warmth and safety.

The cat said, "An agreement is an agreement."

The dog replied, "Let me see that agreement." The cat went quickly up the loft to fetch the agreement, but the agreement, which had been a little greasy, had been nibbled by the mice who were living in the loft, and they went on nibbling away until nothing was left of it but a heap of paper fluff, and as it was as soft as down the mice made their home of it. When the cat came up and saw what the mice had done, her fury knew no bounds, she pursued them madly, killing as many as she could seize, and running after the others with the intent of catching them.

When she came down the dog asked her for the agreement, and as the cat had not brought it, the dog, taking hold of her, shook her until he got tired of shaking her.

Since that time, whenever a dog meets a cat he asks her for the agreement, and as she cannot show it to him he goes for her, and the cat, knowing what the mice had done to her, runs after them when she sees them.

Why Do Cats And Dogs Fight? #2

This is a Slavonic tale

In South Slavonic folk-lore (Krauss, No. 18) there is a parallel to the previous story, but greatly changed from the original form. It is no longer a "creation" legend. It runs as follows:

The dogs used to receive all the meat that fell off the table. This became a habit, and so he and the cat drew up a statement to that effect, and made it a permanent rule. They wrote it on the hide of an ass, and the king of the dogs gave it to the cat, his first chancellor, to take care of it.

The cat hid it away in the rafters of the house. There the skin was found by the mice, who nibbled it until there was scarcely anything left.

One day a dog got badly beaten because he picked up some meat that had fallen from the table. He went and complained to the king, who sent the cat to find the document. The cat could not find it, and saw that the mice had eaten it. Since then there is a continual feud between the cat, the mice and the dog.

Cat Tails – Feline Fairy Tales, Myths And Legends

The Bear, The Dog, And The Cat

This is a Russian tale

This tale has been adapted from Russian Folk-Tales by Aleksander Nikolaevich. The book was published in 1915 by Kegan Paul, Trench, Trubner & Co, Ltd. Aleksander Nikolaevich spent several decades traveling throughout Russia, collecting and recording folk tales from oral tradition. He amassed a vast collection of stories, which he meticulously organized and annotated in his published volumes of Russian Folk-Tales.

Once there lived a peasant who had a good dog, and as the dog grew old it left off barking and guarding the yard and the storehouses. Then its master would no longer nourish it, so the dog went into the wood and lay under a tree to die.

Then a bear came up and asked him, "Hello, Dog, why are you lying here?"

"I have come to die of hunger. You see how unjust people are. As long as you have any strength, they feed you and give you drink, but when your strength dies away and you become old they drive you from the courtyard."

"Well, Dog, would you like something to eat?"

"I certainly should."

"Well, come with me, and I will feed you."

So they went on.

On the way a foal met them.

"Look at me," said the bear, and he began to claw the ground with his paws. "Dog, O dog!"

"What do you want?"

"Look, are my eyes beautiful?"

"Yes, Bear, they are beautiful."

So the bear began clawing at the ground more savagely still. "Dog, O dog, is my hair dishevelled?"

"It is dishevelled, Bear."

"Dog, O dog, is my tail raised?"

"Yes, it is raised."

Then the bear laid hold of the foal by the tail, and the foal fell to the ground. The bear tore her to pieces and said, "Well, Dog, eat as much as you will, and when everything is in order, come and see me."

So the dog lived by himself and had no cares, and when he had eaten all and was again hungry, he ran up to the bear.

"Well, my brother, have you done?"

"Yes, I have done, and again I am hungry."

"What! Are you hungry again? Do you know where your old mistress lives?"

"I do."

"Well, then, come, for I will steal your mistress's child out of the cradle, and then you must chase me away and take the child back. Then you may go back, and she will go on feeding you, as she formerly did, with bread."

So they agreed, and the bear ran up to the hut and stole the child out of the cradle. The child cried, and the woman burst out, and hunted and hunted him, but could not catch him, so they came back, and the mother wept with the other women. Then from somewhere or other the dog appeared, and he drove the bear away, took the child and brought it back.

"Look," said the woman, "it's your old dog and your child!"

So they ran to meet him, and the mother was very glad and joyous. "Now," she said, "I shall never mistreat this old dog."

So they took him in, fed him with milk, gave him bread, and asked him only to taste the things. And they told the peasant, "Now you must keep and feed the dog, for he saved my child from the bear, and you were saying he had no strength!"

This all suited the dog very well, and he ate his fill, and he said, "May God grant health to the bear who did not let me die of hunger!" and he became the bear's best friend.

*

Once there was an evening party given at the peasant's house. At that time the bear came in as the dog's guest. "Hail, Dog, with what luck are you meeting? Is it bread you are eating?"

"Praise be to God," answered the dog, "it is no mere living, it is butter week. And what are you doing? Let us go into the izbá (log cabin). The masters have gone out for a walk and will not see what you are doing. You come into the izbá and go and hide under the stove as fast as you can. I will await you there and will call you."

"Very well."

And so they went into the izbá. The dog saw that his master's guests had drunk too much, and made ready to receive his friend. The bear drank up one glass, then another, and broke it. The guests began singing songs, and the bear wanted to chime in. But the dog persuaded him, saying, "Do not sing, it would only do harm."

But it was no good, for he could not keep the bear silent, and he began singing his song. Then the guests heard the noise, laid hold sticks and began to beat him. He burst out and ran away, and just got away with his life.

Now the peasant also had a cat, which had ceased catching mice, and even playing tricks. Wherever it might crawl it would break something or spill something. The peasant chased the cat out of the house. But the dog saw that it was going to a miserable life without any food, and secretly began bringing it bread and butter and feeding it. Then the mistress looked on, and as soon as she saw this she began beating the dog, beating it hard, very hard, and saying all the time, "Give the cat no beef, nor bread."

Then, three days later, the dog went to the courtyard and saw that the cat was dying of starvation. "What is the matter?" he said.

"I am dying of starvation. I was able to have enough whilst you were feeding me."

"Come with me."

So they went away. The dog went on, until he saw a drove of horses, and he began to scratch the earth with his paws and asked the cat, "Cat, O cat, are my eyes beautiful?"

"No, they are not beautiful."

"Say that they are beautiful!"

So the cat said, "They are beautiful."

"Cat, O cat, is my fur dishevelled?"

"No it is not dishevelled."

"Say, you idiot, that it is dishevelled."

"Well, it is dishevelled."

"Cat, O cat, is my tail raised?"

"No, it is not raised."

"Say, you fool, that it is raised." Then the dog made a dash at a mare, but the mare kicked him back, and the dog died.

So the cat said, "Now I can see that his eyes are very red, and his fur is dishevelled, and his tail is raised. Good-bye, brother Dog, I will go home to die."

The Tigers And The Cat

This is a tale from India

This tale has been adapted from Folklore Of The Santal Parganas by Cecil Henry Bompas. The book was published in 1909 by The Indian Civil Service. Folklore of the Santal Parganas is a seminal work on the folklore and ethnography of the Santal people. The Santal Parganas is a region in eastern India, primarily inhabited by the Santal ethnic group, known for their distinct cultural traditions, including folklore, rituals, and oral literature.

In former days tigers and cats were friends and used to hunt together and share the game they caught, and they did not eat the game raw but used to cook it as men do.

One day some tigers and a cat had killed a deer and they had no fire with which to cook it. Then the tigers said to the cat "You are small, go and beg a light from yonder village."

But the cat said that he was afraid to go, however they urged him saying "You have a thin tail and plump feet, so you can bring it in a trice."

So, as they all insisted on his going, he at last consented, and said "Well, I will go, but don't expect me to be very quick. If I get a good opportunity for fetching the fire, I will come back soon."

The tigers said, "All right, go and run off with a small fire-brand and we will meet you outside the village."

So the cat went off and coming to a house, went inside to pull a firebrand from the hearth. On the fire some milk was boiling, and the cat thought "This smells very nice, I will have a taste of it" and he found it so nice that he made up his mind to drink it all, before he took away the fire-brand.

But in order to lap the milk he had to put his feet on the fireplace, and it was so hot that he burnt his feet and had to get down, so then he sat down and waited till the fire went out and the hearth grew cool, and then he lapped up the milk and ran off with a piece of smouldering wood.

Meanwhile the tigers had got tired of waiting and had eaten the deer raw, and they were very angry at being made to eat raw flesh and swore that they would eat the cat too. When they saw the cat bringing the fire they ran to meet him and abused him and cried out "You have made us eat raw flesh. We will eat you too, dung and all"

On hearing this threat the cat ran back to the village in fear of his life, and the tigers followed in pursuit, but when they got near the village, the village dogs all ran out barking and the tigers were frightened and turned back and the cat was saved.

From that day tigers and leopards have eaten raw flesh, and cats bury their excrement, because of what the tigers had said.

Every day the tigers went to the village in search of the cat, but when the dogs barked they slunk away, for the tigers were very frightened at the sight of the dogs' curly tails. They thought that the tails were nooses and that they would be strangled by them.

One day one of the tigers met a jackal and called to him "Nephew, listen to me. A cat made us eat raw flesh and has escaped into this village and I want to catch it, but the dogs come barking at me. I don't mind that, but I am very frightened of their nooses. Now, you are very like a dog, can you go and tell them not to use their nooses."

The jackal answered, "Uncle, you are quite mistaken; what you see are their tails, not nooses; they will not strangle you with them."

So the tiger took courage and the next day went to the village to hunt for the cat, but he could not find it. And when the dogs barked he got angry and caught and killed one of them, and from that time tigers and leopards eat dogs.

Cat Tails – Feline Fairy Tales, Myths And Legends

The Greedy Cat

This is a Scandinavian tale

This tale has been adapted from Tales From The Fjeld by Peter Christen Asbjørnsen. The book was published in 1908 by G. P. Putnam's Sons, New York. Tales From The Fjeld is a collection of Norwegian folk tales, legends, and fairy tales compiled and edited by Peter Christen Asbjørnsen, in collaboration with Jørgen Moe. Asbjørnsen and Moe are known for their pioneering work in collecting and preserving Norwegian folklore during the 19th century.

Once on a time there was a man who had a cat, and she was so awfully big, and such a beast when it came to eating, that he couldn't keep her any longer. So she was to go down to the river with a stone round her neck, but before she started she was to have a meal of meat. So the man's wife set before the cat a bowl of porridge and a little trough of fat, which the cat gobbled down, and ran off and jumped through the window. Outside stood the good man by the barn door, threshing.

"Good day, good man," said the cat.

"Good day, pussy," said the good man, "have you had any food today?"

"Oh, I've had a little, but I'm really fasting," said the cat. "It was only a bowl of porridge and a trough of fat - and, now I think of it, I'll take you too," and so she took the good man and gobbled him up.

When she had done that, she went into the byre, and there sat the man's wife milking.

"Good day, goody," said the cat.

"Good day, pussy," said the man's wife, "are you here, and have you eaten up your food yet?"

"Oh, I've eaten a little today, but I'm really fasting," said pussy, "it was only a bowl of porridge, and a trough of fat, and the good man - and, now I think of it, I'll take you too," and so she took the man's wife and gobbled her up.

"Good day, you cow at the manger," said the cat to Daisy the cow.

"Good day, pussy," said the bell-cow, "have you had any food today?"

"Oh, I've had a little, but I'm really fasting," said the cat, "I've only had a bowl of porridge, and a trough of fat, and the good man, and his wife - and, now I think of it, I'll take you too," and so she took the cow and gobbled her up.

Then off she set up into the home-field, and there stood a man picking up leaves.

"Good day, you leaf-picker in the field," said the cat.

"Good day, pussy; have you had anything to eat today?" said the leaf-picker.

"Oh, I've had a little, but I'm really fasting," said the cat. "It was only a bowl of porridge, and a trough of fat, and the good man and his wife, and Daisy the cow - and, now I think of it, I'll take you too." So she took the leaf-picker and gobbled him up.

Then she came to a heap of stones, and there stood a stoat and peeped out.

"Good day, Mr. Stoat of Stoneheap," said the cat.

"Good day, Mrs. Pussy; have you had anything to eat today?"

"Oh, I've had a little, but I'm really fasting," said the cat. "It was only a bowl of porridge, and a trough of fat, and the good man, and his wife, and the cow, and the leaf-picker - and, now I think of it, I'll take you too." So she took the stoat and gobbled him up.

When she had gone a bit farther, she came to a hazel-brake, and there sat a squirrel gathering nuts.

"Good day, Sir Squirrel of the Brake," said the cat.

"Good day, Mrs. Pussy; have you had anything to eat today?"

"Oh, I've had a little, but I'm really fasting," said the cat. "It was only a bowl of porridge, and a trough of fat, and the good man, and his wife, and the cow, and the leaf-picker, and the stoat - and, now I think of it, I'll take you too." So she took the squirrel and gobbled him up.

When she had gone a little farther, she saw Reynard the Fox, who was prowling about by the woods.

"Good day, Reynard Slyboots," said the cat.

"Good day, Mrs. Pussy; have you had anything to eat today?"

"Oh, I've had a little, but I'm really fasting," said the cat. "It was only a bowl of porridge, and a trough of fat, and the good man, and his wife, and the cow, and the leaf-picker, and the stoat, and the squirrel - and, now I think of it, I'll take you too." So she took Reynard and gobbled him up.

When she had gone a while farther she met Long Ears the Hare.

"Good day, Mr. Hopper the Hare," said the cat.

"Good day, Mrs. Pussy; have you had anything to eat today?"

"Oh, I've had a little, but I'm really fasting," said the cat. "It was only a bowl of porridge, and a trough of fat, and the good man, and his wife, and the cow, and the leaf-picker, and the stoat, and the squirrel, and the fox - and, now I think of it, I'll take you too." So she took the hare and gobbled him up.

When she had gone a bit farther, she met a wolf.

"Good day, you Greedy Greylegs," said the cat.

"Good day, Mrs. Pussy; have you had anything to eat today?"

"Oh, I've had a little, but I'm really fasting," said the cat. "It was only a bowl of porridge, and a trough of fat, and the good man, and his wife, and the cow, and the leaf-picker, and the stoat, and the squirrel, and the fox and the hare - and, now I think of it, I may as well take you too." So she took and gobbled up Greylegs too.

So she went on into the wood, and when she had gone far and farther than far, over hill and dale, she met a bear-cub.

"Good day, you bare-breeched Bear," said the cat.

"Good day, Mrs. Pussy," said the bear-cub, "have you had anything to eat today?"

"Oh, I've had a little, but I'm really fasting," said the cat. "It was only a bowl of porridge, and a trough of fat, and the good man, and his wife, and the cow, and the leaf-picker, and the stoat, and the squirrel, and the fox, and the hare, and the wolf - and, now I think of it, I may as well take you too," and so she took the bear-cub and gobbled him up.

When the cat had gone a bit farther, she met a she-bear, who was tearing away at a stump till the splinters flew, so angry was she at having lost her cub.

"Good day, you Mrs. Bruin," said the cat.

"Good day, Mrs. Pussy, have you had anything to eat today?"

"Oh, I've had a little, but I'm really fasting," said the cat. "It was only a bowl of porridge, and a trough of fat, and the good man, and his wife, and the cow, and the leaf-picker, and the stoat, and the squirrel, and the fox, and the hare, and the wolf, and the bear-cub - and, now I think of it, I'll take you too," and so she took Mrs. Bruin and gobbled her up too.

When the cat got still farther on, she met Baron Bruin himself.

"Good day, you Baron Bruin," said the cat.

"Good day, Mrs. Pussy," said Bruin, "have you had anything to eat today?"

"Oh, I've had a little, but I'm really fasting," said the cat. "It was only a bowl of porridge, and a trough of fat, and the good man, and his wife, and the cow, and the leaf-picker, and the stoat, and the squirrel, and the fox, and the hare, and the wolf, and the bear-cub, and the she-bear - and, now I think of it, I'll take you too," and so she took Bruin and ate him up too.

So the cat went on and on, and farther than far, till she came to the abodes of men again, and there she met a bridal train on the road.

"Good day, you bridal train on the king's highway," said she.

"Good day, Mrs. Pussy, have you had anything to eat today?"

"Oh, I've had a little, but I'm really fasting," said the cat. "It was only a bowl of porridge, and a trough of fat, and the good man, and his wife, and the cow, and the leaf-picker, and the stoat, and the squirrel, and the fox, and the hare, and the wolf, and the bear-cub, and the she-bear, and the he-bear - and, now I think of it, I'll take you too," and so she rushed at them, and gobbled up both the bride and bridegroom, and the whole train, with the cook and the fiddler, and the horses, and all.

When she had gone still farther, she came to a church, and there she met a funeral.

"Good day, you funeral train," said she.

"Good day, Mrs. Pussy, have you had anything to eat today?"

"Oh, I've had a little, but I'm really fasting," said the cat. "It was only a bowl of porridge, and a trough of fat, and the good man, and his wife, and the cow, and the leaf-picker, and the stoat, and the squirrel, and the fox, and the hare, and the wolf, and the bear-cub, and the she-bear, and the he-bear, and the bride and bridegroom and the whole train - and, now, I don't mind if I take you too," and so she fell on the funeral train and gobbled up both the body and the bearers.

Now when the cat had got the body in her, she was taken up to the sky, and when she had gone a long, long way, she met the moon.

"Good day, Mrs. Moon," said the cat.

"Good day, Mrs. Pussy, have you had anything to eat today?"

"Oh, I've had a little, but I'm really fasting," said the cat. "It was only a bowl of porridge, and a trough of fat, and the good man, and his wife, and the cow, and the leaf-picker, and the stoat, and the squirrel, and the fox, and the hare, and the wolf, and the bear-cub, and the she-bear, and the he-bear, and the bride and bridegroom and the whole train, and the funeral train - and, now I think of it, I don't mind if I take you too," and so she seized hold of the moon, and gobbled her up, both new and full.

So the cat went a long way still, and then she met the sun.

"Good day, you Sun in heaven."

"Good day, Mrs. Pussy," said the sun, "have you had anything to eat today?"

"Oh, I've had a little, but I'm really fasting," said the cat. "It was only a bowl of porridge, and a trough of fat, and the good man, and his wife, and the cow, and the leaf-picker, and the stoat, and the squirrel, and the fox, and the hare, and the wolf, and the bear-cub, and the she-bear, and the he-bear, and the bride and bridegroom, and the whole train, and the funeral train, and the moon - and, now I think of it, I don't mind if I take you too," and so she rushed at the sun in heaven and gobbled him up.

So the cat went far and farther than far, till she came to a bridge, and on it she met a big Billy goat.

"Good day, you Billy goat on Broad-bridge," said the cat.

"Good day, Mrs. Pussy, have you had anything to eat today?" said the Billy goat.

"Oh, I've had a little, but I'm really fasting. I've only had a bowl of porridge, and a trough of fat, and the good man, and his wife in the byre, and Daisy the cow at the manger, and the leaf-picker in the home-field, and Mr. Stoat of Stoneheap, and Sir Squirrel of the Brake, and Reynard Slyboots, and Mr. Hopper the Hare, and Greedy Greylegs the Wolf, and Bare-breech the Bear-cub, and Mrs. Bruin, and Baron Bruin, and a Bridal train on the king's highway, and a Funeral at the church, and Lady Moon in the sky, and Lord Sun in heaven, and, now I think of it, I'll take you too."

"That we'll fight about, said the Billy goat, and butted at the cat till she fell right over the bridge into the river, and there she burst.

So everyone and everything that the cat had gobbled up crept out one after the other, and were just as good as ever. The Goodman of the house, and his wife in the byre, and Daisy the cow at the manger, and the Leaf-picker in the home-field, and Mr. Stoat of Stoneheap, and Sir Squirrel of the Brake, and Reynard Slyboots, and Mr. Hopper the Hare, and Greedy Greylegs the Wolf, and Bare-breech the Bear-cub, and Mrs. Bruin, and Baron Bruin, and the Bridal train on the highway, and the Funeral train at the church, and Lady Moon in the Sky, and Lord Sun in heaven.

Story Of The Foolish Teacher, The Foolish Pupils, And The Cat

This is a Tale From India

This Tale has been adapted from Somadeva Bhatta's book, The Kathá Sarit Ságara, published by the Baptist Mission Press in 1884. "The Kathá Sarit Ságara" (translated as "The Ocean of the Streams of Stories") is a famous 11th-century collection of Indian legends, fairy tales, and folk tales.

In Ujjayiní there lived in a convent a foolish teacher. And he could not sleep, because mice troubled him at night. And wearied with this infliction, he told the whole story to a friend.

The friend, who was a Bráhman, said to that teacher, "You must set up a cat, for it will eat the mice."

The teacher said, "What sort of creature is a cat? Where can one be found? I never came across one."

When the teacher said this, the friend replied, "Its eyes are like glass, its colour is a brownish grey, it has a hairy skin on its back, and it wanders about in roads. So, my friend, you must quickly discover a cat by these signs and have one brought."

After his friend had said this, he went home.

Then that foolish teacher said to his pupils, "You have been present and heard all the distinguishing marks of a cat. So look about for a cat, such as you have heard described, in the roads here."

Accordingly the pupils went and searched hither and thither, but they did not find a cat anywhere.

Then at last they saw a Bráhman boy coming from the opening of a road, his eyes were like glass, his colour brownish grey, and he wore on his back a hairy antelope-skin. And when they saw him they said, "Here we have got the cat according to the description."

So they seized him, and took him to their teacher. Their teacher also observed that he had got the characteristics mentioned by his friend, so he placed him in the convent at night. And the silly boy himself believed that he was a cat, when he heard the description that those fools gave of the animal.

Now it happened that the silly boy was a pupil of that Bráhman, who out of friendship gave that teacher the description of the cat. And that Bráhman came in the morning, and, seeing the boy in the convent, said to those fools, "Who brought this fellow here?"

The teacher and his foolish pupils answered, "We brought him here as a cat, according to the description which we heard from you."

Then the Bráhman laughed and said, "There is considerable difference between a stupid human being, and a cat, which is an animal with four feet and a tail."

When the foolish fellows heard this, they let the boy go and said, "So let us go and search again for a cat such as has been now described to us."

And the people laughed at those fools, saying, "Ignorance makes everyone ridiculous."

The White Cat Of Ecija

This is a Spanish tale

This tale has been adapted from Tales from the Lands of Nuts and Grapes, Spanish and Portuguese Folklore by Charles Sellers. The book was published in 1888 by Swan Sonnenschein & Co., London. Charles Sellers travelled extensively throughout Spain and Portugal, collecting folk tales and legends from oral tradition. He sought out storytellers in rural communities, recording their stories and preserving them for future generations. Sellers' compilation includes a diverse array of narratives, showcasing the breadth and depth of Iberian folklore.

From the gates of the palace, situated on a gentle eminence in the vicinity of Ecija, down to the banks of the Genil, the ground was covered with olive-trees, and the wild aloes formed a natural and strong fence around the property of the White Cat of Ecija, whose origin, dating back to the days of Saracenic rule, was unknown to the liberated Spaniard.

There was a great mystery attaching to the palace and its occupants, and although the servants of the White Cat were to all appearances human beings, still, as they were deaf and dumb, and would not, or could not, understand signs, the neighbours had not been able to discover the secret or mystery.

The palace was a noble building, after the style of the Alcazar at Toledo, but not so large, and the garden at the rear was laid out with many small lakes, round which, at short distances, stood beautifully sculptured statues of young men and women, who seemed to be looking sorrowfully into the water. Only the brain and hand of an exceptionally gifted artist could have so approached perfection as to make the statues look as if alive. At night strings of small lamps were hung round the lakes, and from the interior of the palace proceeded strains of sweet, but very sad music.

Curiosity had long ceased to trouble the neighbours as to the mysterious White Cat and her household, and, with the exception of crossing themselves when they passed by the grounds, they had given up the affair as incomprehensible.

Those, however, who had seen the White Cat, said that she was a beautiful creature; her coat was like velvet, and her eyes were like pearls. One day a knight in armour, and mounted on a coal-black charger, arrived at the principal hostelry in Ecija, and on his shield he bore for his coat of arms a white cat rampant, and, underneath, the device, was written the word, 'Invincible.'

Having partaken of some slight repast, he put spurs to his horse and galloped in the direction of the palace of the White

Cat, but as he was not seen to return through the town, the people supposed that he had left by some other road. The White Cat was seen next day walking about in the grounds, but she seemed more sorrowful than usual.

In another month's time there came another knight fully equipped, and mounted on a grey charger. On his shield he also displayed a white cat, with the device, 'I win or die'. He also galloped off to the palace, or Alcazar, and was not seen to return, but next day the White Cat was still more sorrowful.

In another month a fresh knight appeared. He was a handsome youth, and his bearing was so manly that a crowd collected. He was fully equipped, but on his shield he displayed a simple red cross. He partook of some food, and then cantered out of the town with his lance at rest. He was seen to approach the palace, and as soon as he thrust open the gate with his lance, a terrific roar was heard, and then a sheet of fire flashed from the palace door, and they saw a horrid dragon, whose long tail, as it lashed the air, produced such a wind that it seemed as if a gale had suddenly sprung up.

But the gallant knight was not daunted, and eagerly scanned the dragon as if to see where he might strike him. Suddenly it was seen that the dragon held the White Cat under its talons, so that the Knight of the Cross in charging the dragon had to take care not to strike her. Spurring his horse on, he never pulled up till he had transfixed the dragon with his lance, and, jumping off the saddle, he drew his sword and cut off the monster's head.

No sooner had he done this than he was surrounded by ten enormous serpents, who tried to coil round him, but as fast as they attacked him, he strangled them. Then the serpents turned into twenty black vultures with fiery beaks, and they tried to pick out his eyes, but with his trusty blade he kept them off, and one by one he killed them all, and then found himself surrounded by forty dark-haired and dark-eyed lovely maidens, who would have thrown their arms around him, but that he, fearing their intentions were evil, kept them off. Then, looking on the ground, he saw the White Cat panting, and heard her bid him "strike."

He waited no longer, but struck at them and cut off their heads, and then saw that the ground was covered with burning coal, which would have scorched the White Cat and killed her, had not the gallant knight raised her in his arms. He then placed her on his shield, and as soon as she touched the cross she was seen to change into a beautiful maiden, and all the statues round the lakes left their positions and approached her.

As soon as she could recover herself sufficiently to speak, she addressed the knight as follows, "Gallant sir, I am Mizpah, only daughter of Mudi Ben Raschid, who was governor of this province for many years under the Moorish king, Almandazar the Superb. My mother was daughter of Alcharan, governor of Mazagan, and she was a good wife and kind mother. But my father discovering that she had forsaken the faith of her fathers, and had embraced the religion of the Cross, so worried her to return to her childhood's faith that she died broken-hearted.

Then he married again, and his second wife, my stepmother, was a very wicked woman. She knew that I was a Christian at heart, and that my lover was also a Christian, so one day, when my father was holding a banquet, she said to him, 'Mudi Ben Raschid, the crescent of the Holy Prophet is waning in your family. Your daughter is a renegade!'

"Then he was very much annoyed, and exclaimed that he wished his palace and his riches were made over to the enemy of mankind and I turned into a cat, than that so great a stain should fall on his family. No sooner had he finished speaking than he fell dead and his wicked wife also, and I was turned into a cat. My lover, Haroun, and all my young friends were turned into stone, and my servants were stricken deaf and dumb.

"Many a brave knight has been here to try and deliver me, but they all failed, because they only trusted in themselves, and were therefore defeated. But you, gallant knight, trusted more on the Cross than on yourself, and you have freed me. I am, therefore, the prize of your good sword. Deal with me as you will."

The Knight of the Cross assured her that he came from Compostela, where it was considered a duty to rescue maidens in distress, and that the highest reward coveted was that of doing their duty. He had in various parts of the world been fortunate enough in freeing others, and he had still more work before him. He trusted that the lovely Mizpah might long be spared to Haroun, and, saluting her, he galloped off.

Then the wedding was held, at which all the people from Ecija attended, and the bridegroom, rising, wished prosperity to the good knight, St. James of Compostela, who had been the means of bringing about so much happiness.

Domingo's Cat

This is a Brazilian tale

This story has been adapted from a tale originally told by Elsie Spicer Eells in Tales Of Giants from Brazil, published in 1918 by Dodd, Mead And Company, New York. Following the success of her previous work, Fairy Tales from Brazil,, this book focuses specifically on stories featuring giants, mythical beings of immense size and strength, from Brazilian folklore.

Once upon a time there was a man who was very poor. He was so poor that he had to sell one thing after another to get food to keep from starving. After a while there was nothing left except the cat.

He was very fond of his cat, and he said, "O, Cat, let come what will, I'll never part with you. I would rather starve."

The cat replied, "O good master Domingo, rest in peace. You will never starve as long as you have me. I am going out into the world to make a fortune for us both."

The cat went out into the jungle and dug and dug. Every time he dug he turned up silver pieces. The cat took a number of these home to his master so that he could purchase food. The rest of the pieces of silver the cat carried to the king.

The next day the cat dug up pieces of gold and carried them to the king. The next day he carried pieces of diamonds.

"Where do you get these rich gifts? Who is sending me such wonderful presents?" asked the king.

The cat replied, "It is my master, Domingo."

Now the king had a beautiful daughter. He thought that this man Domingo must be the richest man in the whole kingdom. He decided that his daughter should marry him at once, so he made arrangements for the wedding through the cat.

"I haven't any clothes to wear at the wedding," said Domingo when the cat told him that he was to marry the daughter of the king.

"Never mind about that. Just leave it to me," replied the cat.

The cat went to the king and said, "O King, there has been a terrible fire in the tailor shop where they were making the wedding garments of my master, Domingo. The tailor and all of his assistants were burned to death, and the entire outfit of my master Domingo was destroyed. Hasn't your majesty something which you could lend him to wear at the wedding?"

The king sent the richest garments which his wardrobe afforded. Domingo was clothed in state ready for the wedding.

"I have no palace to which to take my bride," said Domingo to the cat.

"Never mind. I'll see about it at once," replied the cat.

The cat went into the forest to the great castle where the giant dwelt. He marched straight up to the big giant and said, "O Giant, I wish to borrow your castle for my master Domingo. Will you not be so kind as to lend it to me a little while?"

The giant was very much insulted. "No, indeed, I'll not lend my castle to you or your master Domingo or anybody else," he shouted in his most terrible voice.

"Very well, then," replied the cat. He changed the giant to a piece of bacon in the twinkling of an eye and devoured him on the spot.

The giant's palace was a very wonderful palace. There was one room decked with silver, and one room decked with gold, and one room decked with diamonds. A beautiful river flowed by the garden gate.

As Domingo and his bride sailed down the river to the garden gate in the royal barge, they saw the cat sitting in the window singing. After that they never saw him again. He disappeared in the jungle and went to make some other poor man rich.

Perhaps he will come your way some day. Who knows?

Cat Tails – Feline Fairy Tales, Myths And Legends

The Cats Who Made Their Master Rich

This is an Italian tale

This tale has been adapted from Roman Legends: A Collection Of The Fables And Folk-Lore Of Rome by Rachel Harriette Busk. The book was published in 1877 by Estes And Lauriat, Boston. The book features a variety of Italian and Roman legends, myths, and folklore, drawing from both classical sources and popular oral traditions. These stories encompass a wide range of themes, including mythology, history, religion, and everyday life in Italy. The tales often involve gods and goddesses, legendary heroes, mythical creatures, and historical figures.

In America, once upon a time, there were no cats.

Mice there were in plenty, mice everywhere, and not peeping out of holes now and then, but infesting everything, swarming over every room, and when a family sat down to meals, the mice rushed upon the table and disputed the victuals with them.

Then someone thought of a plan.

He freighted three ships; full, full of cats, and off to America he went with them. There he sold them for their weight in gold and more, and whiff, the mice were swept away, and he made a great fortune.

A great fortune, all out of cats!'

The Master Cat; Or, Puss In Boots

This is a French tale

This tale has been adapted from The All Sorts Of Stories Book by Andrew Lang. The book was published in 1911 by Longman, Green And Company, London. Lang was a Scottish poet, novelist, literary critic, and contributor to the field of anthropology. Lang is perhaps best known for his "Fairy Books" series, which includes collections of fairy tales from around the world. The original of this tale was first told by Charles Perrault.

There was a miller who left no more estate to the three sons he had than his mill, his ass, and his cat. The partition was soon made. Neither scrivener nor attorney was sent for, as they would soon have eaten up all the poor patrimony. The eldest had the mill, the second the ass, and the youngest nothing but the cat. The poor young fellow was quite comfortless at having so poor a lot.

"My brothers," said he, "may get their living handsomely enough by joining their stocks together, but for my part, when I have eaten up my cat, and made me a muff of his skin, I must die of hunger."

The Cat, who heard all this, but made as if he did not, said to him with a grave and serious air, "Do not afflict yourself, my good master. You have nothing else to do but to give me a bag and get a pair of boots made for me that I may scamper through the dirt and the brambles, and you shall see that you have not so bad a portion in me as you imagine."

The Cat's master did not build very much upon what he said. He had often seen him play a great many cunning tricks to catch rats and mice, as when he used to hang by the heels, or hide himself in the meal, and make as if he were dead, so that he did not altogether despair of his affording him some help in his miserable condition. When the Cat had what he asked for he booted himself very gallantly, and putting his bag about his neck, he held the strings of it in his two forepaws and went into a warren where was great abundance of rabbits. He put bran and sow-thistle into his bag, and stretching out at length, as if he had been dead, he waited for some young rabbits, not yet acquainted with the deceits of the world, to come and rummage his bag for what he had put into it.

Scarce was he lain down but he had what he wanted. A rash and foolish young rabbit jumped into his bag, and Monsieur Puss, immediately drawing close the strings, took and killed him without pity. Proud of his prey, he went with it to the palace and asked to speak with his majesty. He was shown upstairs into the King's apartment, and, making a low reverence, said to him, "I have brought you, sir, a rabbit of the warren, which my noble lord the Marquis of Carabas (for that was the title which puss was pleased to give his master) has commanded me to present to your majesty from him."

"Tell your master," said the king, "that I thank him and that he does me a great deal of pleasure."

Another time he went and hid himself among some standing corn, holding his bag open, and when a brace of partridges ran into it he drew the strings and so caught them both. He went and made a present of these to the king, as he had done before of the rabbit which he took in the warren. The king, in like manner, received the partridges with great pleasure, and ordered him some money for drink.

The Cat continued for two or three months in carrying to his Majesty, from time to time, game of his master's taking. One day in particular, when he knew for certain that he was to take the air along the river-side, with his daughter, the most beautiful princess in the world, the Cat said to his master, "If you will follow my advice your fortune is made. You have nothing else to do but go and wash yourself in the river, in that part I shall show you, and leave the rest to me."

The Marquis of Carabas did what the Cat advised him to, without knowing why or wherefore. While he was washing the King passed by, and the Cat began to cry out, "Help! Help! My Lord Marquis of Carabas is going to be drowned."

At this noise the King put his head out of the coach-window, and, finding it was the Cat who had so often brought him such good game, he commanded his guards to run immediately to the assistance of his Lordship the Marquis of Carabas. While they were drawing the poor Marquis out of the river, the Cat came up to the coach and told the King that, while his master was washing, there came by some rogues, who went off with his clothes, though he had cried out, "Thieves! Thieves!" several times, as loud as he could.

This cunning Cat had actually hidden his masters poor clothes under a great stone. The King immediately commanded the officers of his wardrobe to run and fetch one of his best suits for the Lord Marquis of Carabas.

The King caressed him after a very extraordinary manner, and as the fine clothes he had given him extremely set off his good looks (for he was well made and very handsome in his person), the King's daughter took a secret inclination to him, and the Marquis of Carabas had no sooner cast two or three respectful and somewhat tender glances but she fell in love with him to distraction. The King asked him to join them in the coach and take part of the airing.

The Cat, quite overjoyed to see his project begin to succeed, marched on before, and, meeting with some countrymen, who were mowing a meadow, he said to them, "Good people, you who are mowing, if you do not tell the King that the meadow you mow belongs to my Lord Marquis of Carabas, you shall be chopped as small as herbs for the pot."

The King did not fail asking of the mowers to whom the meadow they were mowing belonged.

"To my Lord Marquis of Carabas," answered they altogether, for the Cat's threats had made them terribly afraid.

"You see, sir," said the Marquis, "this is a meadow which never fails to yield a plentiful harvest every year."

The Master Cat, who went still on before, met with some reapers, and said to them, "Good people, you who are reaping, if you do not tell the King that all this corn belongs to the Marquis of Carabas, you shall be chopped as small as herbs for the pot."

The King, who passed by a moment after, would needs know to whom all that corn, which he then saw, did belong.

"To my Lord Marquis of Carabas," replied the reapers, and the King was very well pleased with it, as well as the Marquis, whom he congratulated thereupon. The Master Cat, who went always before, said the same words to all he met, and the King was astonished at the vast estates of my Lord Marquis of Carabas.

Monsieur Puss came at last to a stately castle, the master of which was an ogre, the richest had ever been known, for all the lands which the King had then gone over belonged to this castle. The Cat, who had taken care to inform himself who this ogre was and what he could do, asked to speak with him, saying he could not pass so near his castle without having the honour of paying his respects to him.

The ogre received him as civilly as an ogre could do, and made him sit down.

"I have been assured," said the Cat, "that you have the gift of being able to change yourself into all sorts of creatures you have a mind to; you can, for example, transform yourself into a lion, or elephant, and the like."

"That is true," answered the ogre very briskly, "and to convince you, you shall see me now become a lion."

Puss was so sadly terrified at the sight of a lion so near him that he immediately got into the gutter, not without abundance of trouble and danger, because of his boots, which were of no use at all to him in walking upon the roof tiles. A little while after, when Puss saw that the ogre had resumed his natural form, he came down, and admitted he had been very much frightened.

"I have been, moreover, informed," said the Cat, "but I know not how to believe it, that you have also the power to take on you the shape of the smallest animals, for example, to change yourself into a rat or a mouse, but I must admit to you I take this to be impossible."

"Impossible!" cried the ogre, "you shall see that presently."

And at the same time he changed himself into a mouse, and began to run about the floor. Puss no sooner perceived this but he fell upon him and ate him up.

Meanwhile the King, who saw, as he passed, this fine castle, had a mind to go into it. Puss, who heard the noise of his Majesty's coach running over the draw-bridge, ran out, and said to the King, "Your Majesty is welcome to this castle of my Lord Marquis of Carabas."

"What! My Lord Marquis," cried the King, "and does this castle also belong to you? There can be nothing finer than this court and all the stately buildings which surround it. Let us go into it, if you please."

The Marquis gave his hand to the Princess, and followed the King, who went first. They passed into a spacious hall, where they found a magnificent collation, which the ogre had prepared for his friends, who were that very day to visit him, but dared not enter, knowing the King was there. His Majesty was perfectly charmed with the good qualities of my Lord Marquis of Carabas, as was his daughter, who had fallen violently in love with him, and, seeing the vast estate he possessed, said to him, after having drunk five or six glasses of good, rich wine, "It will be owing to yourself only, my Lord Marquis, if you are not my son-in-law."

The Marquis, making several low bows, accepted the honour which his Majesty conferred upon him, and forthwith, that very same day, married the Princess.

Puss became a great lord, and never ran after mice anymore except for his own diversion.

The Cat Of Norrhult

A Swedish Tale – a version of a previous tale, The Cat On The Dovrefell

This tale has been adapted from Swedish Fairy Tales by Herman Hofberg, published by Belford-Clarke Co., Chicago in 1890. Herman Hofberg (1823–1883) was a notable Swedish writer, historian, and librarian. He is best known for his contributions to the documentation and preservation of Swedish history and culture.

On the estate of Norrhult, in the parish of Rumskulla, the people in olden times were very much troubled by Trolls and ghosts. The disturbances finally became so unbearable that they were compelled to desert house and home, and seek an asylum with their neighbours. One old man was left behind, and he, because he was so feeble that he could not move with the rest.

Sometime thereafter, there came one evening a man having with him a bear, and he asked for lodgings for himself and his companion. The old man consented, but expressed doubts about his guest being able to endure the disturbances that were likely to occur during the night.

The stranger replied that he was not afraid of noises, and laid himself down, with his bear, near the old man's bed.

Only a few hours had passed, when a multitude of Trolls came into the hut and began their usual clatter. Some of them built the fire in the fireplace, others set the kettle upon the fire, and others again put into the kettle a mess of lizards, frogs, and. worms.

When the mess was cooked, the table was laid and the Trolls sat down to the feast. One of them threw a worm to the bear, and said, "Will you have a fish, Kitty?"

Another went to the bear keeper and asked him if he would not have some of their food. At this the latter let loose the bear, which struck about him so lustily that soon the whole swarm of Trolls was flying through the door.

Sometime after, the door was again opened, and a Troll with a mouth so large that it filled the whole opening peeked in. "Seek him!" said the bear keeper, and the bear soon hunted him away also.

In the morning the stranger gathered the people of the village around him and directed them to raise a cross upon the estate, and to engrave a prayer on Cross Mountain, where the Trolls dwelt, so that they would be freed from their troublesome visitors.

Seven years later a resident of Norrhult went to Norrköping. On his way home he met a man who asked him where he came from, and, upon being informed, claimed to be a neighbour, and invited the peasant to ride with him on his black horse. Away they went at a lively trot along the road, the peasant supposed, but in fact they were high up in the air. When it became quite dark the horse stumbled so that the peasant came near to falling off.

"It is well you were able to hold on," said the horseman. "That was the point of the steeple of Linköping's cathedral that the horse stumbled against. Listen!" he continued. "Seven years ago I visited Norrhult. Back then you had a vicious cat that fought off the Trolls. Is it still alive?"

"Yes, truly, and many more," said the peasant.

After a time the rider checked his horse and bade the peasant dismount. When the latter looked around him he found himself at Cross Mountain, near his home.

Sometime later another Troll came to the peasant's cottage and asked if that great savage cat still lived there.

"Look out!" said the peasant, "she is lying there on the oven, and has seven young ones, all worse than she."

"Oh!" cried the Troll, and rushed for the door. From that time no Trolls have ever visited Norrhult.

Why The Cat Always Falls Upon Her Feet

This is a tale from India

This tale has been adapted from The Book Of Nature Myths by Florence Holbrook. The book was published in 1902 by Houghton Mifflin Company, Boston and New York. The Book of Nature Myths was intended for young readers and served as an educational tool for teaching about nature and mythology. Holbrook's retellings of the myths are engaging and accessible, making them suitable for children to read independently or for teachers to use in the classroom.

Some magicians are cruel, but others are gentle and good to all the creatures of the earth. One of these good magicians was one day traveling in a great forest. The sun rose high in the heavens, and he lay down at the foot of a tree. Soft, green moss grew all about him. The sun shining through the leaves made flecks of light and shadow upon the earth. He heard the song of the bird and the lazy buzz of the wasp. The wind rustled the leafy boughs above him. All the music of the forest lulled him to slumber, and he closed his eyes.

As the magician lay asleep, a great serpent came softly from the thicket. It lifted high its shining crest and saw the man at the foot of the tree. "I will kill him!" it hissed. "I could have eaten that cat last night if he had not called, 'Watch, little cat, watch!' I will kill him, I will kill him!"

Closer and closer the deadly serpent moved. The magician stirred in his sleep. "Watch, little cat, watch!" he said softly.

The serpent drew back, but the magician's eyes were shut, and it went closer. It hissed its war-cry. The sleeping magician did not move. Suddenly the serpent was upon him, but far up in the high branches of the tree above his head the little cat lay hidden. She had seen the serpent when it came from the thicket.

She watched it as it went closer and closer to the sleeping man, and she heard it hiss its war-cry. The little cat's body quivered with anger and with fear, for she was so little and the serpent was so big. "The magician was very good to me," she thought, and she leaped down upon the serpent.

Oh, how angry the serpent was! It hissed, and the flames shot from its eyes. It struck wildly at the brave little cat, but now the cat had no fear. Again and again she leaped upon the serpent's head, and at last the creature lay dead beside the sleeping man whom it had wished to kill.

When the magician awoke, the little cat lay on the earth, and not far away was the dead serpent. He knew at once what the cat had done, and he said, "Little cat, what can I do to show you honour for your brave fight? Your eyes are quick to see, and your ears are quick to hear. You can run very swiftly. I know what I can do for you. You shall be known over the earth as the friend of man, and you shall always have a home in the home of man. And one thing more, little cat. You leaped from the high tree to kill the deadly serpent, and now as long as you live, you shall leap where you will, and you shall always fall upon your feet."

Cat Tails – Feline Fairy Tales, Myths And Legends

The Pike and the Cat

A Tale From Russia

This tale has been adapted from Kate Douglas Wiggin's and Nora Archibald Smith's book, The Talking Beasts, published by Houghton Mifflin Company, New York & Boston in 1911. "The Talking Beasts" remains a valuable collection of fables that continues to educate and entertain, reflecting her commitment to literature and moral education.

A conceited Pike took it into its head to exercise the functions of a cat. I do not know whether the Evil One had plagued it with envy, or whether, perhaps, it had grown tired of fishy fare, but, at all events, it thought fit to ask the Cat to take it out to the chase, with the intention of catching a few mice in the warehouse.

"But, my dear friend," Vaska the Cat said to the Pike, "do you understand that kind of work? Take care, gossip, that you don't incur disgrace. It isn't without reason that they say: 'The work ought to be in the master's power.'"

"Why really, gossip, what a tremendous affair it is! Mice, indeed! Why, I have been in the habit of catching perches!"

"Oh, very well. Come along!"

And off they went. They each lay in ambush. The Cat thoroughly enjoyed itself, made a hearty meal, and then went to look after its comrade.

Alas! The Pike, almost destitute of life, lay there gasping, its tail nibbled away by the mice. So the Cat, seeing that its comrade had undertaken a task quite beyond its strength, dragged it back, half dead, to its pond.

Cat Tails – Feline Fairy Tales, Myths And Legends

The White Cat

This is a French tale

This tale has been adapted from The Blue Fairy Book by Andrew Lang. The book was published in 1889 by Longman, Green And Company, London. Lang was a Scottish poet, novelist, literary critic, and contributor to the field of anthropology. Lang is perhaps best known for his "Fairy Books" series, which includes collections of fairy tales from around the world. The original of this tale was first told as La Chatte Blanch by Madame la Comtesse d'Aulnoy

Once upon a time there was a king who had three sons, who were all so clever and brave that he began to be afraid that they would want to reign over the kingdom before he was dead. Now the King, though he felt that he was growing old, did not at all wish to give up the government of his kingdom while he could still manage it very well, so he thought the best way to live in peace would be to divert the minds of his sons by promises which he could always get out of when the time came for keeping them.

So he sent for them all, and, after speaking to them kindly, he added, "You will quite agree with me, my dear children, that my great age makes it impossible for me to look after my affairs of state as carefully as I once did. I begin to fear that this may affect the welfare of my subjects, therefore I wish that one of you should succeed to my crown, but in return for such a gift as this it is only right that you should do something for me. Now, as I think of retiring into the country, it seems to me that a pretty, lively, faithful little dog would be very good company for me, so, without any regard for your ages, I promise that the one who brings me the most beautiful little dog shall succeed me at once."

The three Princes were greatly surprised by their father's sudden fancy for a little dog, but as it gave the two younger ones a chance they would not otherwise have had of being king, and as the eldest was too polite to make any objection, they accepted the commission with pleasure. They bade farewell to the King, who gave them presents of silver and precious stones, and appointed to meet them at the same hour, in the same place, after a year had passed, to see the little dogs they had brought for him.

Then they went together to a castle which was about a league from the city, accompanied by all their particular friends, to whom they gave a grand banquet, and the three brothers promised to be friends always, to share whatever good fortune befell them, and not to be parted by any envy or jealousy, and so they set out, agreeing to meet at the same castle at the appointed time, to present themselves before the

King together. Each one took a different road, and the two eldest met with many adventures, but it is about the youngest that you are going to hear. He was young, and gay, and handsome, and knew everything that a prince ought to know, and as for his courage, there was simply no end to it.

Hardly a day passed without his buying several dogs, big and little, greyhounds, mastiffs, spaniels, and lapdogs. As soon as he had bought a pretty one he was sure to see a still prettier one, and then he had to get rid of all the others and buy that one, as, being alone, he found it impossible to take thirty or forty thousand dogs about with him. He journeyed from day to day, not knowing where he was going, until at last, just at nightfall, he reached a great, gloomy forest. He did not know his way, and, to make matters worse, it began to thunder, and the rain poured down. He took the first path he could find, and after walking for a long time he fancied he saw a faint light, and began to hope that he was coming to some cottage where he might find shelter for the night. At length, guided by the light, he reached the door of the most splendid castle he could have imagined. This door was of gold covered with carbuncles, and it was the pure red light which shone from them that had shown him the way through the forest. The walls were of the finest porcelain in all the most delicate colours, and the Prince saw that all the stories he had ever read were pictured upon them, but as he was terribly wet, and the rain still fell in torrents, he could not stay to look about anymore, but came back to the golden door. There he saw a deer's foot hanging by a chain of diamonds, and he began to wonder who could live in this magnificent castle.

"They must feel very secure against robbers," he said to himself. "What is to hinder anyone from cutting off that chain and digging out those carbuncles, and making himself rich for life?"

He pulled the deer's foot, and immediately a silver bell sounded and the door flew open, but the Prince could see nothing but numbers of hands in the air, each holding a torch. He was so much surprised that he stood quite still, until he felt himself pushed forward by other hands, so that, though he was somewhat uneasy, he could not help going on. With his hand on his sword, to be prepared for whatever might happen, he entered a hall paved with lapis-lazuli, while two lovely voices sang:

"The hands you see floating above

Will swiftly your bidding obey;

If your heart dreads not conquering Love,

In this place you may fearlessly stay."

The Prince could not believe that any danger threatened him when he was welcomed in this way, so, guided by the mysterious hands, he went toward a door of coral, which opened of its own accord, and he found himself in a vast hall of mother-of-pearl, out of which opened a number of other rooms, glittering with thousands of lights, and full of such beautiful pictures and precious things that the Prince felt quite bewildered. After passing through sixty rooms the hands that conducted him stopped, and the Prince saw a most comfortable-looking arm-chair drawn up close to the chimney-corner. At the same moment the fire lighted itself, and the pretty, soft, clever hands took off the Prince's wet, muddy clothes, and presented him with fresh ones made of the richest stuffs, all embroidered with gold and emeralds. He could not help admiring everything he saw, and the deft way in which the hands waited on him, though they sometimes appeared so suddenly that they made him jump.

When he was quite ready, and I can assure you that he looked very different from the wet and weary Prince who had stood outside in the rain, and pulled the deer's foot, the hands led him to a splendid room, upon the walls of which were painted the histories of Puss in Boots and a number of other famous cats. The table was laid for supper with two golden plates, and golden spoons and forks, and the sideboard was covered with dishes and glasses of crystal set with precious stones. The Prince was wondering who the second place could be for, when suddenly in came about a dozen cats carrying guitars and rolls of music, who took their places at one end of the room, and under the direction of a cat who beat time with a roll of paper began to mew in every imaginable key, and to draw their claws across the strings of the guitars, making the strangest kind of music that could be heard. The Prince hastily stopped up his ears, but even then the sight of these comical musicians sent him into fits of laughter.

"What funny thing shall I see next?" he said to himself, and instantly the door opened, and in came a tiny figure covered by a long black veil. It was conducted by two cats wearing black mantles and carrying swords, and a large party of cats followed, who brought in cages full of rats and mice.

The Prince was so much astonished that he thought he must be dreaming, but the little figure came up to him and threw back its veil, and he saw that it was the loveliest little white cat it is possible to imagine. She looked very young and very sad, and in a sweet little voice that went straight to his heart she said to the Prince, "King's son, you are welcome, for the Queen of the Cats is glad to see you."

"Lady Cat," replied the Prince, "I thank you for receiving me so kindly, but surely you are no ordinary pussy-cat? Indeed, the way you speak and the magnificence of your castle prove it plainly."

"King's son," said the White Cat, "I beg you to spare me these compliments, for I am not used to them. But now," she added, "let supper be served, and let the musicians be silent, as the Prince does not understand what they are saying."

So the mysterious hands began to bring in the supper, and first they put on the table two dishes, one containing stewed pigeons and the other a fricassee of fat mice. The sight of the latter made the Prince feel as if he could not enjoy his supper at all, but the White Cat, seeing this, assured him that the dishes intended for him were prepared in a separate kitchen, and he might be quite certain that they contained neither rats nor mice, and the Prince felt so sure that she would not deceive him that he had no more hesitation in beginning. Presently he noticed that on the little paw that was next him the White Cat wore a bracelet containing a portrait, and he begged to be allowed to look at it. To his great surprise he found it represented an extremely handsome young man, who was so like himself that it might have been his own portrait!

The White Cat sighed as he looked at it, and seemed sadder than ever, and the Prince dared not ask any questions for fear of displeasing her; so he began to talk about other things, and found that she was interested in all the subjects he cared for himself, and seemed to know quite well what was going on in the world. After supper they went into another room, which was fitted up as a theatre, and the cats acted and danced for their amusement, and then the White Cat said good-night to him, and the hands conducted him into a room he had not seen before, hung with tapestry worked with butterflies' wings of every colour. There were mirrors that reached from the ceiling to the floor, and a little white bed with curtains of gauze tied up with ribbons. The Prince went to bed in silence, as he did not quite know how to begin a conversation with the hands that waited on him, and in the morning he was awakened by a noise and confusion outside of his window, and the hands came and quickly dressed him in hunting costume. When he looked out all the cats were assembled in the courtyard, some leading greyhounds, some blowing horns, for the White Cat was going out hunting. The hands led a wooden horse up to the Prince, and seemed to expect him to mount it, at which he was very indignant, but it was no use for him to object, for he speedily found himself upon its back, and it pranced gaily off with him.

The White Cat herself was riding a monkey, which climbed even up to the eagles' nests when she had a fancy for the young eaglets. Never was there a pleasanter hunting party, and when they returned to the castle the Prince and the White Cat supped together as before, but when they had finished she offered him a crystal goblet, which must have contained a magic draught, for, as soon as he had swallowed its contents, he forgot everything, even the little dog that he was seeking for the King, and only thought how happy he was to be with the White Cat! And so the days passed, in every kind of amusement, until the year was nearly gone. The Prince had forgotten all about meeting his brothers: he did not even know what country he belonged to, but the White Cat knew when he ought to go back, and one day she said to him, "Do you know that you have only three days left to look for the little dog for your father, and your brothers have found lovely ones?"

Then the Prince suddenly recovered his memory, and cried, "What can have made me forget such an important thing? My whole fortune depends upon it, and even if I could in such a short time find a dog pretty enough to gain me a kingdom, where should I find a horse who would carry me all that way in three days?" And he began to be very vexed.

But the White Cat said to him: "King's son, do not trouble yourself. I am your friend, and will make everything easy for you. You can still stay here for a day, as the good wooden horse can take you to your country in twelve hours."

"I thank you, beautiful Cat," said the Prince, "but what good will it do me to get back if I have not a dog to take to my father?"

"See here," answered the White Cat, holding up an acorn, "there is a prettier one in this than in the Dog star!"

"Oh! White Cat dear," said the Prince, "how unkind you are to laugh at me now!"

"Only listen," she said, holding the acorn to his ear.

And inside it he distinctly heard a tiny voice say, "Bow-wow!"

The Prince was delighted, for a dog that can be shut up in an acorn must be very small indeed. He wanted to take it out and look at it, but the White Cat said it would be better not to open the acorn till he was before the King, in case the tiny dog should be cold on the journey. He thanked her a thousand times, and said good-by quite sadly when the time came for him to set out.

"The days have passed so quickly with you," he said, "I only wish I could take you with me now."

But the White Cat shook her head and sighed deeply in answer.

After all the Prince was the first to arrive at the castle where he had agreed to meet his brothers, but they came soon after, and stared in amazement when they saw the wooden horse in the courtyard jumping like a hunter.

The Prince met them joyfully, and they began to tell him all their adventures, but he managed to hide from them what he had been doing, and even led them to think that a turnspit dog which he had with him was the one he was bringing for the King. Fond as they all were of one another, the two eldest could not help being glad to think that their dogs certainly had a better chance. The next morning they started in the same chariot. The elder brothers carried in baskets two such tiny, fragile dogs that they hardly dared to touch them. As for the turnspit, he ran after the chariot, and got so covered with mud that one could hardly see what he was like at all.

When they reached the palace everyone crowded round to welcome them as they went into the King's great hall, and when the two brothers presented their little dogs nobody could decide which was the prettier. They were already arranging between themselves to share the kingdom equally, when the youngest stepped forward, drawing from his pocket the acorn the White Cat had given him. He opened it quickly, and there upon a white cushion they saw a dog so small that it could easily have been put through a ring. The Prince laid it upon the ground, and it got up at once and began to dance.

The King did not know what to say, for it was impossible that anything could be prettier than this little creature. Nevertheless, as he was in no hurry to part with his crown, he told his sons that, as they had been so successful the first time, he would ask them to go once again, and seek by land and sea for a piece of muslin so fine that it could be drawn through the eye of a needle. The brothers were not very willing to set out again, but the two eldest consented because it gave them another chance, and they started as before. The youngest again mounted the wooden horse, and rode back at full speed to his beloved White Cat. Every door of the castle stood wide open, and every window and turret was illuminated, so it looked more wonderful than before. The hands hastened to meet him, and led the wooden horse off to the stable, while he hurried in to find the White Cat. She was asleep in a little basket on a white satin cushion, but she very soon started up when she heard the Prince, and was overjoyed at seeing him once more.

"How could I hope that you would come back to me King's son?" she said. And then he stroked and petted her, and told her of his successful journey, and how he had come back to ask her help, as he believed that it was impossible to find what the King demanded. The White Cat looked serious, and said she must think what was to be done, but that, luckily, there were some cats in the castle who could spin very well, and if anybody could manage it they could, and she would set them the task herself.

And then the hands appeared carrying torches, and conducted the Prince and the White Cat to a long gallery which overlooked the river, from the windows of which they saw a magnificent display of fireworks of all sorts, after which they had supper, which the Prince liked even better than the fireworks, for it was very late, and he was hungry after his long ride. And so the days passed quickly as before. It was impossible to feel dull with the White Cat, and she had quite a talent for inventing new amusements. Indeed, she was cleverer than a cat has any right to be. But when the Prince asked her how it was that she was so wise, she only said, "King's son, do not ask me. Guess what you please. I may not tell you anything."

The Prince was so happy that he did not trouble himself at all about the time, but presently the White Cat told him that the year was gone, and that he need not be at all anxious about the piece of muslin, as they had made it very well.

"This time," she added, "I can give you a suitable escort", and on looking out into the courtyard the Prince saw a superb chariot of burnished gold, enamelled in flame colour with a thousand different devices. It was drawn by twelve snow-white horses, harnessed four abreast, and their trappings were flame-coloured velvet, embroidered with diamonds. A hundred chariots followed, each drawn by eight horses, and filled with officers in splendid uniforms, and a thousand guards surrounded the procession.

"Go!" said the White Cat, "and when you appear before the King in such state he surely will not refuse you the crown which you deserve. Take this walnut, but do not open it until you are before him, then you will find in it the piece of stuff you asked me for."

"Lovely Blanchette," said the Prince, "how can I thank you properly for all your kindness to me? Only tell me that you wish it, and I will give up for ever all thought of being king, and will stay here with you always."

"King's son," she replied, "it shows the goodness of your heart that you should care so much for a little white cat, who is good for nothing but to catch mice, but you must not stay."

So the Prince kissed her little paw and set out. You can imagine how fast he travelled when I tell you that they reached the King's palace in just half the time it had taken the wooden horse to get there. This time the Prince was so late that he did not try to meet his brothers at their castle, so they thought he could not be coming, and were rather glad of it, and displayed their pieces of muslin to the King proudly, feeling sure of success. And indeed the stuff was very fine, and would go through the eye of a very large needle, but the King, who was only too glad to make a difficulty, sent for a particular needle, which was kept among the Crown jewels, and had such a small eye that everybody saw at once that it was impossible that the muslin should pass through it.

The Princes were angry, and were beginning to complain that it was a trick, when suddenly the trumpets sounded and the youngest Prince came in. His father and brothers were quite astonished at his magnificence, and after he had greeted them he took the walnut from his pocket and opened it, fully expecting to find the piece of muslin, but instead there was only a hazel-nut. He cracked it, and there lay a cherry-stone. Everybody was looking on, and the King was chuckling to himself at the idea of finding the piece of muslin in a nutshell.

However, the Prince cracked the cherry-stone, but everyone laughed when he saw it contained only its own kernel. He opened that and found a grain of wheat, and in that was a millet seed. Then he himself began to wonder, and muttered softly, "White Cat, White Cat, are you making fun of me?"

In an instant he felt a cat's claw give his hand quite a sharp scratch, and hoping that it was meant as an encouragement he opened the millet seed, and drew out of it a piece of muslin four hundred ells long, woven with the loveliest colours and most wonderful patterns, and when the needle was brought it went through the eye six times with the greatest ease! The King turned pale, and the other Princes stood silent and sorrowful, for nobody could deny that this was the most marvellous piece of muslin that was to be found in the world.

Presently the King turned to his sons, and said, with a deep sigh, "Nothing could console me more in my old age than to realize your willingness to gratify my wishes. Go then once more, and whoever at the end of a year can bring back the loveliest princess shall be married to her, and shall, without further delay, receive the crown, for my successor must certainly be married."

The Prince considered that he had earned the kingdom fairly twice over but still he was too well bred to argue about it, so he just went back to his gorgeous chariot, and, surrounded by his escort, returned to the White Cat faster than he had come. This time she was expecting him, the path was strewn with flowers, and a thousand braziers were burning scented woods which perfumed the air. Seated in a gallery from which she could see his arrival, the White Cat waited for him.

"Well, King's son," she said, "here you are once more, without a crown."

"Madam," said he, "thanks to your generosity I have earned one twice over, but the fact is that my father is so loth to part with it that it would be no pleasure to me to take it."

"Never mind," she answered, "it's just as well to try and deserve it. As you must take back a lovely princess with you next time I will be on the look-out for one for you. In the meantime let us enjoy ourselves. Tonight I have ordered a battle between my cats and the river rats on purpose to amuse you."

So this year slipped away even more pleasantly than the preceding ones. Sometimes the Prince could not help asking the White Cat how it was she could talk. "Perhaps you are a fairy," he said. "Or has some enchanter changed you into a cat?"

But she only gave him answers that told him nothing. Days go by so quickly when one is very happy that it is certain the Prince would never have thought of its being time to go back, when one evening as they sat together the White Cat said to him that if he wanted to take a lovely princess home with him the next day he must be prepared to do what she told him.

"Take this sword," she said, "and cut off my head!"

"I!" cried the Prince, "I cut off your head! Blanchette darling, how could I do it?"

"I entreat you to do as I tell you, King's son," she replied.

The tears came into the Prince's eyes as he begged her to ask him anything but that, to set him any task she pleased as a proof of his devotion, but to spare him the grief of killing his dear Pussy. But nothing he could say altered her determination, and at last he drew his sword, and desperately, with a trembling hand, cut off the little white head. But imagine his astonishment and delight when suddenly a lovely princess stood before him, and, while he was still speechless with amazement, the door opened and a good company of knights and ladies entered, each carrying a cat's skin! They hastened with every sign of joy to the Princess, kissing her hand and congratulating her on being once more restored to her natural shape.

She received them graciously, but after a few minutes begged that they would leave her alone with the Prince, to whom she said, "You see, Prince, that you were right in supposing me to be no ordinary cat. My father reigned over six kingdoms. The Queen, my mother, whom he loved dearly, had a passion for traveling and exploring, and when I was only a few weeks old she obtained his permission to visit a certain mountain of which she had heard many marvellous tales, and set out, taking with her a number of her attendants. On the way they had to pass near an old castle belonging to the fairies. Nobody had ever been into it, but it was reported to be full of the most wonderful things, and my mother remembered to have heard that the fairies had in their garden such fruits as were to be seen and tasted nowhere else. She began to wish to try them for herself, and turned her steps in the direction of the garden.

"On arriving at the door, which blazed with gold and jewels, she ordered her servants to knock loudly, but it was useless; it seemed as if all the inhabitants of the castle must be asleep or dead. Now the more difficult it became to obtain the fruit, the more the Queen was determined that have it she would. So she ordered that they should bring ladders, and get over the wall into the garden, but though the wall did not look very high, and they tied the ladders together to make them very long, it was quite impossible to get to the top.

"The Queen was in despair, but as night was coming on she ordered that they should encamp just where they were, and went to bed herself, feeling quite ill, she was so disappointed. In the middle of the night she was suddenly awakened, and saw to her surprise a tiny, ugly old woman seated by her bedside, who said to her, 'I must say that we consider it somewhat troublesome of your Majesty to insist upon tasting our fruit, but to save you annoyance, my sisters and I will consent to give you as much as you can carry away, on one condition - that is, that you shall give us your little daughter to bring up as our own.'

"'Ah! My dear madam,' cried the Queen, 'is there nothing else that you will take for the fruit? I will give you my kingdoms willingly.'

"'No,' replied the old fairy, 'we will have nothing but your little daughter. She shall be as happy as the day is long, and we will give her everything that is worth having in fairy-land, but you must not see her again until she is married.'

"'Though it is a hard condition,' said the Queen, 'I consent, for I shall certainly die if I do not taste the fruit, and so I should lose my little daughter either way.'

"So the old fairy led her into the castle, and, though it was still the middle of the night, the Queen could see plainly that it was far more beautiful than she had been told, which you can easily believe, Prince," said the White Cat, "when I tell you that it was this castle that we are now in. 'Will you gather the fruit yourself, Queen?' said the old fairy, 'or shall I call it to come to you?'

"'I beg you to let me see it come when it is called,' cried the Queen. 'That will be something quite new.'

"The old fairy whistled twice, then she cried, "'Apricots, peaches, nectarines, cherries, plums, pears, melons, grapes, apples, oranges, lemons, gooseberries, strawberries, raspberries, come!'

"And in an instant they came tumbling in one over another, and yet they were neither dusty nor spoilt, and the Queen found them quite as good as she had fancied them. You see they grew upon fairy trees.

"The old fairy gave her golden baskets in which to take the fruit away, and it was as much as four hundred mules could carry. Then she reminded the Queen of her agreement, and led her back to the camp, and next morning she went back to her kingdom, but before she had gone very far she began to repent of her bargain, and when the King came out to meet her she looked so sad that he guessed that something had happened, and asked what the matter was. At first the Queen was afraid to tell him, but when, as soon as they reached the palace, five frightful little dwarfs were sent by the fairies to fetch me, she was obliged to confess what she had promised.

"The King was very angry, and had the Queen and myself shut up in a great tower and safely guarded, and drove the little dwarfs out of his kingdom, but the fairies sent a great dragon who ate up all the people he met, and whose breath burnt up everything as he passed through the country, and at last, after trying in vain to rid himself of this monster, the King, to save his subjects, was obliged to consent that I should be given up to the fairies.

"This time they came themselves to fetch me, in a chariot of pearl drawn by sea-horses, followed by the dragon, who was led with chains of diamonds. My cradle was placed between the old fairies, who loaded me with caresses, and away we whirled through the air to a tower which they had built on purpose for me. There I grew up surrounded with everything that was beautiful and rare, and learning everything that is ever taught to a princess, but without any companions but a parrot and a little dog, who could both talk, and receiving every day a visit from one of the old fairies, who came mounted upon the dragon.

"One day, however, as I sat at my window I saw a handsome young prince, who seemed to have been hunting in the forest which surrounded my prison, and who was standing and looking up at me. When he saw that I observed him he saluted me with great deference. You can imagine that I was delighted to have someone new to talk to, and in spite of the height of my window our conversation was prolonged till night fell, then my prince reluctantly bade me farewell. But after that he came again many times and at last I consented to marry him, but the question was how I was to escape from my tower. The fairies always supplied me with flax for my spinning, and by great diligence I made enough cord for a ladder that would reach to the foot of the tower, but, alas, just as my prince was helping me to descend it, the crossest and ugliest of the old fairies flew in. Before he had time to defend himself my unhappy lover was swallowed up by the dragon.

"As for me, the fairies, furious at having their plans defeated, for they intended me to marry the king of the dwarfs, and I utterly refused, changed me into a white cat. When they brought me here I found all the lords and ladies of my father's court awaiting me under the same enchantment, while the people of lesser rank had been made invisible, all but their hands.

"As they laid me under the enchantment the fairies told me all my history, for until then I had quite believed that I was their child, and warned me that my only chance of regaining my natural form was to win the love of a prince who resembled in every way my unfortunate lover."

"And you have won it, lovely Princess," interrupted the Prince.

"You are indeed wonderfully like him," resumed the Princess, "in voice, in features, and everything, and if you really love me all my troubles will be at an end."

"And mine too," cried the Prince, throwing himself at her feet, "if you will consent to marry me."

"I love you already better than anyone in the world," she said, "but now it is time to go back to your father, and we shall hear what he says about it."

So the Prince gave her his hand and led her out, and they mounted the chariot together; it was even more splendid than before, and so was the whole company. Even the horses' shoes were of rubies with diamond nails, and I suppose that is the first time such a thing was ever seen.

As the Princess was as kind and clever as she was beautiful, you may imagine what a delightful journey the Prince found it, for everything the Princess said seemed to him quite charming.

When they came near the castle where the brothers were to meet, the Princess got into a chair carried by four of the guards; it was hewn out of one splendid crystal, and had silken curtains, which she drew round her that she might not be seen.

The Prince saw his brothers walking upon the terrace, each with a lovely princess, and they came to meet him, asking if he had also found a wife. He said that he had found something much rarer, a white cat! At which they laughed very much, and asked him if he was afraid of being eaten up by mice in the palace. And then they set out together for the town. Each prince and princess rode in a splendid carriage; the horses were decked with plumes of feathers, and glittered with gold. After them came the youngest prince, and last of all the crystal chair, at which everybody looked with admiration and curiosity. When the courtiers saw them coming they hastened to tell the King.

"Are the ladies beautiful?" he asked anxiously.

And when they answered that nobody had ever before seen such lovely princesses he seemed quite annoyed.

However, he received them graciously, but found it impossible to choose between them.

Then turning to his youngest son he said, "Have you come back alone, after all?"

"Your Majesty," replied the Prince, "will find in that crystal chair a little white cat, which has such soft paws, and mews so prettily, that I am sure you will be charmed with it."

The King smiled, and went to draw back the curtains himself, but at a touch from the Princess the crystal shivered into a thousand splinters, and there she stood in all her beauty. Her fair hair floated over her shoulders and was crowned with flowers, and her softly falling robe was of the purest white. She saluted the King gracefully, while a murmur of admiration rose from all around.

"Sire," she said, "I do not come to deprive you of the throne you fill so worthily. I already have six kingdoms, so permit me to bestow one upon you, and upon each of your sons. I ask nothing but your friendship, and your consent to my marriage with your youngest son. We shall still have three kingdoms left for ourselves."

The King and all the courtiers could not conceal their joy and astonishment, and the marriage of the three Princes was celebrated at once. The festivities lasted several months, and then each king and queen departed to their own kingdom and lived happily ever after.

Cat Tails – Feline Fairy Tales, Myths And Legends

The Cat's Elopement

This a Japanese Tale

Adapted from the original book, Japanische Marchen und Sagen, by David Brauns. This version is taken from The Pink Fairy Book by Andrew Lang, and published by Longmans, Green And Co, London in 1897.

Once upon a time there lived a cat of marvellous beauty, with a skin as soft and shining as silk, and wise green eyes, that could see even in the dark. His name was Gon, and he belonged to a music teacher, who was so fond and proud of him that he would not have parted with him for anything in the world.

Now not far from the music master's house there dwelt a lady who possessed a most lovely little pussy cat called Koma. She was such a little dear altogether, and blinked her eyes so daintily, and ate her supper so tidily, and when she had finished she licked her pink nose so delicately with her little tongue, that her mistress was never tired of saying, "Koma, Koma, what should I do without you?"

Well, it happened one day that these two, when out for an evening stroll, met under a cherry tree, and in one moment fell madly in love with each other. Gon had long felt that it was time for him to find a wife, for all the ladies in the neighbourhood paid him so much attention that it made him quite shy, but he was not easy to please, and did not care about any of them. Now, before he had time to think, Cupid had entangled him in his net, and he was filled with love towards Koma. She fully returned his passion, but, like a woman, she saw the difficulties in the way, and consulted sadly with Gon as to the means of overcoming them. Gon entreated his master to set matters right by buying Koma, but her mistress would not part from her. Then the music master was asked to sell Gon to the lady, but he declined to listen to any such suggestion, so everything remained as before.

At length the love of the couple grew to such a pitch that they determined to please themselves, and to seek their fortunes together. So one moonlight night they stole away, and ventured out into an unknown world. All day long they marched bravely on through the sunshine, till they had left their homes far behind them, and towards evening they found themselves in a large park.

The wanderers by this time were very hot and tired, and the grass looked very soft and inviting, and the trees cast cool deep shadows, when suddenly an ogre appeared in this Paradise, in the shape of a big, big dog! He came springing towards them showing all his teeth, and Koma shrieked, and rushed up a cherry tree. Gon, however, stood his ground boldly, and prepared to give battle, for he felt that Koma's eyes were upon him, and that he must not run away. But, alas, his courage would have availed him nothing had his enemy once touched him, for he was large and powerful, and very fierce. From her perch in the tree Koma saw it all, and screamed with all her might, hoping that someone would hear, and come to help. Luckily a servant of the princess to whom the park belonged was walking by, and he drove off the dog, and picking up the trembling Gon in his arms, carried him to his mistress.

So poor little Koma was left alone, while Gon was borne away full of trouble, not in the least knowing what to do. Even the attention paid him by the princess, who was delighted with his beauty and pretty ways, did not console him, but there was no use in fighting against fate, and he could only wait and see what would turn up.

The princess, Gon's new mistress, was so good and kind that everybody loved her, and she would have led a happy life, had it not been for a serpent who had fallen in love with her, and was constantly annoying her by his presence. Her servants had orders to drive him away as often as he appeared, but as they were careless, and the serpent very sly, it sometimes happened that he was able to slip past them, and then frighten the princess by appearing before her.

One day she was seated in her room, playing on her favourite musical instrument, when she felt something gliding up her sash, and saw her enemy making his way to kiss her cheek. She shrieked and threw herself backwards, and Gon, who had been curled up on a stool at her feet, understood her terror, and with one bound seized the snake by his neck. He gave him one bite and one shake, and flung him on the ground, where he lay, never to worry the princess anymore. Then she took Gon in her arms, and praised and caressed him, and saw that he had the nicest bits to eat, and the softest mats to lie on, and he would have had nothing in the world to wish for if only he could have seen Koma again.

Time passed on, and one morning Gon lay before the house door, basking in the sun. He looked lazily at the world stretched out before him, and saw in the distance a big ruffian of a cat teasing and ill-treating quite a little one. He jumped up, full of rage, and chased away the big cat, and then he turned to comfort the little one, when his heart nearly burst with joy to find that it was Koma.

At first Koma did not know him again, he had grown so large and stately, but when it dawned upon her who it was, her happiness knew no bounds. And they rubbed their heads and their noses again and again, while their purring might have been heard a mile off.

Paw in paw they appeared before the princess, and told her the story of their life and its sorrows. The princess wept for sympathy, and promised that they should never more be parted, but should live with her to the end of their days.

By-and-bye the princess herself got married, and brought a prince to dwell in the palace in the park. And she told him all about her two cats, and how brave Gon had been, and how he had delivered her from her enemy the serpent.

And when the prince heard, he swore they should never leave them, but should go with the princess wherever she went. So it all fell out as the princess wished, and Gon and Koma had many children, and so had the princess, and they all played together, and were friends to the end of their lives.

The Greedy Palm-Cat

This is a Sri Lankan tale

This tale has been adapted from Village Folk-Tales Of Ceylon Volume 3 by Henry Parker. The book was published in 1914 by Luzac & Co, India. The book contains a selection of traditional folk tales and legends from Sri Lanka. These stories are drawn from various regions of the island and reflect the cultural diversity and rich storytelling tradition of the Sinhalese and Tamil communities. The tales encompass a wide range of themes, including mythology, folklore, superstition, morality, and everyday life.

In a certain city, three farmers cleared a plot of land for cultivation. After clearing it, they decided, "Let's plant some plantains."

They planted the plantains, but as the fruits began to mature, the flowers started falling off before the fruits could ripen.

Puzzled, they inspected the plants and found that only the fresh fruits were intact while the rest were missing. They couldn't figure out if someone was destroying their crops. To solve the mystery, they came up with a plan. They brought in a plantain tree and inserted poison into its fruits.

As the flowers fell and the fruits ripened, releasing a sweet fragrance, a female palm-cat arrived with her kitten. The kitten looked up at the tree, and the mother warned, "Farmer, this is not safe."

The young palm-cat replied, "What harm is there in just looking up if I don't climb the tree?"

Ignoring the warning, it climbed the tree.

The mother cautioned again, "Don't do it."

The young palm-cat responded, "What harm is there in climbing if I don't touch the fruit?"

But it did touch the fruit and examined it.

The mother asked, "What are you doing?"

The young one replied, "What harm is there in touching it if I don't eat it?"

The young palm-cat peeled the fruit.

The mother asked again, "What are you doing?"

The young one replied, "What harm is there in peeling it if I don't eat it?"

Then it sniffed the fruit.

The mother asked, "What are you doing?"

The young one replied, "What harm is there in smelling it if I don't eat it?"

Finally, it put the fruit in its mouth.

The mother warned, "What are you doing?"

The young one replied, "What harm is there in putting it in my mouth if I don't swallow it?"

But when it swallowed the fruit, it fell down and died. The mother palm-cat left, mourning her loss, and the thief of the garden had been caught.

Cat Tails – Feline Fairy Tales, Myths And Legends

The Cat and the Mouse

This is a Persian tale

This story has been adapted from a tale originally told by Hartwell James in The Cat And The Mouse, published in 1906 by Henry Altemus Company, Philadelphia. The Cat and the Mouse follows in the tradition of Aesop's fables, using anthropomorphic animals to convey lessons about behaviour, morality, and human nature in a format accessible to children.

ACCORDING to the decree of Heaven, there once lived in the Persian city of Kerman a cat that looked like a dragon, a longsighted cat who hunted like a lion, a cat with fascinating eyes and long whiskers and sharp teeth. Its body was like a drum, its beautiful fur like ermine skin.

Nobody was happier than this cat, neither the newly-wedded bride, nor the hospitable master of the house when he looks round on the smiling faces of his guests.

This cat moved in the midst of friends, boon companions of the saucepan, the cup, and the milk jug of the court, and of the dinner table when the cloth is spread.

Perceiving the wine cellar open, one day, the cat ran gleefully into it to see if he could catch a mouse, and hid himself behind a wine jar. At that moment a mouse ran out of a hole in the wall, quickly climbed the jar, and putting his head into it, drank so long and so deeply that he became drunk, talked very stupidly, and fancied he was as bold as a lion.

"Where is the cat?" he shouted, "that I may off with his head. I would cut off his head as if on the battlefield. A cat in front of me would fare worse than any dog who might happen to cross my path."

The cat ground his teeth with rage while hearing this. Quicker than the eye could follow, he made a spring, seized the mouse in his claws, and said, "Oh, little mouse, now will you take off my head?"

"I am your servant," replied the mouse, "forgive my sin. I was drunk. I am your slave, a slave whose ear is pierced and on whose shoulder the yoke is."

"Tell fewer lies," replied the cat. "Was there ever such a liar? I heard all you said and you shall pay for your sin with your life. I will make your life less than that of a dead dog."

So the cat killed and ate the mouse, but afterwards, being sorry for what he had done, he ran to the Mosque, and passed his hands over his face, poured water on his paws, and anointed himself as he had seen the faithful do at the appointed hours of prayer.

Then he began to recite the beautiful chapter to Allah in the Holy Book of the Persians, and to make his confession. "I have repented, and will not again tear the body of a mouse with my teeth. I will give bread to the deserving poor. Forgive my sin, O great Forgiver, for have I not come to you bowed down with sorrow?"

He repeated this so many times and with so much feeling that he really thought he meant it, and finally wept for grief.

A little mouse happened to be behind the pulpit, and overhearing the cat's vows, speedily carried the glad but surprising news to the other mice. Breathlessly he related how that the cat had become a true Muslim, and how that he had seen him in the Mosque weeping and lamenting, and saying, "Oh, Creator of the world, put away my sin, for I have offended like a big fool." Then the mouse went on to describe how that the cat had a rosary of beads, and made pious reflections in the spirit of a true penitent.

The mice began to make merry when they heard this startling news, for they were exceedingly glad. Seven chosen mice, each the headman of a mouse village, arose and gave thanks that the cat should have entered the fold of the true believers.

All danced and shouted, "Ah, ah! Hu, hu!" and drank red wine and white wine until they were very merry. Two rang bells, two played castanets, and two sang. One carried a tray behind his back laden with good things, so that all could help themselves. Some smoked water-pipes, while another acted like a clown, and others played various tunes on different musical instruments.

A few days after the feast, the King of the mice said to them, "Oh, friends, all of you bring costly presents worthy of the cat!" Then the mice scattered in search of gifts, and soon returned, each bearing something worthy of presentation, even to a nobleman.

One brought a bottle of wine, another a dish full of raisins, while others came with salted nuts and melon seeds, lumps of cheese, basins of sugar-candy, pistachio nuts, little cakes iced with sugar, bottles of lemon juice, Indian shawls, hats, cloaks and many other things.

Discreetly they bore their gifts before the King of the Cats. When in the royal presence, they made humble obeisances, touching their foreheads on the ground, and saluting him, said, "Oh, master, liberator of the lives of all, we have brought gifts worthy of your service. We beseech you to accept them."

Then the cat thought to himself, "I am rewarded for becoming a pious Muslim. Though I have endured much hunger, yet this day finds me freely and amply provided for. Not for many days have I broken my fast. It is clear that Allah is appeased."

Then he turned to the mice, and bade them come nearer, calling them his friends. And they went forward trembling. So frightened were they that they were hardly aware of what they were doing. When they were close the cat made a sudden spring upon them.

Five mice he caught, each one the chief of a village, two with his front paws, two with his hind ones, and one in his mouth. The remaining mice barely escaped with their lives.

Picking up one of their murdered brothers, they quickly carried the sad news to the rest of the mice, saying: "Why do you sit still, oh mice? Throw dust on your heads, oh young men, for the cruel cat has seized five of our unsuspecting companions with teeth and claws and has killed them."

Then for the space of five days they rent their clothes as do the mourners, and cast dust on their heads. Then they said, "We must go and tell our King all that has befallen the mice. We must not fail to tell him this calamity."

Whereupon they all rose up and went their way in deep sorrow, one beating the muffled drum, one tolling the bell, and all had shawls around their necks, their tears the while running in little streams down their whiskers.

Arrived where the King was sitting on his throne, the mice paid homage to him, saying: "Master, we are subjects and you are King. Behold the cat has treated us cruelly since he became a pious follower of The Prophet. Whereas, before his conversion he was wont to catch only one of us in a year, now that he is a sincere Muslim his appetite has so increased that only five at a time will satisfy him."

Whereupon the King fell into such a violent rage that he resembled a saucepan boiling over. But to the deputation of mice he spoke very kindly, calling them his newly-arrived and welcome guests, and to comfort them vowed that he would give the cat such a chastisement that the news of it should circulate through the world.

Then, observing their grief, he commanded that the dead mouse should be buried with all pomp and ceremony. Accordingly they made lamentation for a whole week, as though it had been for one of royal degree, and having prepared delicious sweetmeats, they placed them in baskets and carried them with streaming eyes to the grave.

After the burial service, the King ordered the army to assemble on a given day on the great sandy plain that stretches as far as the eye can see around the city. Then he addressed them, saying, "Oh, mice and soldiers, inasmuch as the cat has so cruelly ill-treated our countrymen, he being a heretic and an evil doer, and brutal in nature, we must now go to the city of Kerman and fight him."

So three hundred and thirty thousand mice went forth, armed with swords, guns, and spears, and with flags and pennons bravely flying. A passing Arab from the desert, skilfully balancing himself on the back of a swift-traveling camel by means of a long pole, spied the great army in motion, and was so overcome with astonishment that he lost his balance and fell off. Several regiments of mice were put out of action by his fall, but nothing daunted, the army pressed on.

When the army was ready for battle, the King again addressed them saying, "O young men, an ambassador must be sent to the cat, one who is able, discreet, and eloquent."

Then they all shouted, "The King's orders shall be carried out! Upon our heads be it."

Now, there was present a learned and eloquent mouse, the ruler of a province, and he it was that the King commanded to go as an ambassador to the cat in the city of Kerman. Almost before his name was out of the King's mouth, he had jumped out of his place in the ranks, and, traveling as swiftly as the winds of the desert, he went in boldly before the cat and said,

"As an ambassador from the King of the Mice am I come, bowed down with grief and fatigue. Know this, my master has determined to wage war, and even now comes with his army to take off your head."

The cat roared out in reply, "Go tell your King to eat dust! I come not out of this city except at my good pleasure!"

Then he sent messengers to bring up quickly some fighting and hunting cats to Kerman from Khorassan, the land of the sun.

As soon as the cat's army was ready, the King of the Cats gave them marching orders, promising to come himself to the battle on the next day. The cats came out on horseback, each one like a hungry tiger. The mice also mounted their steeds, armed to the teeth, and boiling with rage. Shouting "Allah! Allah!" the armies fell upon each other with unsheathed swords.

So many cats and mice were killed that there was no room for the horses' feet. The cats fought valiantly, their fierce attacks carrying them through the first line of the mice, then through the second, and many Amirs and chiefs were killed. The mice, thinking the battle lost, turned to flee, crying out, "Throw dust upon your heads, young men!"

But afterwards, rallying again, they faced their pursuers and attacked the right wing of the cat's army, shouting their battle cry of "Allah! Allah!"

In the thickest of the fray a mounted mouse speared the King of the Cats, so that he fell fainting to the ground. Before he could rise, the mouse leaped upon him and brought him captive to the King of the Mice. So the cats were defeated on that day and sullenly retreated to the city of Kerman.

Having bound the cat, the mice beat him until he became unconscious. Then the plain echoed with the beating of tom-toms and shouts of joy. Then the King of the Mice seated himself on his throne and ordered the cat to be brought before him.

"Scoundrel!" he said to him, "Why have you eaten up my army? Hear now the King of the Mice."

The cat hung his head in fear, and remained silent. After a few minutes, he said, "I am your servant, even to death."

Then the King replied, "Carry this black-faced dog to the execution ground. I will come in person without delay to kill him in revenge for the blood of my slaughtered subjects."

So he mounted his elephant, and his guard marched proudly before him. The cat, with his paws tied together, stood weeping. Upon arriving at the execution grounds and discerning that the cat was not yet executed, the King said angrily to the hangman: "Why is it this prisoner is still alive? Hang him immediately!"

At that very moment a horseman came galloping furiously from the city and begged the King, saying, "Forgive this miserable cat; in future he will do you no harm."

However, the King turned a deaf ear to his entreaties, ordering that the cat be killed at once. The mice hesitated, being unwilling, through fear, to carry out the order.

Of course, this made the King very angry. "O foolish mice!" he cried, "You will all take pity on the cat, in order that he may again make a sacrifice of you."

Directly the cat saw the horseman, his courage revived. With one bound he sprang from his place as does the tiger on his prey, burst his bonds asunder, and seized five unfortunate mice. The other mice, filled with dismay and terror, ran here and there, crying wildly, "Allah! Allah! Shoot him! Cut off his head, as did Rostam his enemies on the day of battle!"

When the King of the Mice saw what, had happened, he fainted, whereupon the cat leaped on him, pulled off his crown, and placing the rope over his head, hanged him, so that he died immediately.

Then he darted here and there, seizing and slaying, and dashing mice to the earth, till the whole army of mice was routed, and there was none left to oppose him.

The Cottager And His Cat

This is an Icelandic tale

This tale has been adapted from The Crimson Fairy Book by Andrew Lang. The book was published in 1906 by Longman, Green And Company, London. Lang was a Scottish poet, novelist, literary critic, and contributor to the field of anthropology. Lang is perhaps best known for his "Fairy Books" series, which includes collections of fairy tales from around the world

Once upon a time there lived an old man and his wife in a dirty, tumble-down cottage, not very far from the splendid palace where the king and queen dwelt. In spite of the wretched state of the hut, which many people declared was too bad even for a pig to live in, the old man was very rich, for he was a great miser, and lucky besides, and would often go without food all day sooner than change one of his beloved gold pieces.

But after a while he found that he had starved himself once too often. He fell ill, and had no strength to get well again, and in a few days he died, leaving his wife and one son behind him.

The night following his death, the son dreamed that an unknown man appeared to him and said, "Listen to me. Your father is dead and your mother will soon die, and all their riches will belong to you. Half of his wealth is ill-gotten, and this you must give back to the poor from whom he squeezed it. The other half you must throw into the sea. Watch, however, as the money sinks into the water, and if anything should swim, catch it and keep it, even if it is nothing more than a bit of paper."

Then the man vanished, and the youth awoke.

The remembrance of his dream troubled him greatly. He did not want to part with the riches that his father had left him, for he had known all his life what it was to be cold and hungry, and now he had hoped for a little comfort and pleasure. Still, he was honest and good-hearted, and if his father had come wrongfully by his wealth he felt he could never enjoy it, and at last he made up his mind to do as he had been bidden. He found out who were the people who were poorest in the village, and spent half of his money in helping them, and the other half he put in his pocket. From a rock that jutted right out into the sea he flung it in. In a moment it was out of sight, and no man could have told the spot where it had sunk, except for a tiny scrap of paper floating on the water. He stretched down carefully and managed to reach it, and on opening it found six shillings wrapped inside. This was now all the money he had in the world.

The young man stood and looked at it thoughtfully. "Well, I can't do much with this," he said to himself, but, after all, six shillings were better than nothing, and he wrapped them up again and slipped them into his coat.

He worked in his garden for the next few weeks, and he and his mother contrived to live on the fruit and vegetables he got out of it, and then she too died suddenly. The poor fellow felt very sad when he had laid her in her grave, and with a heavy heart he wandered into the forest, not knowing where he was going. By-and-by he began to get hungry, and seeing a small hut in front of him, he knocked at the door and asked if they could give him some milk. The old woman who opened it begged him to come in, adding kindly, that if he wanted a night's lodging he might have it without its costing him anything.

Two women and three men were at supper when he entered, and silently made room for him to sit down by them. When he had eaten he began to look about him, and was surprised to see an animal sitting by the fire different from anything he had ever noticed before. It was grey in colour, and not very big, but its eyes were large and very bright, and it seemed to be singing in an odd way, quite unlike any animal in the forest.

"What is the name of that strange little creature?" asked he.

And they answered, "We call it a cat."

"I should like to buy it, if it is not too dear," said the young man, "it would be company for me."

And they told him that he might have it for six shillings, if he cared to give so much. The young man took out his precious bit of paper, handed them the six shillings, and the next morning bade them farewell, with the cat lying snugly in his cloak.

For the whole day they wandered through meadows and forests, till in the evening they reached a house. The young fellow knocked at the door and asked the old man who opened it if he could rest there that night, adding that he had no money to pay for it.

"Then I must give it to you," answered the man, and led him into a room where two women and two men were sitting at supper. One of the women was the old man's wife, the other his daughter. He placed the cat on the mantel shelf, and they all crowded round to examine this strange beast, and the cat rubbed itself against them, and held out its paw, and sang to them, and the women were delighted, and gave it everything that a cat could eat, and a great deal more besides.

After hearing the youth's story, and how he had nothing in the world left him except his cat, the old man advised him to go to the palace, which was only a few miles distant, and take counsel of the king, who was kind to everyone, and would certainly be his friend. The young man thanked him, and said he would gladly take his advice, and early next morning he set out for the royal palace.

He sent a message to the king to beg for an audience, and received a reply that he was to go into the great hall, where he would find his Majesty.

The king was at dinner with his court when the young man entered, and he signed to him to come near. The youth bowed low, and then gazed in surprise at the crowd of little black creatures who were running about the floor, and even on the table itself. Indeed, they were so bold that they snatched pieces of food from the King's own plate, and if he drove them away, tried to bite his hands, so that he could not eat his food, and his courtiers fared no better.

"What sort of animals are these?" asked the youth of one of the ladies sitting near him.

"They are called rats," answered the king, who had overheard the question, "and for years we have tried some way of putting an end to them, but it is impossible. They come into our very beds."

At this moment something was seen flying through the air. The cat was on the table, and with two or three shakes a number of rats were lying dead round him. Then a great scuffling of feet was heard, and in a few minutes the hall was clear.

For some minutes the King and his courtiers only looked at each other in astonishment. "What kind of animal is that which can work magic of this sort?" asked he.

And the young man told him that it was called a cat, and that he had bought it for six shillings.

And the King answered: "Because of the luck you have brought me, in freeing my palace from the plague which has tormented me for many years, I will give you the choice of two things. Either you shall be my Prime Minister, or else you shall marry my daughter and reign after me. Say, which shall it be?"

"The princess and the kingdom," said the young man.

And so it was.

The Lazy Cat

This is a Hungarian tale

This adaptation is taken from a story originally collected by János Kriza, János Erdélyi, Gyula Pap, and others, and adapted by the Reverend William Henry Jones and Lewis L. Kropf in The Folk Tales of the Magyars, published by Elliot Stock for the Folklore Society in 1889.

A lad married a lazy rich girl, and he made a vow that he would never beat her. The lass never did any work but went about from house to house gossiping and making all kinds of mischief, but still her husband never scolded her.

One morning as he was going out to his work he said to the cat, "You cat, I command you to do everything that is needed in the house. While I am away put everything in order, cook the dinner, and do some spinning, if you don't, I'll give you such a thrashing as you won't forget."

The cat listened to his speech half asleep, blinking on the hearth. The woman thought to herself, "My husband has gone mad." So she said, "Why do you order the cat to do all these things, which she knows nothing about?"

"Whether she does or whether she doesn't it's all the same to me, wife. I have no one else whom I can ask to do anything, and if she does not do all that I have ordered her to do you will see that I will give her such a thrashing as she will never forget."

With this he went out to work, and the wife began to talk to the cat and said, "You had better get your work done, or he will beat you," but the cat did not work, and the wife went from house-to-house gossiping.

When she came home the cat was asleep on the hearth, and the fire had gone out, so she said, "Make the fire up, cat, and get your work done, or you will get a sound thrashing," but the cat did not work.

In the evening the master came home and found that nothing was done and that his orders were not carried out, so he took hold of the cat by its tail and fastened it to his wife's back, and began to beat till his wife cried out, "Don't beat that cat anymore! Don't beat that cat anymore! It is not her fault. She cannot help it. She does not understand these things."

"Will you promise then that you will do it all in her stead?" inquired her husband.

"I will do it all and even more than you order," replied his wife, "if you will only leave off beating that cat."

The woman then ran off home to complain to her mother of all these things, and said, "I have promised that I will do all the work instead of the cat, in order to prevent my husband beating her to death on my back."

And then her father spoke up and said, "If you have promised to do it you must do it. If not, the cat will get a thrashing tomorrow." And he sent her back to her husband.

Next time the master again told the cat what she had to do, and she did nothing again. So she got another beating on the wife's back, who ran home again to complain, but her father drove her back, and she ran so fast that her foot did not touch the ground as she went.

On the third morning again the master commenced to give his commands to the cat, who, however, was too frightened to listen, and did no work that day, but this time the mistress did her work for her. She forgot nothing she had promised. She lighted the fire, fetched water, cooked the food, swept the house, and put everything in order, for she was frightened lest her husband should beat the poor cat again, for the wretched animal in its agony stuck its claws into her back, and, besides, the end of the two-tailed whip reached further than the cat's back, so that with every stroke she received one as well as the cat.

When her husband came home everything was in order, and he kept muttering, "Don't be afraid, cat, I won't thrash you this time," and his wife laid the cloth joyfully, dished up the food, and they had a good meal in peace.

After that the cat had no more beatings, and the mistress became such a good housewife that you could not wish for a better.

Cat Tails – Feline Fairy Tales, Myths And Legends

Pussy Willow

This is an American tale

This tale is adapted from The emerald Story Book by Ada M. Skinner and Eleanor L. Skinner, published by Duffield And Co., New York, in 1915. The story "Pussy Willow" by Kate Louise Brown is a literary tale rather than a traditional folk tale, and it originates from the United States. Kate Louise Brown was an American author who wrote children's literature in the late 19th and early 20th centuries.

All winter Miss Pussy had been shut up in her house by the brook, but one bright morning in early spring, the door of her house opened. Then she stepped out to see the world.

The swelling buds were rocking to and fro on the branches, the grass blades were peeping above the ground, and a few brave flowers were opening their sleepy eyes.

"Dear me!" cried Pussy, "the wind is sharp and cold, even if it is a bright day."

"Why, whom have we here?" asked the brook in great surprise. "True as I live, it is Miss Pussy Willow! Good morning, Pussy, you are out bright and early, but why do you wear that fur hood? Summer is coming and the days grow warmer."

"Oh, Mother Nature told me to wear it in case of toothache."

Everybody was glad to see Pussy. The little brook, the grass, the buds, and the little spring birds. But they were all very curious to know why she wore her fur hood.

Poor Pussy! She was tempted more than once to take it off, so much was said about it, but she didn't. She thought best to mind Mother Nature.

Now, it grieves me to say Mr. Robin was very bold and saucy. He whispered some unkind things to Pussy's friends one day. The next morning, when Pussy opened her eyes, the birds, the buds, the brook, the grass, and the flowers began to whisper to themselves: "Do you suppose Pussy Willow has to wear her hood because she has no hair? Poor Pussy Willow!"

Poor Pussy Willow! Brave Pussy felt very sad. All she said was, "Wait and see."

How surprised everyone was a few days after this! There was Pussy Willow with no fur hood on her head, but bright golden curls were dancing up and down in the breeze.

"Pussy Willow is not a baldhead. She wears beautiful golden curls," cried all her friends. Mr. Robin hid his head and flew away, very much ashamed.

Cat Tails – Feline Fairy Tales, Myths And Legends

The Troll Turned Cat

This is a Scandinavian tale

This tale has been adapted from The Fairy Mythology by Thomas Keightley. The book was published in 1892 by George Bell and Sons, London and New York. First published in 1828, this seminal work explores the origins, evolution, and cultural significance of fairy beliefs across various cultures and historical periods.

About a quarter of a mile from Soröe lies Pedersborg, and a little farther on is the town of Lyng. Just between these towns is a hill called Bröndhöi (Spring-hill), said to be inhabited by the Troll-people.

There goes a story that there was once among these Troll-people of Bröndhöi an old cross-grained curmudgeon of a Troll, whom the rest nick-named Knurremurre (Rumble-grumble), because he was evermore the cause of noise and uproar within the hill.

This Knurremurre having discovered what he thought to be too great a degree of intimacy between his young wife and a young Troll of the society, took this in such ill part, that he vowed vengeance, swearing he would have the life of the young one. The latter, accordingly, thought it would be his best course to be off out of the hill till better times, so, turning himself into a noble tortoiseshell tom-cat, he quitted his old residence one fine morning, and journeyed down to the neighbouring town of Lyng, where he established himself in the house of an honest but poor man named Plat.

Here he lived for a long time comfortable and easy, with nothing to annoy him, and was as happy as any tom-cat or Troll crossed in love could be. Every day he got plenty of milk and good groute to eat, and lay the whole day long at his ease in a warm arm-chair behind the stove.

One evening Plat happened to come home rather late, and as he entered the room the cat was sitting in his usual place, scraping meal-groute out of a pot, and licking the pot itself carefully.

"Listen, my lovely cat," said Plat, as he came in at the door, "till I tell you what happened to me on the road. Just as I was coming past Bröndhöi, a Troll came out, and he called out to me, and said, "Listen, Plat, tell your cat, that Knurremurre is dead."

The moment the cat heard these words, he tumbled the pot down on the floor, sprang out of the chair, and stood up on his hind-legs. Then, as he hurried out of the door, he cried out with exultation, "What! Is Knurremurre dead? Then I may go home as fast as I please."

And so saying he scampered off to the hill, to the amazement of honest Plat, and it is likely that he lost no time in making his advances to the young widow.

The Hypocritical Cat

This is a tale from India

This tale has been adapted from The Giant Crab and Other Tales from Old India by W. H. D. Rouse. The book was published in 1897 by David Nutt, London. The book features a variety of folk tales, fairy tales, and legends from ancient India. These stories encompass a wide range of themes, including mythical creatures, heroic deeds, magical quests, and moral lessons. Many of the tales are drawn from Hindu mythology, including stories from the Mahabharata, the Ramayana, and the Puranas.

Once upon a time there was a troop of Rats that used to live in holes by a river side. A certain Cat often saw them going to and fro, and longed to have them to eat. But he was not strong enough to attack them all together, and besides, that would not have suited his purpose, because most of them would have run away.

So he used to stand early in the morning, not far from their holes, with his face towards the sun, snuffing up the air, and standing on one leg.

The Rats wondered why he did that, so one day they all trooped up to him in a body, and asked the reason.

"What is your name, sir?" they began.

"Holy is my name," said the Cat.

"Why do you stand on one leg?"

"Because if I stood on all four, the earth could not bear my weight."

"And why do you keep your mouth open?"

"Because I feed on the air, and never eat anything else."

"And why do you face the sun?"

"Because I worship the sun."

"What a pious Cat!" the Rats all thought. Ever after that, when they started out in the morning, they did not fail first to make their bow to the Cat one by one, and to show thus their respect for his piety.

This was just what our Cat wanted. Every day, as they filed past, he waited till the tail of the string came up, then like lightning pounced upon the hindmost, and gobbled him up in a trice, after which he stood on one leg as before, licking his lips greedily.

For a while all went well with the Cat's plan, but at last the Chief of the Rats noticed that the troop seemed to grow smaller. Here and there he missed some familiar face. He could not make it out, but at last a thought came into his mind, that perhaps the pious Cat might know more about it than he chose to tell.

Next day accordingly, he posted himself at the tail of the troop, where he could see everything that went on, and as the Rats one by one bowed before the Cat, he watched the Cat out of the corner of his eye.

As he came up, the Cat prepared for his pounce. But our Rat was ready for him, and dodged out of the way.

"Aha!" said the Rat, "so that is your piety! Feeds on the air, does he! And worships the sun, eh? What a humbug!"

And with one spring he was at the Cat's throat, and his sharp teeth stuck fast in the Cat's throat. The other Rats heard the scuffle, and came trooping back, and it was crunch and munch, till not a vestige remained of the hypocritical Cat. Those who came first had cat to eat, and those who came last went sniffing about at the mouths of their friends, and asking what the taste of cat meat was like. And ever after the Rats lived in peace and happiness.

Belling The Cat

This is a Greek tale

This tale has been adapted from The Junior Classics, Volume 1, Fairy And Wonder Tales by William Patten. The book was published in 1912 by P. F. Collier & Son, New York. The Junior Classics, Volume 1: Fairy and Wonder Tales is the first volume in a collection of classic literature curated and edited for young readers by William Patten. Published in 1912, this anthology aimed to introduce children to a diverse selection of fairy tales and wonder tales from around the world, presenting them in an accessible and engaging format.

Long ago, the mice held a general council to consider what measures they could take to outwit their common enemy, the Cat. Some said this, and some said that, but at last a young mouse got up and said he had a proposal to make, which he thought would meet the case.

"You will all agree," he said, "that our chief danger consists in the sly and treacherous manner in which the enemy approaches us. Now, if we could receive some signal of her approach, we could easily escape from her. I venture, therefore, to propose that a small bell be procured, and it should be attached by a ribbon round the neck of the Cat. By this means we should always know when she was about, and could easily retire while she was in the neighbourhood."

This proposed met with general applause, until an old mouse got up and said, "That is all very well, but who is to bell the Cat?"

The mice looked at one another and nobody spoke. Then the old mouse said, "it is easy to propose impossible remedies!"

Cat Tails – Feline Fairy Tales, Myths And Legends

Brother Rabbit and Mr. Wildcat

This is an African-American tale

This tale has been adapted from Nights With Uncle Remus by Joel Chandler Harris. The book was published in 1883 by Houghton Mifflin Company, New York & Boston. "Brother Rabbit and Mr. Wildcat" is one of the many stories included in Joel Chandler Harris's Uncle Remus series, a collection of African American folktales that Harris adapted and published in the late 19th century. These stories are often framed as being told by Uncle Remus, a fictional elderly black man, to a young white boy on a Southern plantation.

"Uncle Remus," asked the little boy after a pause, "where did Brother Rabbit go when he got out of the hollow tree?"

"Well, sir," said Uncle Remus, "you might not believe it, but as soon as that tricky creature got out of that tree, he found himself in more trouble, and he was almost scared out of his skin.

"When Brother Rabbit got out of the hollow tree, he threw some sass back at old Brother Buzzard and then took off down the big road instead of heading home to check on his family. He was going along—lickety-clickety, clickety-lickety—when, before he knew it, he felt something drop down on him. And there he was. Bless your soul, when Brother Rabbit finally gathered his wits, he realized it was old Mr. Wildcat hugging him from behind and whispering in his ear."

"What did he whisper, Uncle Remus?" the little boy asked.

"Oh, this and that," replied Uncle Remus, sidestepping the question.

"But what did he say?" the boy insisted.

"Here's how it happened," said Uncle Remus, ignoring the boy's curiosity. "Brother Rabbit was galloping down the road, and old Mr. Wildcat was stretched out, taking a nap on a tree limb hanging across the road. He heard Brother Rabbit coming lickety-clickety down the road, so he got himself ready. When Brother Rabbit danced under the limb, all Mr. Wildcat had to do was drop right down on him, and there he was. Mr. Wildcat hugged him tight and laughed while whispering in his ear."

"Well, Uncle Remus, what did he *say*?" the little boy persisted.

The old man made a sweeping gesture with his left hand that could mean anything or nothing, and then continued his story.

"Old Mr. Wildcat hugged Brother Rabbit close and whispered in his ear. Brother Rabbit kicked and squirmed. After a while, he caught his breath and said, 'Oh! Oh Lordy-lordy! What have I done now?'

"Mr. Wildcat rubbed his wet nose on Brother Rabbit's ear, sending chills up his back. Then he said, 'Oh Brother Rabbit, I just love you! You've been fooling all my cousins and kinfolk, and it wasn't long ago that you sent Cousin Fox to me, and I almost tore him in two. Oh, Brother Rabbit! I just love you,' he said.

"Then he laughed, and his teeth clicked together right near Brother Rabbit's ear.

Brother Rabbit said, 'Well, Mr. Wildcat, I thought you might like to have Brother Fox for supper, which is why I sent him to where you were. It's a sad thing when folks can't be friends without something or other getting in the way, and if that's the case, I won't be friends with anyone anymore, no, I won't.'

"Mr. Wildcat wiped his nose on Brother Rabbit's ear and seemed to be thinking.

Brother Rabbit kept talking. He said, 'All this time, have I ever bothered you, Mr. Wildcat?'

"'No, Brother Rabbit, I can't say that you have.'

"'No, Mr. Wildcat, I haven't. And more than that, I've done my best to help you out. And even though you've jumped on me and scared me terribly, I'm still willing to do you a good turn. I hear some wild turkeys yelping out there, and if you'll let me go this time, I'll go call them up, and you can pretend to be dead. When they come over to check you out, you can jump up and catch a whole bunch of them before they get away.'

"Mr. Wildcat stopped to think, because if there's one kind of meat he loves, it's turkey meat. Then he asked Brother Rabbit if he was joking. Brother Rabbit said if he were sitting somewhere alone, he might joke, but how could he joke when Mr. Wildcat had him hugged so tight? This sounded so convincing that it wasn't long before Mr. Wildcat agreed if Brother Rabbit was serious. And after a while, bless your soul, if you had come along there, you'd have seen old Mr. Wildcat stretched out on the ground, looking like he'd been dead a month, and you'd have heard old Brother Rabbit yelping out in the bushes just like a real turkey hen."

The little boy, always eager for a demonstration, asked Uncle Remus how Brother Rabbit could yelp like a turkey hen. In response, Uncle Remus found a reed on his mantelpiece, which he intended to use as a pipe stem. He put one end of the reed in his mouth and enclosed the other end in his hands. By sucking air through the reed and adjusting the tone with his hands, the old man produced a remarkable imitation of a turkey hen's call, much to the boy's delight.

"Ah, Lord!" exclaimed Uncle Remus, after repeating the call until the boy was satisfied. "Many a time, I've gone out in the woods with old master before daybreak and called wild turkeys right up to where we could have killed them with a stick. When we first moved here from Virginia, they used to come right up to where the barn is now, and I've even seen old master kill them right out there by the front gate. But town folks have been coming around here with their pointer dogs until now, if you want to see a turkey track, you have to go down to the Oconee, and that's two miles away."

"Did the Wildcat catch the turkeys?" the little boy asked when it seemed Uncle Remus was about to drift off into his own memories.

"Goodness gracious!" exclaimed the old man. "Here I am running on, and there lies Mr. Wildcat waiting for Brother Rabbit to help bring up those turkeys. And it didn't take long either, because, bless your soul, old Brother Rabbit was a yelper, I tell you.

"Sure enough, after a while, here they came, with old Brother Gibley Gobbler leading the way. Brother Rabbit ran to meet them and gave them a wink about old Mr. Wildcat. By the time they got to where he was lying, Brother Gibley Gobbler and all his folks were deep in a big argument. One said he was dead, another said he wasn't, one said he was stiff, and another said he wasn't, and so on. They stretched out their necks and stepped high with their feet, but they didn't get too close to Mr. Wildcat.

"He lay there and didn't move. The wind ruffled his fur, but he didn't move. The sun shone down on him, but he didn't move. The turkeys gobbled and yelped, but they didn't get any closer. They argued and hollered, but they didn't get any closer. They stretched their necks and lifted their feet high, but they didn't get any closer.

"This went on until, finally, Mr. Wildcat got tired of waiting and jumped up to dash at the nearest turkey. But that turkey was ready, and when Mr. Wildcat came at him, he just flew up in the air, and Mr. Wildcat ran under him. Then he ran at another one, and that one flew up. They kept doing this until it wasn't long before Mr. Wildcat was so stiff in the joints and short of breath that he just had to lay down on the ground and rest.

"And when he did that, old Brother Gibley Gobbler and all his folks went about their business. But ever since that day, they've been constantly arguing with themselves and everybody who comes by. If you don't believe me," Uncle Remus added with an air of finality, "just holler at the first Gobbler you meet, and if he refuses to holler back, you can use my head for a hole in the wall. What more could you ask?"

"What happened to Brother Rabbit, Uncle Remus?" asked the little boy.

"Well, sir, Brother Rabbit left those lowlands. While the arguing was going on, he bowed his goodbyes and then just took off. The next day, old Brother Gibley Gobbler sent him a turkey wing to make a fan out of, and Brother Rabbit sent it to Miss Meadows and the girls. And I'll have you know," continued the old man, chuckling to himself, "they were quite impressed with it."

The Clever Cat

This is a Hungarian tale

This tale has been adapted from The Orange Fairy Book by Andrew Lang. The book was published in 1906 by Longman, Green And Company, London. Lang was a Scottish poet, novelist, literary critic, and contributor to the field of anthropology. Lang is perhaps best known for his "Fairy Books" series, which includes collections of fairy tales from around the world.

Once upon a time there lived an old man who dwelt with his son in a small hut on the edge of the plain. He was very old, and had worked very hard, and when at last he was struck down by illness he felt that he should never rise from his bed again.

So, one day, he bade his wife summon their son, when he came back from his journey to the nearest town, where he had been to buy bread.

"Come here, my son," said he, "I know myself well to be dying, and I have nothing to leave you but my falcon, my cat and my greyhound, but if you make good use of them you will never lack food. Be good to your mother, as you have been to me. And now farewell!"

Then he turned his face to the wall and died.

There was great mourning in the hut for many days, but at length the son rose up, and calling to his greyhound, his cat and his falcon, he left the house saying that he would bring back something for dinner. Wandering over the plain, he noticed a troop of gazelles, and pointed to his greyhound to give chase. The dog soon brought down a fine fat beast, and slinging it over his shoulders, the young man turned homewards. On the way, however, he passed a pond, and as he approached a cloud of birds flew into the air. Shaking his wrist, the falcon seated on it darted into the air, and swooped down upon the quarry he had marked, which fell dead to the ground. The young man picked it up, and put it in his pouch and then went towards home again.

Near the hut was a small barn in which he kept the produce of the little patch of corn, which grew close to the garden. Here a rat ran out almost under his feet, followed by another and another, but quick as thought the cat was upon them and not one escaped her.

When all the rats were killed, the young man left the barn. He took the path leading to the door of the hut, but stopped on feeling a hand laid on his shoulder.

"Young man," said an ogre (for such was the stranger), "you have been a good son, and you deserve the piece of luck which has befallen you this day. Come with me to that shining lake over there, and fear nothing."

Wondering a little at what might be going to happen to him, the youth did as the ogre bade him, and when they reached the shore of the lake, the ogre turned and said to him, "Step into the water and shut your eyes! You will find yourself sinking slowly to the bottom, but take courage, all will go well. Only bring up as much silver as you can carry, and we will divide it between us."

So the young man stepped bravely into the lake, and felt himself sinking, sinking, till he reached firm ground at last. In front of him lay four heaps of silver, and in the midst of them a curious white shining stone, marked over with strange characters, such as he had never seen before. He picked it up in order to examine it more closely, and as he held it the stone spoke.

"As long as you hold me, all your wishes will come true," it said. "But hide me in your turban, and then call to the ogre that you are ready to come up."

In a few minutes the young man stood again by the shores of the lake.

"Well, where is the silver?" asked the ogre, who was awaiting him.

"Ah, my father, how can I tell you! So bewildered was I, and so dazzled with the splendours of everything I saw, that I stood like a statue, unable to move. Then hearing steps approaching I got frightened, and called to you, as you know."

"You are no better than the rest," cried the ogre, and turned away in a rage.

When he was out of sight the young man took the stone from his turban and looked at it. "I want the finest camel that can be found, and the most splendid garments," said he.

"Shut your eyes then," replied the stone. And he shut them, and when he opened them again the camel that he had wished for was standing before him, while the festal robes of a desert prince hung from his shoulders. Mounting the camel, he whistled the falcon to his wrist, and, followed by his greyhound and his cat, he started homewards.

His mother was sewing at her door when this magnificent stranger rode up, and, filled with surprise, she bowed low before him.

"Don't you know me, mother?" he said with a laugh. And on hearing his voice the good woman nearly fell to the ground with astonishment.

"How have you got that camel and those clothes?" asked she. "Can a son of mine have committed murder in order to possess them?"

"Do not be afraid. They are quite honestly come by," answered the youth. "I will explain all by-and-by, but now you must go to the palace and tell the king I wish to marry his daughter."

At these words the mother thought her son had certainly gone mad, and stared blankly at him. The young man guessed what was in her heart, and replied with a smile, "Fear nothing. Promise all that he asks, for it will be fulfilled somehow."

So she went to the palace, where she found the king sitting in the Hall of Justice listening to the petitions of his people. The woman waited until all had been heard and the hall was empty, and then went up and knelt before the throne.

"My son has sent me to ask for the hand of the princess," said she.

The king looked at her and thought that she was mad, but, instead of ordering his guards to turn her out, he answered gravely, "Before he can marry the princess he must build me a palace of ice, which can be warmed with fires, and wherein the rarest singing- birds can live!"

"It shall be done, your Majesty," said she, and got up and left the hall.

Her son was anxiously awaiting her outside the palace gates, dressed in the clothes that he wore every day.

"Well, what have I got to do?" he asked impatiently, drawing his mother aside so that no one could overhear them.

"Oh, something quite impossible, and I hope you will put the princess out of your head," she replied.

"Well, but what is it?" persisted he.

"Nothing but to build a palace of ice wherein fires can burn that shall keep it so warm that the most delicate singing-birds can live in it!"

"I thought it would be something much harder than that," exclaimed the young man. "I will see about it at once." And leaving his mother, he went into the country and took the stone from his turban.

"I want a palace of ice that can be warmed with fires and filled with the rarest singing-birds!"

"Shut your eyes, then," said the stone, and he shut them, and when he opened them again there was the palace, more beautiful than anything he could have imagined, the fires throwing a soft pink glow over the ice.

"It is fit even for the princess," thought he to himself.

As soon as the king awoke next morning he ran to the window, and there across the plain he beheld the palace.

"That young man must be a great wizard. He may be useful to me." And when the mother came again to tell him that his orders had been fulfilled he received her with great honour, and bade her tell her son that the wedding was fixed for the following day.

The princess was delighted with her new home, and with her husband also, and several days slipped happily by, spent in turning over all the beautiful things that the palace contained. But at length the young man grew tired of always staying inside walls, and he told his wife that the next day he must leave her for a few hours, and go out hunting.

"You will not mind?" he asked.

She answered as became a good wife, "Yes, of course I shall mind, but I will spend the day in planning out some new dresses, and then it will be so delightful when you come back, you know!"

So the husband went off to hunt, with the falcon on his wrist, and the greyhound and the cat behind him, for the palace was so warm that even the cat did not mind living in it.

No sooner had he gone, than the ogre who had been watching his chance for many days, knocked at the door of the palace.

"I have just returned from a far country," he said, "and I have some of the largest and most brilliant stones in the world with me. The princess is known to love beautiful things, perhaps she might like to buy some?"

Now the princess had been wondering for many days what trimming she should put on her dresses, so that they should outshine the dresses of the other ladies at the court balls. Nothing that she thought of seemed good enough, so, when the message was brought that the ogre and his wares were below, she at once ordered that he should be brought to her chamber.

Oh, what beautiful stones he laid before her. What lovely rubies, and what rare pearls! No other lady would have jewels like those, of that the princess was quite sure, but she cast down her eyes so that the ogre might not see how much she longed for them.

"I fear they are too costly for me," she said carelessly, "and besides, I have hardly need of any more jewels just now."

"I have no particular wish to sell them myself," answered the ogre, with equal indifference. "But I have a necklace of shining stones which was left me by father, and one, the largest, engraved with weird characters, is missing. I have heard that it is in your husband's possession, and if you can get me that stone you shall have any of these jewels that you choose. But you will have to pretend that you want it for yourself, and, above all, do not mention me, for he sets great store by it, and would never part with it to a stranger!

Tomorrow I will return with some jewels yet finer than those I have with me today. So, madam, farewell!"

Left alone, the princess began to think of many things, but chiefly as to whether she would persuade her husband to give her the stone or not. At one moment she felt he had already bestowed so much upon her that it was a shame to ask for the only object he had kept back. No, it would be mean, and she could not do it! But then, those diamonds, and those strings of pearls! After all, they had only been married a week, and the pleasure of giving it to her ought to be far greater than the pleasure of keeping it for himself. And she was sure it would be!

Well, that evening, when the young man had supped off his favourite dishes which the princess took care to have specially prepared for him, she sat down close beside him, and began stroking his head. For some time she did not speak, but listened attentively to all the adventures that had befallen him that day.

"But I was thinking of you all the time," said he at the end, "and wishing that I could bring you back something you would like. But, alas! what is there that you do not possess already?"

"How good of you not to forget me when you are in the midst of such dangers and hardships," she answered. "Yes, it is true I have many beautiful things, but if you want to give me a present, and tomorrow is my birthday, there *is* one thing that I wish for very much."

"And what is that? Of course you shall have it directly!" he asked eagerly.

"It is that bright stone which fell out of the folds of your turban a few days ago," she answered, playing with his finger; "the little stone with all those funny marks upon it. I never saw any stone like it before."

The young man did not answer at first, then he said, slowly, "I have promised, and therefore I must perform. But will you swear never to part from it, and to keep it safely about you always? More I cannot tell you, but I beg you earnestly to take heed to this."

The princess was a little startled by his manner, and began to be sorry that she had every listened to the ogre. But she did not like to draw back, and pretended to be immensely delighted at her new toy, and kissed and thanked her husband for it.

"After all I needn't give it to the ogre," thought she as she dropped off to sleep.

Unluckily the next morning the young man went hunting again, and the ogre, who was watching, knew this, and did not come till much later than before. At the moment that he knocked at the door of the palace the princess had tired of all her employments, and her attendants were at their wits' end how to amuse her, when a tall servant dressed in scarlet came to announce that the ogre was below, and desired to know if the princess would speak to him.

"Bring him here at once!" cried she, springing up from her cushions, and forgetting all her resolves of the previous night. In another moment she was bending with rapture over the glittering gems.

"Have you got it?" asked the ogre in a whisper, for the princess's ladies were standing as near as they dared to catch a glimpse of the beautiful jewels.

"Yes, here," she answered, slipping the stone from her sash and placing it among the rest. Then she raised her voice, and began to talk quickly of the prices of the chains and necklaces, and after some bargaining, to deceive the attendants, she declared that she liked one string of pearls better than all the rest, and that the ogre might take away the other things, which were not half as valuable as he supposed.

"As you please, madam," said he, bowing himself out of the palace.

Soon after he had gone a curious thing happened. The princess carelessly touched the wall of her room, which was wont to reflect the warm red light of the fire on the hearth, and found her hand quite wet. She turned round, and was it her fancy or did the fire burn more dimly than before? Hurriedly she passed into the picture gallery, where pools of water showed here and there on the floor, and a cold chill ran through her whole body. At that instant her frightened ladies came running down the stairs, crying, "Madam! Madam! What has happened? The palace is disappearing under our eyes!"

"My husband will be home very soon," answered the princess, who, though nearly as much frightened as her ladies, felt that she must set them a good example. "Wait till then, and he will tell us what to do."

So they waited, seated on the highest chairs they could find, wrapped in their warmest garments, and with piles of cushions under their feet, while the poor birds flew with numbed wings here and there, till they were so lucky as to discover an open window in some forgotten corner. Through this they vanished, and were seen no more.

At last, when the princess and her ladies had been forced to leave the upper rooms, where the walls and floors had melted away, and to take refuge in the hall, the young man came home. He had ridden back along a winding road from which he did not see the palace till he was close upon it, and stood horrified at the spectacle before him. He knew in an instant that his wife must have betrayed his trust, but he would not reproach her, as she must be suffering enough already. Hurrying on, he sprang over all that was left of the palace walls, and the princess gave a cry of relief at the sight of him.

"Come quickly," he said, "or you will be frozen to death!" And a dreary little procession set out for the king's palace, the greyhound and the cat bringing up the rear.

At the gates he left them, though his wife begged him to allow him to stay.

"You have betrayed me and ruined me," he said sternly. "I go to seek my fortune alone." And without another word he turned and left her.

With his falcon on his wrist, and his greyhound and cat behind him, the young man walked a long way, inquiring of everyone he met whether they had seen his enemy the ogre. But nobody had. Then he bade his falcon fly up into the sky, up, up, and up, and try to see if his sharp eyes could discover the old thief. The bird had to go so high that he did not return for some hours, but he told his master that the ogre was lying asleep in a splendid palace in a far country on the shores of the sea. This was delightful news to the young man, who instantly bought some meat for the falcon, bidding him make a good meal.

"Tomorrow," said he, "you will fly to the palace where the ogre lies, and while he is asleep you will search all about him for a stone on which is engraved strange signs. This you will bring to me. In three days I shall expect you back here.'

"Well, I must take the cat with me," answered the bird.

The sun had not yet risen before the falcon soared high into the air, the cat seated on his back, with his paws tightly clasping the bird's neck.

"You had better shut your eyes or you may get giddy," said the bird, and the cat, who had never before been off the ground except to climb a tree, did as she was bid.

All that day and all that night they flew, and in the morning they saw the ogre's palace lying beneath them.

"Dear me," said the cat, opening her eyes for the first time, "that looks to me very like a rat city down there, let us go down to it. They may be able to help us."

So they alighted in some bushes in the heart of the rat city. The falcon remained where he was, but the cat lay down outside the principal gate, causing terrible excitement among the rats.

At length, seeing she did not move, one rat bolder than the rest put its head out of an upper window of the castle, and said, in a trembling voice, "Why have you come here? What do you want? If it is anything in our power, tell us, and we will do it."

"If you would have let me speak to you before, I would have told you that I come as a friend," replied the cat. "I shall be greatly obliged if you would send four of the strongest and most cunning among you, to do me a service.'

"Oh, we shall be delighted," answered the rat, much relieved. "But if you will inform me what it is you wish them to do I shall be better able to judge who is most fitted for the post."

"I thank you," said the cat. "Well, what they have to do is this... Tonight they must burrow under the walls of the castle and go up to the room were an ogre lies asleep. Somewhere about him he has hidden a stone, on which are engraved strange signs. When they have found it they must take it from him without his waking, and bring it to me."

"Your orders shall be obeyed," replied the rat. And he went out to give his instructions.

About midnight the cat, who was still sleeping before the gate, was awakened by some water flung at her by the head rat, who could not make up his mind to open the doors.

"Here is the stone you wanted," said he, when the cat started up with a loud mew. 'If you will hold up your paws I will drop it down." And so he did. "And now farewell," continued the rat. "You have a long way to go, and will do well to start before daybreak."

"Your counsel is good," replied the cat, smiling to itself, and putting the stone in her mouth she went off to seek the falcon.

Now all this time neither the cat nor the falcon had had any food, and the falcon soon got tired carrying such a heavy burden. When night arrived he declared he could go no further, but would spend it on the banks of a river.

"And it is my turn to take care of the stone," said he, "or it will seem as if you had done everything and I nothing."

"No, I got it, and I will keep it," answered the cat, who was tired and cross, and they began a fine quarrel. But, unluckily, in the midst of it, the cat raised her voice, and the stone fell into the ear of a big fish which happened to be swimming by, and though both the cat and the falcon sprang into the water after it, they were too late.

Half drowned, and more than half choked, the two faithful servants scrambled back to land again. The falcon flew to a tree and spread his wings in the sun to dry, but the cat, after giving herself a good shake, began to scratch up the sandy banks and to throw the bits into the stream.

"What are you doing that for?" asked a little fish. "Do you know that you are making the water quite muddy?"

"That doesn't matter at all to me," answered the cat. 'I am going to fill up all the river, so that the fishes may die."

"That is very unkind, as we have never done you any harm," replied the fish. "Why are you so angry with us?"

"Because one of you has got a stone of mine, a stone with strange signs upon it, which dropped into the water. If you will promise to get it back for me, why, perhaps I will leave your river alone."

"I will certainly try," answered the fish in a great hurry, "but you must have a little patience, as it may not be an easy task." And in an instant his scales could be seen flashing quickly along.

The fish swam as fast as he could to the sea, which was not far distant, and calling together all his relations who lived in the neighbourhood, he told them of the terrible danger which threatened the dwellers in the river.

"None of us has got it," said the fishes, shaking their heads, "but in the bay over there is a tunny who, although he is so old, always goes everywhere. He will be able to tell you about it, if anyone can." So the little fish swam off to the tunny, and again related his story.

"Why I was up that river only a few hours ago!" cried the tunny, "and as I was coming back something fell into my ear, and there it is still, for I went to sleep, when I got home and forgot all about it. Perhaps it may be what you want." And stretching up his tail he whisked out the stone.

"Yes, I think that must be it," said the fish with joy. And taking the stone in his mouth he carried it to the place where the cat was waiting for him.

"I am much obliged to you," said the cat, as the fish laid the stone on the sand, "and to reward you, I will let your river alone." And she mounted the falcon's back, and they flew to their master.

Ah, how glad he was to see them again with the magic stone in their possession. In a moment he had wished for a palace, but this time it was of green marble, and then he wished for the princess and her ladies to occupy it. And there they lived for many years, and when the old king died the princess's husband reigned in his stead.

The Heron, The Cat & The Bramble

This is a Welsh tale

Adapted from Welsh Folk-Lore by Elias Owen, published in 1896 by Woodall, Minshall and Co, and based on Elias' prize essay of the National Eisteddfod, 1887.

The heron as it flies slowly towards the source of a river is said to be going up the river to bring the water down, in other words, this flight is a sign of coming rain. The same thing is said of the crane.

*

The heron, the cat, and the bramble bought the tithe of a certain parish. The heron bought the hay, mowed it, harvested it, and cocked it, and intended carrying it the following day, but in the night a storm came on, and carried the hay away, and ever since then the heron frequents the banks of the rivers and lakes, looking for her hay that was carried away, and saying "Pay me my tithe."

The cat bought the oats, cut them, and even threshed them, and left them in the barn, intending the following day to take them to the market for sale. But when she went into the barn, early the next morning, she found the floor covered with rats and mice, which had devoured the oats, and the cat flew at them and fought with them, and drove them from the barn, and this is why she is at enmity with rats and mice even to our day.

*

The bramble bought the wheat, and was more fortunate than the heron and cat, for the wheat was bagged, and taken to the market and sold, but sold on trust, and the bramble never got the money, and this is why it takes hold of everyone and says, "Pay me my tithe," for it forgot to whom the wheat had been sold.

Cat Tails – Feline Fairy Tales, Myths And Legends

The Hen And The Cat

This is an Ethiopian tale

This tale has been adapted from Talking Beasts by Kate Douglas Wiggin and Nora Archibald Smith. The book was published in 1922 by Houghton Mifflin Company, Boston and New York. Talking Beasts features a series of short stories in which animals possess the ability to talk and interact with humans. Each story explores themes such as friendship, kindness, courage, and the importance of understanding and respecting animals.

A cat woke up in her house and went to a hen, saying, "Let's be friends!"

The hen replied, "Do you really want to be friends with me?"

The cat said, "Yes," and left. After a while, she sent her child to the hen with a message, "Tell the hen to get up early tomorrow morning and come with me to a nearby town."

The cat's child went to the hen's house and greeted her. The hen asked, "Are you here in peace, child of the cat?"

The cat's child replied, "Yes, my mother sent me."

The hen said, "What did your mother send you to tell me?"

After the cat's child delivered the message, the hen agreed to go and sent her child back home. Then, the hen called her own child and said, "Go ask the cat what time we should leave for the nearby town." As the child was leaving, the hen called it back and said, "Listen carefully to what the cat says and come back to tell me."

The hen's child went to the cat and greeted her. The cat asked, "Why did your mother send you?"

The hen's child replied, "My mother wants to know how early we should leave for the town."

The cat said, "Tell your mother to come at dawn, for what should eat her?"

The hen's child returned home and reported the cat's message. The hen said, "Lie down and rest, I've heard what the cat said."

The hen and her child slept until the rooster crowed. When the cat heard the rooster, she got ready and waited, thinking, "May she come so we can go!" The rooster crowed again, but the hen stayed home, and soon it was day.

The cat went to the hen's house and said, "Hen, you sent your child to ask what time to get up, and I said to come at dawn. Didn't your child tell you? Why are you still home when it's already day?"

The hen replied, "Sister Cat, if you want to be friends, I can't get up and go out at night."

The cat asked, "What are you afraid of? What's out there?"

The hen listened, got ready, and called her children, saying, "Let's go with the cat to the town!"

They set off, but soon the cat grabbed two of the hen's children. The hen saw this and said, "Sister Cat, we've barely started and you're already taking my children?"

The cat replied, "They are too weak to walk, so I carried them."

The hen said, "If this is how you act, our friendship is over."

The cat replied, "If you don't want to be friends, go home."

As the hen turned to leave, the cat jumped and seized the hen's head. The hen cried for help, and the townspeople heard her, ran over, and found the cat holding the hen's head. Seeing the people, the cat let go and ran into the forest.

The hen stood there, and the townspeople said, "Foolish hen, why did you try to befriend a cat? If we hadn't heard you, she would have killed you and taken your children."

The hen replied, "Thank you for saving me from the cat."

The townspeople said, "Today you've been saved, but never try to befriend a cat again. The cat is too cunning. Beware!"

And so, the friendship between cats and fowls ended.

The Cat And The Sparrows

This is a tale from India

his tale has been adapted from The Talking Thrush by William Crooke and W. H. D. Rouse. The book was published in 1922 by E. P. Dutton, New York. William Crooke and W. H. D. Rouse carefully selected and organized the stories in the anthology to provide a balanced representation of Indian folklore. The collection includes tales from various linguistic and cultural traditions, including Sanskrit, Tamil, Bengali, and Punjabi, among others. Crooke and Rouse's goal was to introduce readers to the rich tapestry of Indian storytelling and inspire appreciation for its cultural heritage.

THERE was once a pair of Sparrows that lived in a tree. They used to hop about all over the place, picking up seeds or anything they could find to eat. One day, when they came back with their pickings, the Cock Sparrow had found some rice, and the Hen a few lentils. They put it all in an earthen pot, and then proceeded to cook their dinner. Then they divided the mess into two equal parts.

The Cock was rather greedy, so he would not wait while his wife put out the fire and got ready to join in the meal. No! He gobbled up his share at once, before she could begin.

When at last the poor Hen came up, her greedy mate would not let her rest even then. "Go and get me a drink of water," he said quite rudely.

She was a very kind wife, so without taking any notice of his rudeness, off she went for the water.

While she was gone the Cock-sparrow's eyes fell on his wife's share of the dinner. "Ah," he thought, "how I should like another bit! Well, why shouldn't I have it? A man does all the work, and women don't want much to eat at any time." So without any more ado, he just set to, and gobbled up his wife's share.

Back came the Hen-sparrow with a drink of water for her husband. When he had drunk it up (and I am afraid he forgot to say thank you), she turned round to look for her dinner. Lo and behold, there was none. What could have become of it? As she was wondering, she happened to look at her husband. He looked so guilty that there could be no manner of doubt where her dinner was.

"You greedy bird," she said, "why have you eaten my dinner?"

"I haven't touched your dinner," said the Cock angrily.

"I'm sure you have," she said, "or you would not look so guilty. Why, you are actually blushing." And so indeed he was, for the tip of his beak was quite red.

However, he still denied it, and grew angrier and angrier, as people do when they know they are in the wrong. They had a terrible quarrel. At last the Hen-sparrow said, "Well, I know a way to find out whether you are telling lies or not. You come along with me." And she made him go with her to the well.

Across the top of the well she stretched a piece of string, and she sat on the middle of the string, and began to chirp, "If I am telling lies, I pray I may fall in." But though she sat there a long time, chirping away, she did not fall in.

Then came the Cock-sparrow's turn. He perched on the string and began to chirrup, "If I am telling lies, may I fall into the well too", but hardly had he got the words out of his mouth, when, splash, down he went.

Then the Hen was very sorry that she had proposed this plan, and she began to weep and cheep, and said, "Alas, alas, why didn't I leave it alone? What does it matter if he eats my dinner, so long as I have my dear husband? Now I have killed him by my folly."

Just at that moment up came a Cat.

"What's the matter?" said the Cat.

"Cheep, cheep, cheep," went the Hen-sparrow. "My husband has fallen into the well, and I don't know how to get him out."

"If I get him out," said the Cat, "will you let me eat him?"

"Of course you may," said the Hen-sparrow.

So the Cat climbed down, and pulled out the Cock-sparrow. When she had brought him to the edge of the well, she said, "Now I'm going to eat him as you promised."

"Oh, all right," said the Hen. "But stop a minute, your mouth is dirty. I am sure you have been eating mice. Now haven't you?"

"Why, yes," said the Cat, "so I have."

"Well," said the Hen-sparrow, "you must get yourself clean. We birds are clean creatures, and you must positively wash your mouth before you begin."

Away went the Cat, and washed her mouth clean, and came back again.

The Hen-sparrow looked at her carefully. "You have not washed your whiskers," said she, "they are still dirty."

The Cat went obediently and washed her whiskers. Meanwhile the Cock-sparrow had been sitting on the edge of the well in the sun, and by this time his feathers were quite dry. So his Hen chirped to him, "Now, dear, you can fly, let's be off."

And off they flew together, and the Cat was left licking her chops and wishing she had not been such a fool.

Cat Tails – Feline Fairy Tales, Myths And Legends

The Contessa's Cat

This is an Italian tale

This tale has been adapted from Roman Legends A Collection Of The Fables And Folk-Lore Of Rome by Rachel Harriette Busk. The book was published in 1877 by Estes And Lauriat, Boston. The book features a variety of Italian and Roman legends, myths, and folklore, drawing from both classical sources and popular oral traditions. These stories encompass a wide range of themes, including mythology, history, religion, and everyday life in Italy. The tales often involve gods and goddesses, legendary heroes, mythical creatures, and historical figures.

There was a very rich Contessa who was a widow and lived all alone, with no companion but only a cat, after her husband died. The greatest care was taken of this cat, and every day a chicken was boiled on purpose for him.

One day the Contessa went out to spend the day at a friend's villa in the Campagna, and she said to the waiting woman, "Mind the cat has his chicken just the same as if I were at home."

"Yes! Signora Contessa, leave that to me," answered the woman, but the Countess was no sooner gone out than she said to the man-servant, "The cat has the chicken every day, but suppose we have it today?"

The man said, "To be sure!" And they ate the chicken themselves, giving the cat only the inside, but they threw the bones down in the usual corner, to make it appear as if he had eaten the whole chicken.

The cat said nothing, but looked on with great eyes, full of meaning.

When the Contessa came back that evening the cat, instead of going out to meet her as he always did, remained still in his place and said nothing.

"What's the matter with the cat? Hasn't he had his chicken?" asked the Contessa, immediately.

"Yes! Signora Contessa," answered the cameriera. "See, there are the bones on the floor, where he always leaves them."

The Contessa could not deny the testimony of her eyes, so she said nothing more but went up to bed.

The cat followed her as he always did, for he slept on her bed, but he followed at a distance, without purring or rubbing himself against her. The Contessa saw something was wrong, but she didn't know what to make of it, and went to bed as usual.

That night the cat throttled the Contessa, and killed her. The cat is very intelligent in his own interest, but he is a traitor.

*

'It would have been more intelligent,' I observed, 'if he had throttled the waiting woman in this instance.'

Not at all. The cat's reasoning was this: If you had not gone out and left me to the mercy of menials, this would not have happened, therefore it was you who had to die.

This is quite true, for cats are always traitors. Dogs are faithful, cats are traitors.

The Cat Who Guarded The Precepts

This is a Sri Lankan tale

This tale has been adapted from Village Folk-Tales Of Ceylon Volume 1 by Henry Parker. The book was published in 1910 by Luzac & Co, India. The book contains a selection of traditional folk tales and legends from Sri Lanka. These stories are drawn from various regions of the island and reflect the cultural diversity and rich storytelling tradition of the Sinhalese and Tamil communities. The tales encompass a wide range of themes, including mythology, folklore, superstition, morality, and everyday life.

A cat discovered a sun-dried fish inside a bag of rice. As he approached to eat it, a rosary fell around his neck. With the rosary on, he walked away and encountered a jungle hen, who quickly ran off.

The cat called after her, saying, "I am following the Buddhist Precepts. Tummal Kitti, come here and join me."

As he continued, they met a ground cuckoo. The cat called out, "Kaccale, who sings 'bug-bug', I am keeping the Precepts. Come with me."

Next, they met a hare. The cat invited him too, "Tokka the Devil-dancer, come join us. I am observing the Precepts."

They all arrived at a rock cave, which the cat used as a monk's residence. Inside, the cat accused Tummal Kitti of defiling the cave by scratching the ground. He declared, "I must kill her," and the hare agreed, saying, "That's right."

The cat killed Tummal Kitti and asked, "It's not wrong to eat the dead, is it?"

The hare replied, "No, it's not," so the cat ate her.

Later, the cat accused the ground cuckoo of drinking palm spirit until his eyes turned red. He announced, "I must kill him," and did so. Again, he justified eating the dead.

Finally, the cat accused the hare of defiling the cave with dung and declared, "I must kill you."

The hare responded, "Killing me is virtuous and proper, but let me first perform a great and a little gallop."

The cat agreed.

The hare ran around the cave, saying, "That's the small gallop."

He ran again, jumped over the cat's head, and as he ran off, he shouted, "That's the great gallop," and escaped.

The King Of The Cats

This is an Irish tale

This tale has been adapted from Ancient Legends, Mystic Charms and Superstitions of Ireland by Jane Francesca Wilde. The book was published in 1919 by Chatto and Windus, London. The book delves into various aspects of Irish folklore, including myths, legends, folk tales, superstitions, and beliefs surrounding magic and the supernatural. It covers a wide range of topics, from ancient gods and heroes to fairies, witches, and ghostly apparitions.

A most important personage in feline history is the King of the Cats. In your house a cat may be a common looking fellow enough, with no distinguishing mark of exalted rank about him, so that it is very difficult to verify his genuine claims to royalty. Therefore the best way is to cut off a tiny little bit of his ear. If he is really the royal personage, he will immediately speak out and declare who he is, and perhaps, at the same time, tell you some very disagreeable truths about yourself, not at all pleasant to have discussed by the house cat.

A man once, in a fit of passion, cut off the head of the domestic pussy, and threw it on the fire. On which the head exclaimed, in a fierce voice, "Go tell your wife that you have cut off the head of the King of the Cats, but wait! I shall come back and be avenged for this insult," and the eyes of the cat glared at him horribly from the fire.

And so it happened, for that day a year later, while the master of the house was playing with a pet kitten, it suddenly flew at his throat and bit him so severely that he died soon after.

A story is current also, that one night an old woman was sitting up very late spinning, when a knocking came to the door.

"Who is there?" she asked.

No answer, but still the knocking went on.

"Who is there?" she asked a second time.

No answer, and the knocking continued.

"Who is there?" she asked the third time, in a very angry passion.

Then there came a small voice. "Ah, Judy, let me in, for I am cold and hungry. Open the door, Judy, and let me sit by the fire, for the night is cold out here. Judy, let me in, let me in!"

Judy's heart was touched, for she thought it was some small child that had lost its way, and she rose up from her spinning, and went and opened the door, when in walked a large black cat with a white breast, and two white kittens after her.

They all made over to the fire and began to warm and dry themselves, purring all the time very loudly, but Judy said never a word, and only went on spinning.

Then the black cat spoke at last. "Judy don't stay up so late again, for the fairies wanted to hold a council here tonight, and to have some supper, but you have prevented them, so they were very angry and determined to kill you, and only for myself and my two daughters here you would be dead by this time. So take my advice, don't interfere with the fairy hours again, for the night is theirs, and they hate to look on the face of a mortal when they are out for pleasure or business. So I ran on to tell you, and now give me a drink of milk, for I must be off."

And after the milk was finished the cat stood up, and called her daughters to come away. "Good-night, Judy," she said. "You have been very civil to me, and I'll not forget it. Good-night, good-night."

With that the black cat and the two kittens whisked up the chimney, but Judy looking down saw something glittering on the hearth, and taking it up she found it was a piece of silver, more than she ever could make in a month by her spinning, and she was glad in her heart, and never again sat up so late to interfere with the fairy hours, but the black cat and her daughters came no more to the house.

Cat Tails – Feline Fairy Tales, Myths And Legends

The Demon Cat

This is an Irish tale

This tale has been adapted from Ancient Legends, Mystic Charms and Superstitions of Ireland by Jane Francesca Wilde. The book was published in 1919 by Chatto and Windus, London. The book delves into various aspects of Irish folklore, including myths, legends, folk tales, superstitions, and beliefs surrounding magic and the supernatural. It covers a wide range of topics, from ancient gods and heroes to fairies, witches, and ghostly apparitions.

The cat of the foregoing legend had evidently charming manners, and was well intentioned, but there are other cats of evil and wicked ways, that are, in fact, demons or witches, who assume the cat-form, in order to get easy entrance to a house, and spy over everything.

There was a woman in Connemara, the wife of a fisherman, and as he always had very good luck, she had plenty of fish at all times stored away in the house ready for market. But to her great annoyance she found that a great cat used to come in at night and devour all the best and finest fish. So she kept a big stick by her and determined to watch.

One day, as she and a woman were spinning together, the house suddenly became quite dark, and the door was burst open as if by the blast of the tempest, when in walked a huge black cat, who went straight up to the fire, then turned round and growled at them.

"Why, surely this is the devil!" said a young girl, who was nearby, sorting the fish.

"I'll teach you how to call me names," said the cat; and, jumping at her, he scratched her arm till the blood came. "There now," he said, "you will be more civil another time when a gentleman comes to see you." And with that he walked over to the door and shut it to prevent any of them going out, for the poor young girl, while crying loudly from fright and pain, had made a desperate rush to get away.

Just then a man was going by, and hearing the cries he pushed open the door and tried to get in, but the cat stood on the threshold and would let no one pass. On this, the man attacked him with his stick, and gave him a sound blow, The cat, however, was more than his match in the fight, for it flew at him and tore his face and hands so badly that the man at last took to his heels and ran away as fast as he could.

"Now it's time for my dinner," said the cat, going up to examine the fish that was laid out on the tables. "I hope the fish is good today. Now don't disturb me, nor make a fuss; I can help myself." With that he jumped up and began to devour all the best fish, while he growled at the woman.

"Away, out of this, you wicked beast!" she cried, giving it a blow with the tongs that would have broken its back, only it was a devil, "out of this! No fish shall you have today."

But the cat only grinned at her, and went on tearing and spoiling and devouring the fish, evidently not a bit the worse for the blow. On this, both the women attacked it with sticks, and struck hard blows enough to kill it, on which the cat glared at them, and spit fire, then making a leap, it tore their hands and arms till the blood came, and the frightened women rushed shrieking from the house.

But presently the mistress returned, carrying with her a bottle of holy water, and looking in, she saw the cat still devouring the fish, and not keeping watch. So she crept over quietly and threw the holy water on it without a word. No sooner was this done than a dense black smoke filled the place, through which nothing was seen but the two red eyes of the cat, burning like coals of fire. Then the smoke gradually cleared away, and she saw the body of the creature burning slowly till it became shrivelled and black like a cinder, and finally disappeared. And from that time the fish remained untouched and safe from harm, for the power of the Evil One was broken, and the demon cat was seen no more.

Cat Tails – Feline Fairy Tales, Myths And Legends

The Cat Who Became Head-Forester

This is a Russian tale

This tale has been adapted from Arthur Ransome's book, Old Peter's Russian Tales, published by Frederick A. Stokes Co, New York, in 1916. "The Cat Who Became Head-Forester" is a traditional Russian folktale, part of a rich tradition of Slavic folklore. The story belongs to the larger corpus of Russian fairy tales (known as "skazki"), which often feature animals, magical transformations, and clever protagonists who overcome difficult circumstances.

If you drop Vladimir by mistake, you know he always falls on his feet. And if Vladimir tumbles off the roof of the hut, he always falls on his feet. Cats always fall on their feet, on their four paws, and never hurt themselves. And as in tumbling, so it is in life. No cat is ever unfortunate for very long. The worse things look for a cat, the better they are going to be.

Well, once upon a time, not so very long ago, an old peasant had a cat and did not like him. He was a tom-cat, always fighting, and he had lost one ear, and was not very pretty to look at. The peasant thought he would get rid of his old cat, and buy a new one from a neighbour. He did not care what became of the old tom-cat with one ear, so long as he never saw him again. It was no use thinking of killing him, for it is a life's work to kill a cat, and it's likely enough that the cat would come alive at the end.

So the old peasant he took a sack, and he bundled the tom-cat into the sack, and he sewed up the sack and slung it over his back, and walked off into the forest. Off he went, trudging along in the summer sunshine, deep into the forest. And when he had gone very many versts into the forest, he took the sack with the cat in it and threw it away among the trees.

"You stay there," he said, "and if you do get out in this desolate place, much good may it do you, old quarrelsome bundle of bones and fur!"

And with that he turned round and trudged home again, and bought a nice-looking, quiet cat from a neighbour in exchange for a little tobacco, and settled down comfortably at home with the new cat in front of the stove; and there he may be to this day, so far as I know. My story does not bother with him, but only with the old tom-cat tied up in the sack away there out in the forest.

The bag flew through the air, and plumped down through a bush to the ground. And the old tom-cat landed on his feet inside it, very much frightened but not hurt. He thought, this bag, this flight through the air, this bump, mean that my life is going to change. Very well...there is nothing like something new now and again.

And presently he began tearing at the bag with his sharp claws. Soon there was a hole he could put a paw through. He went on, tearing and scratching, and there was a hole he could put two paws through. He went on with his work, and soon he could put his head through, all the easier because he had only one ear. A minute or two after that he had wriggled out of the bag, and stood up on his four paws and stretched himself in the forest.

"The world seems to be larger than the village," he said. "I will walk on and see what there is in it."

He washed himself all over, curled his tail proudly up in the air, cocked the only ear he had left, and set off walking under the forest trees.

"I was the head-cat in the village," he said to himself. "If all goes well, I shall be head here too." And he walked along as if he were the Tzar himself.

Well, he walked on and on, and he came to an old hut that had belonged to a forester. There was nobody there, nor had been for many years, and the old tom-cat made himself quite at home. He climbed up into the loft under the roof, and found a little rotten hay.

"A very good bed," he said, and curled up and fell asleep.

When he woke he felt hungry, so he climbed down and went off in the forest to catch little birds and mice. There were plenty of them in the forest, and when he had eaten enough he came back to the hut, climbed into the loft, and spent the night there very comfortably.

You would have thought he would be content. Not he. He was a cat. He said, "This is a good enough lodging. But I have to catch all my own food. In the village they fed me every day, and I only caught mice for fun. I ought to be able to live like that here. A person of my dignity ought not to have to do all the work for himself."

Next day he went walking in the forest. And as he was walking he met a fox, a vixen, a very pretty young thing, gay and giddy like all girls. And the fox saw the cat, and was very much astonished.

"All these years," she said, for though she was young she thought she had lived a long time, "all these years I've lived in the forest, but I've never seen a wild beast like that before. What a strange-looking animal! And with only one ear. How handsome!"

And she came up and made her bows to the cat, and said, "Tell me, great lord, who you are. What fortunate chance has brought you to this forest? And by what name am I to call your Excellency?"

Oh, the fox was very polite. It is not every day that you meet a handsome stranger walking in the forest.

The cat arched his back, and set all his fur on end, and said, very slowly and quietly, "I have been sent from the far forests of Siberia to be Head-forester over you. And my name is Cat Ivanovitch."

"O Cat Ivanovitch!" said the pretty young fox, and she made more bows. "I did not know. I beg your Excellency's pardon. Will your Excellency honour my humble house by visiting it as a guest?"

"I will," said the cat. "And what do they call you?"

"My name, your Excellency, is Lisabeta Ivanovna."

"I will come with you, Lisabeta," said the cat.

And they went together to the fox's earth. Very snug, very neat it was inside, and the cat curled himself up in the best place, while Lisabeta Ivanovna, the pretty young fox, made ready a tasty dish of game. And while she was making the meal ready, and dusting the furniture with her tail, she looked at the cat. At last she said, shyly, "Tell me, Cat Ivanovitch, are you married or single?"

"Single," said the cat.

"And I too am unmarried," said the pretty young fox, and she went busily on with her dusting and cooking.

Presently she looked at the cat again.

"What if we were to marry, Cat Ivanovitch? I would try to be a good wife to you."

"Very well, Lisabeta," said the cat, "I will marry you."

The fox went to her store and took out all the dainties that she had, and made a wedding feast to celebrate her marriage to the great Cat Ivanovitch, who had only one ear, and had come from the far Siberian forests to be Head-forester. Then they ate up everything there was in the place.

Next morning the pretty young fox went off busily into the forest to get food for her grand husband. But the old tom-cat stayed at home, and cleaned his whiskers and slept. He was a lazy one, was that cat, and proud.

The fox was running through the forest, looking for game, when she met an old friend, the handsome young wolf, and he began making polite speeches to her.

"What had become of you, gossip?" he asked. "I've been to all the best earths and not found you at all."

"Let be, fool," said the fox very shortly. "Don't talk to me like that. What are you jesting about? Formerly I was a young, unmarried fox, but now I am a wedded wife."

"Whom have you married, Lisabeta Ivanovna?"

"What," says the fox, "you have not heard that the great Cat Ivanovitch, who has only one ear, has been sent from the far Siberian forests to be Head-forester over all of us? Well, I am now the Head-forester's wife."

"No, I had not heard, Lisabeta Ivanovna. And when can I pay my respects to his Excellency?"

"Not now, not now," said the fox. "Cat Ivanovitch will be raging angry with me if I let anyone come near him. Presently he will be taking his food. Look you. Get a sheep, and make it ready, and bring it as a greeting to him, to show him that he is welcome and that you know how to treat him with respect. Leave the sheep nearby, and hide yourself so that he shall not see you, for, if he did, things might be awkward."

"Thank you, thank you, Lisabeta Ivanovna," said the wolf, and off he went to look for a sheep.

The pretty young fox went idly on, taking the air, for she knew that the wolf would save her the trouble of looking for food. Presently she met the bear.

"Good-day to you, Lisabeta Ivanovna," said the bear; "as pretty as ever, I see you are."

"Bandy-legged one," said the fox, "fool, don't come worrying me. Formerly I was a young, unmarried fox, but now I am a wedded wife."

"I beg your pardon," says the bear, "but whom have you married, Lisabeta Ivanovna?"

"The great Cat Ivanovitch has been sent from the far Siberian forests to be Head-forester over us all. And Cat Ivanovitch is now my husband," said the fox.

"Is it forbidden to have a look at his Excellency?"

"It is forbidden," said the fox. "Cat Ivanovitch will be raging angry with me if I let anyone come near him. Presently he will be taking his food. Get along with you quickly, and make ready an ox, and bring it by way of welcome to him. The wolf is bringing a sheep. And look, leave the ox nearby, and hide yourself so that the great Cat Ivanovitch shall not see you, or else, brother, things may be awkward."

The bear shambled off as fast as he could go to get an ox.

The pretty young fox, enjoying the fresh air of the forest, went slowly home to her earth, and crept in very quietly, so as not to awake the great Head-forester, Cat Ivanovitch, who had only one ear and was sleeping in the best place.

Presently the wolf came through the forest, dragging a sheep he had killed. He did not dare to go too near the fox's earth, because of Cat Ivanovitch, the new Head-forester. So he stopped, well out of sight, and stripped off the skin of the sheep, and arranged the sheep so as to seem a nice, tasty morsel. Then he stood still, thinking what to do next. He heard a noise, and looked up. There was the bear, struggling along with a dead ox.

"Good-day, brother Michael Ivanovitch," said the wolf.

"Good-day, brother Levon Ivanovitch," said the bear. "Have you seen the fox, Lisabeta Ivanovna, with her husband, the Head-forester?"

"No, brother," said the wolf. "For a long time I have been waiting to see them."

"Go on and call out to them," said the bear.

"No, Michael Ivanovitch," said the wolf, "I will not go. You go, for you are bigger and bolder than I."

"No, no, Levon Ivanovitch, I will not go. There is no use in risking one's life without need."

Suddenly, as they were talking, a little hare came running by. The bear saw him first, and roared out, "Hi, Squinteye! Trot along here."

The hare came up, slowly, two steps at a time, trembling with fright.

"Now then, you squinting rascal," said the bear, "do you know where the fox lives, over there?"

"I know, Michael Ivanovitch."

"Get along there quickly, and tell her that Michael Ivanovitch the bear and his brother Levon Ivanovitch the wolf have been ready for a long time, and have brought presents of a sheep and an ox, as greetings to his Excellency..."

"His Excellency, mind," said the wolf. "Don't forget."

The hare ran off as hard as he could go, glad to have escaped so easily. Meanwhile the wolf and the bear looked about for good places in which to hide.

"It will be best to climb trees," said the bear. "I shall go up to the top of this fir."

"But what am I to do?" said the wolf. "I can't climb a tree for the life of me. Brother Michael, Brother Michael, hide me somewhere or other before you climb up. I beg you, hide me, or I shall certainly be killed."

"Crouch down under these bushes," said the bear, "and I will cover you with the dead leaves."

"May you be rewarded," said the wolf; and he crouched down under the bushes, and the bear covered him up with dead leaves, so that only the tip of his nose could be seen.

Then the bear climbed slowly up into the fir tree, into the very top, and looked out to see if the fox and Cat Ivanovitch were coming.

They were coming, oh yes, they were coming! The hare ran up and knocked on the door, and said to the fox, "Michael Ivanovitch the bear and his brother Levon Ivanovitch the wolf have been ready for a long time, and have brought presents of a sheep and an ox as greetings to his Excellency."

"Get along, Squinteye," said the fox; "we are just coming." And so the fox and the cat set out together.

The bear, up in the top of the tree, saw them, and called down to the wolf, "They are coming, Brother Levon, they are coming, the fox and her husband. But what a little one he is, to be sure!"

"Quiet, quiet," whispered the wolf. "He'll hear you, and then we are done for."

The cat came up, and arched his back and set all his furs on end, and threw himself on the ox, and began tearing the meat with his teeth and claws. And as he tore he purred. And the bear listened, and heard the purring of the cat, and it seemed to him that the cat was angrily muttering, "Small, small, small...."

And the bear whispered, "He's no giant, but what a glutton! Why, we couldn't get through a quarter of that, and he finds it not enough. Heaven help us if he comes after us!"

The wolf tried to see, but could not, because his head, all but his nose, was covered with the dry leaves. Little by little he moved his head, so as to clear the leaves away from in front of his eyes. Try as he would to be quiet, the leaves rustled, so little, ever so little, but enough to be heard by the one ear of the cat.

The cat stopped tearing the meat and listened. "I haven't caught a mouse to-day," he thought.

Once more the leaves rustled. The cat leapt through the air and dropped with all four paws, and his claws out, on the nose of the wolf. How the wolf yelped! The leaves flew like dust, and the wolf leapt up and ran off as fast as his legs could carry him.

Well, the wolf was frightened, I can tell you, but he was not so frightened as the cat. When the great wolf leapt up out of the leaves, the cat screamed and ran up the nearest tree, and that was the tree where Michael Ivanovitch the bear was hiding in the topmost branches.

"Oh, he has seen me. Cat Ivanovitch has seen me," thought the bear. He had no time to climb down, and the cat was coming up in long leaps.

The bear trusted to Providence, and jumped from the top of the tree. Many were the branches he broke as he fell, and many were the bones he broke when he crashed to the ground. He picked himself up and stumbled off, groaning.

The pretty young fox sat still, and cried out, "Run, run, Brother Levon!... Quicker on your pins, Brother Michael! His Excellency is behind you, his Excellency is close behind!"

Ever since then all the wild beasts have been afraid of the cat, and the cat and the fox live merrily together, and eat fresh meat all the year round, which the other animals kill for them and leave a little way off.

And that is what happened to the old tom-cat with one eye, who was sewn up in a bag and thrown away in the forest.

Cat Tails – Feline Fairy Tales, Myths And Legends

Seanchan The Bard And The King Of The Cats

This is an Irish tale

This tale has been adapted from Ancient Legends, Mystic Charms and Superstitions of Ireland by Jane Francesca Wilde. The book was published in 1919 by Chatto and Windus, London. The book delves into various aspects of Irish folklore, including myths, legends, folk tales, superstitions, and beliefs surrounding magic and the supernatural. It covers a wide range of topics, from ancient gods and heroes to fairies, witches, and ghostly apparitions.

In ancient Ireland the men of learning were esteemed beyond all other classes. All the great ollaves and professors and poets held the very highest social position, and took precedence of the nobles, and ranked next to royalty. The leading men amongst them lived luxuriously in the great Bardic House, and when they went abroad through the country they travelled with a train of minor bards, fifty or more, and were entertained free of cost by the kings and chiefs, who considered themselves highly honoured by the presence of so distinguished a company at their court. If the receptions were splendid and costly, the praise of the entertainer was chanted by all the poets at the feast, but if any slight were offered, then the Ard-Filé poured forth his stinging satire in such bitter odes, that many declared they would sooner die than incur the anger of the poets or be made the subject of their scathing satire.

All the learned men and professors, the ollaves of music, poetry, oratory, and of the arts and sciences generally, formed a great Bardic Association, who elected their own president, with the title of Chief Poet of all Ireland, and they also elected chief poets for each of the provinces. Learned women, likewise, and poetesses, were included in the Bardic Association, with distinct and recognized privileges, both as to revenue and costly apparel. Legal enactments even were made respecting the number of colours allowed to be worn in their mantles, the poet being allowed six colours, and the poetess five in her robe and mantle, the number of colours being a distinct recognition and visible sign of rank, and therefore very highly esteemed.

But, in time, as a consequence of their many and great privileges, the pride and insolence of the learned class, the ollaves, poets, and poetesses, became so insufferable, that even the kings trembled before them. This is shown in the Ossianic tale, from which we may gather that Seanchan the Bard, when entertained at the court of King Guaire, grew jealous of the attention paid to the nobles while he was present. So he sulked at the festival, and made himself eminently disagreeable, as will be seen by the following legend:

*

When Seanchan, the renowned Bard, was made *Ard-Filé*, or Chief Poet of Ireland, Guaire, the king of Connaught, to do him honour, made a great feast for him and the whole Bardic Association. And all the professors went to the king's house, the great ollaves of poetry and history and music, and of the arts and sciences, and the learned, aged females, Grug and Grag and Grangait, and all the chief poets and poetesses of Ireland, an amazing number. But Guaire the king entertained them all splendidly, so that the ancient pathway to his palace is still called "The Road of the Dishes."

And each day he asked, "How fares it with my noble guests?" But they were all discontented, and wanted things he could not get for them. So he was very sorrowful, and prayed to God to be delivered from "the learned men and women, a vexatious class."

Still the feast went on for three days and three nights. And they drank and made merry. And the whole Bardic Association entertained the nobles with the choicest music and professional accomplishments.

But Seanchan sulked and would neither eat nor drink, for he was jealous of the nobles of Connaught. And when he saw how much they consumed of the best meats and wine, he declared he would taste no food till they and their servants were all sent away out of the house.

And when Guaire asked him again, "How fares my noble guest, and this great and excellent people?" Seanchan answered, "I have never had worse days, nor worse nights, nor worse dinners in my life." And he ate nothing for three whole days.

Then the king was sorely grieved that the whole Bardic Association should be feasting and drinking while Seanchan, the chief poet of Erin, was fasting and weak. So he sent his favourite serving-man, a person of mild manners and cleanliness, to offer special dishes to the bard.

"Take them away," said Seanchan, "I'll have none of them."

"And why, oh, Royal Bard?" asked the servitor.

"Because you are an Your grandfather was chip-nailed. I have seen him. I shall eat no food from your hands."

Then the king called a beautiful maiden to him, his foster daughter, and said, "Lady, take this wheaten cake and this dish of salmon to the illustrious poet, and serve him yourself." So the maiden went.

But when Seanchan saw her he asked, "Who sent you here, and why have you brought me food?"

"My lord the king sent me, oh, Royal Bard," she answered, "because I am pretty to look upon, and he ordered me to serve you with food myself."

"Take it away," said Seanchan, "you are an ugly girl, I know of none uglier. I have seen your grandmother. She sat on a wall one day and pointed out the way with her hand to some travelling lepers. How could I touch your food?" So the maiden went away in sorrow.

And then Guaire the king was indeed angry, and he exclaimed, "My curse is on the mouth that uttered that! May the kiss of a leper be on Seanchan's lips before he dies!"

Now there was a young serving-girl there, and she said to Seanchan, "There is a hen's egg in the place, my lord, may I bring it to you, oh, Chief Bard?"

"It will suffice," said Seanchan, "bring it that I may eat."

But when she went to look for it, the egg was gone.

"You have eaten it," said the bard, in anger.

"Not so, my lord," she answered, "but the mice, the nimble race, have carried it away."

"Then I will satirize them in a poem," said Seanchan, and forthwith he chanted so bitter a satire against them that ten mice fell dead at once in his presence.

"'Tis well," said Seanchan, "but the cat is the one most to blame, for it was her duty to suppress the mice. Therefore I shall satirize the tribe of the cats, and their chief lord, Irusan, son of Arusan. For I know where he lives with his wife Spitfire, and his daughter Sharp-tooth, with her brothers, the Purrer and the Growler. But I shall begin with Irusan himself, for he is king, and answerable for all the cats."

And he said:

"Irusan, monster of claws,

who strikes at the mouse,

but lets it go, weakest of cats.

The otter did well who bit off

the tips of your progenitor's ears,

so that every cat since is jagged-eared.

Let your tail hang down.

It is right, for the mouse jeers at you."

Now Irusan heard these words in his cave, and he said to his daughter, Sharp-tooth: "Seanchan has satirized me, but I will be avenged."

"No, father," she said, "bring him here alive, that we may all take our revenge."

"I shall go then and bring him," said Irusan, "so send your brothers after me."

Now when it was told to Seanchan that the King of the Cats was on his way to come and kill him, he was afraid, and sought out Guaire and all the nobles to stand by and protect him. And before long a vibrating, impressive, impetuous sound was heard, like a raging tempest of fire in full blaze.

And when the cat appeared he seemed to them of the size of a bullock, and this was his appearance: rapacious, panting, jagged-eared, snub-nosed, sharp-toothed, nimble, angry, vindictive, glare-eyed, terrible, sharp-clawed. Such was his similitude. But he passed on amongst the courtiers, not minding till he came to Seanchan, and him he seized by the arm and jerked him up on his back, and made off the way he came before anyone could touch him, for he had no other object in view but to get hold of the poet.

Now Seanchan, being in evil plight, had recourse to flattery. "Oh, Irusan," he exclaimed, "how truly splendid you are, such running, such leaps, such strength, and such agility! But what evil have I done, oh, Irusan, son of Arusan? Spare me, I entreat. I invoke the saints between you and me, oh, great King of the Cats."

But not a bit did the cat let go his hold for all this fine talk. He went straight on to Clonmacnoise where there was a forge, and St. Kieran happened to be there standing at the door.

"What!" exclaimed the saint, "is that the Chief Bard of Erin on the back of a cat? Has Guaire's hospitality ended in this?"

And he ran for a red-hot bar of iron that was in the furnace, and struck the cat on the side with it, so that the iron passed through him, and he fell down lifeless.

"Now my curse on the hand that gave that blow!" said the bard, when he got upon his feet.

"Why?" asked St. Kieran.

"Because," answered Seanchan, "I would rather Irusan had killed me, and eaten me every bit, so that I might bring disgrace on Guaire for the bad food he gave me, for it was all owing to his wretched dinners that I got into this plight."

And when all the other kings heard of Seanchan's misfortunes, they sent to beg that he would visit their courts. But he would have neither kiss nor welcome from them, and went on his way to the bardic mansion, where the best of good living was always to be had. And ever after the kings were afraid to offend Seanchan.

So as long as he lived he had the chief place at the feast, and all the nobles there were made to sit below him, and Seanchan was content. And in time he and Guaire were reconciled, and Seanchan and all the ollaves, and the whole Bardic Association, were feasted by the king for thirty days in noble style, and had the choicest of viands and the best of French wines to drink, served in goblets of silver. And in return for his splendid hospitality the Bardic Association decreed, unanimously, a vote of thanks to the king. And they praised him in poems as "Guaire the Generous," by which name he was ever after known in history, for the words of the poet are immortal.

Cat Tails – Feline Fairy Tales, Myths And Legends

Why Do Cats Eat Mice?

This is a Romanian tale

This tale has been adapted from Rumanian Bird and Beast Stories translated by Moses Gaster. The book was published in 1915 by Sidgwick & Jackson, Ltd., London. The book features a variety of folk tales from Romania that centre around birds and beasts, including both domestic and wild animals. These stories often anthropomorphize animals, imbuing them with human-like qualities, emotions, and behaviours. The tales explore themes such as friendship, loyalty, cunning, and bravery, offering readers insight into Romanian folklore and cultural values.

When Adam and Eve had lived for some time together, Adam suddenly noticed a change in his wife's demeanour. Watching her narrowly, he found that she had fallen in love with the devil. She had introduced him into the house, which she had built close to the seashore. Adam, as a wise man, kept his peace, but he thought day and night what was he to do to get rid of the devil and to save his wife? At last he thought that the only way would be to take his wife away into some distant land across the sea, where the devil could not follow him. But how were they to cross that sea? At last he discovered that the best way to cross the sea would be to make a boat, and then, when it was ready, he would take his wife quietly and they would both sail away. But the devil has nothing to do but to watch other people's doings, and to put a spoke into the wheel wherever he can. He was therefore not to be outdone in as simple a manner as Adam thought. He saw that Adam was cutting wood, and making timber and laths, and joining them together, but whenever he asked Adam what he was doing he would not answer him.

So at last he came to Eve and told her: "Look here, that husband of yours is preparing some trick, and it is meant against you and me. You better find out what is in Adam's mind. What is he doing, and what is the meaning of it?"

Eve, in order to please the devil, asked Adam what he was doing, but he knew it was no good giving a secret into the keeping of a woman. So he kept his counsel to himself.

At last, when the devil saw the boat, he told Eve, "I know what Adam means, he wants to take you away and leave me here alone. That you must not allow, but when everything is ready and he is coming to fetch you, ask him to allow you to bring the house-snake with you. He will not refuse you, and I will take the form of the snake, and so you will carry me with you into the boat. Then we shall see who will be the cleverer, Adam or I."

So when Adam came to fetch Eve, she asked him to be allowed to bring also the house-snake with her. Adam, good-hearted fellow as he was, did not refuse her. What did the devil do? He took the form of the snake, and to make sure of being carried into the boat, he coiled himself round Eve's bosom, and so was carried by her into the boat, chuckling all the while at the stupidity of Adam. Adam had no suspicion who the passenger was, he had brought with him.

One day, after he had sailed a long time, Adam, tired from his work, laid down to rest, when he suddenly felt that the boat was sinking. Up he jumped, trimmed the sail, and looked round to see whether the boat had sprung a leak and was making water, for he could not understand why the boat should suddenly sink and let the water in. The devil, thinking that Adam was asleep and not able to watch his tricks, had made himself heavy like lead in the hope of sinking the ship and drowning Adam. But he had reckoned without his host, for Adam woke up in the nick of time and caught the Wicked One at his evil deeds.

When the devil saw that Adam was awake, he changed himself quickly into a mouse. Adam did not trouble, but thought his time would come. The devil, who cannot keep quiet but must do mischief whenever he can, was not content to be left in peace, and be carried across the water, so he started gnawing away at one of the planks of the ship to make a hole and drown Adam. His misfortune was that, just when the plank at which he was gnawing had got as thin as a sheet of paper, Adam surprised the Black One at his work. What did he do? He took off his fur glove and threw it at the mouse.

The fur glove changed into a cat which, seizing the mouse, killed it and ate it up. And thus the cat got the devil into it. And that is why the cat's hair bristles and makes sparks, and the eyes of the cat glisten in the dark. These are sparks of the devil in the cat.

King Arthur And The Cat

This is an Irish tale

This tale has been adapted from Ancient Legends, Mystic Charms and Superstitions of Ireland by Jane Francesca Wilde. The book was published in 1919 by Chatto and Windus, London. The book delves into various aspects of Irish folklore, including myths, legends, folk tales, superstitions, and beliefs surrounding magic and the supernatural. It covers a wide range of topics, from ancient gods and heroes to fairies, witches, and ghostly apparitions.

Merlin told the king that the people beyond the Lake of Lausanne greatly desired his help, "for there lives a devil that destroys the country. It is a cat so great and ugly that it is horrible to look on."

One time a fisher came to the lake with his nets, and he promised to give our Lord the first fish he took. It was a fish worth thirty shillings, and when he saw it so fair and great, he said to himself softly, "God shall not have this, but I will surely give Him the next." Now, the next was still better, and he said, "Our Lord may wait yet awhile, but the third shall be His without doubt." So he cast his net, but drew out only a little kitten, as black as any coal.

And when the fisher saw it he said he had need of it at home for rats and mice, and he nourished it and kept it in his house till it strangled him and his wife and children. Then the cat fled to a high mountain and destroyed and slew all that came in his way, and was great and terrible to behold.

When the king heard this he made ready and rode to the Lac de Lausanne and found the country desolate and void of people, for neither man nor woman would inhabit the place for fear of the cat.

And the king was lodged a mile from the mountain, with Sir Gawain and Merlin and others. And they climbed the mountain, Merlin leading the way. And when they reached the summit, Merlin said to the king, "Sir, in that rock lives the cat;" and he showed him a great cave, large and deep, in the mountain.

"And how shall the cat come out?" said the king.

"That you shall you see very soon," said Merlin. "But look and be ready to defend, for soon he will attack you."

"Then draw back," said the king, "for I will prove his power."

And when they withdrew, Merlin whistled loud, and the cat leaped out of the cave, thinking it was some wild beast, for he was hungry and fasting, and he ran boldly to the king, who was ready with his spear, and thought to smite him through the body. But the fiend seized the spear in his mouth and broke it in two.

Then the king drew his sword, holding his shield before him. And as the cat leaped at his throat, he struck him so fiercely that the creature fell to the ground, but it soon was up again, and ran at the king so hard that his claws gripped through the hauberk to the flesh, and the red blood followed the claws.

Now the king was almost falling to earth, but when he saw the red blood he was greatly angered, and with his sword in his right hand and his shield at his breast, he ran at the cat, who sat licking his claws, all wet with blood. But when he saw the king coming towards him, he leapt up to seize him by the throat, as before, and stuck his fore-feet so firmly in the shield that they stayed there, and the king cut him on the legs, so that he cut them off to the knees, and the cat fell to the ground.

Then the king ran at him with his sword, but the cat stood on his hind-legs and grinned with his teeth, and coveted the throat of the king, and the king tried to hit him on the head, but the cat strained his hind feet and leaped at the king's breast, and fixed his teeth in the flesh, so that the blood streamed down from breast and shoulder.

Then the king struck him fiercely on the body, and the cat fell head downwards, but the feet stayed fixed in the hauberk. And the king ripped them away, at which the cat fell to the ground, where she howled and brayed so loudly that it was heard through all the host, and she began to creep towards the cave, but the king stood between her and the cave, and when she tried to catch him with her teeth he struck her dead.

Then Merlin and the others ran to him and asked how he was feeling.

"Well, blessed be our Lord!" said the king, "for I have slain this devil, but, truly, I never had such doubt of myself, not even when I slew the giant on the mountain, therefore I thank the Lord."

(This was the great giant of St. Michael's Mount, who supped all the season on seven knave children chopped in a charger of white silver, with powder of precious spices, and goblets full of Portugal wine.)

"Sir," said the barons, "you have great cause for thankfulness."

Then they looked on the feet that were left in the shield and in the hauberk, and said, "Such feet were never seen before!" And they took the shield and showed it to the host with great joy.

So the king kept the shield with the cat's feet, but the other feet he had laid in a coffin to be buried. And the mountain was called from that day, "The Mountain of the Cat," and the name will never be changed while the world endures.

Whittington And His Cat

This is an English tale

This tale has been adapted from English Fairy Tales by Joseph Jacobs. The book was published in 1890 by David Nutt, London. The book contains a diverse selection of fairy tales and folk stories that originate from various regions of England. Jacobs gathered these tales from oral tradition, folklore sources, and literary sources, aiming to preserve and showcase the rich heritage of English storytelling.

In the reign of the famous King Edward III there was a little boy called Dick Whittington, whose father and mother died when he was very young. As poor Dick was not old enough to work, he was very badly off. He got very little for his dinner, and sometimes nothing at all for his breakfast, for the people who lived in the village were very poor indeed, and could not spare him much more than the parings of potatoes, and now and then a hard crust of bread.

Now Dick had heard a great many very strange things about the great city called London, for the country people at that time thought that folks in London were all fine gentlemen and ladies, and that there was singing and music there all day long, and that the streets were all paved with gold.

One day a large waggon and eight horses, all with bells at their heads, drove through the village while Dick was standing by the sign-post. He thought that this waggon must be going to the fine town of London, so he took courage, and asked the waggoner to let him walk with him by the side of the waggon. As soon as the waggoner heard that poor Dick had no father or mother, and saw by his ragged clothes that he could not be worse off than he was, he told him he might go if he would, so off they set together.

So Dick got safe to London, and was in such a hurry to see the fine streets paved all over with gold, that he did not even stay to thank the kind waggoner, but ran off as fast as his legs would carry him, through many of the streets, thinking every moment to come to those that were paved with gold, for Dick had seen a guinea three times in his own little village, and remembered what a deal of money it brought in change, so he thought he had nothing to do but to take up some little bits of the pavement, and should then have as much money as he could wish for.

Poor Dick ran till he was tired, and had quite forgotten his friend the waggoner, but at last, finding it grow dark, and that every way he turned he saw nothing but dirt instead of gold, he, sat down in a dark corner and cried himself to sleep.

Little Dick was all night in the streets, and next morning, being very hungry, he got up and walked about, and asked everybody he met to give him a halfpenny to keep him from starving, but nobody stayed to answer him, and only two or three gave him a halfpenny; so that the poor boy was soon quite weak and faint for the want of food.

In this distress he asked charity of several people, and one of them said crossly: "Go to work, you idle rogue."

"That I will," said Dick, "I will go to work for you, if you will let me." But the man only cursed at him and went on.

At last a good-natured looking gentleman saw how hungry he looked. "Why don't you go to work my lad?" he asked Dick.

"That I would, but I do not know how to get any," answered Dick.

"If you are willing, come along with me," said the gentleman, and took him to a hay-field, where Dick worked briskly, and lived merrily till the hay was made.

After this he found himself as badly off as before, and being almost starved again, he laid himself down at the door of Mr. Fitzwarren, a rich merchant. Here he was soon seen by the cook-maid, who was an ill-tempered creature, and happened just then to be very busy dressing dinner for her master and mistress, so she called out to poor Dick: "What business have you there, you lazy rogue? There is nothing else but beggars. If you do not take yourself away, we will see how you will like a sousing of some dish-water, for I have some here hot enough to make you jump."

Just at that time Mr. Fitzwarren himself came home to dinner, and when he saw a dirty ragged boy lying at the door, he said to him: "Why do you lie there, my boy? You seem old enough to work. I am afraid you are inclined to be lazy."

"No, indeed, sir," said Dick to him, "that is not the case, for I would work with all my heart, but I do not know anybody, and I believe I am very sick for the want of food."

"Poor fellow, get up; let me see what ails you."

Dick now tried to rise, but was obliged to lie down again, being too weak to stand, for he had not eaten any food for three days, and was no longer able to run about and beg a halfpenny of people in the street. So the kind merchant ordered him to be taken into the house, and have a good dinner given him, and be kept to do what work he was able to do for the cook.

Little Dick would have lived very happy in this good family if it had not been for the ill-natured cook. She used to say, "You are under me, so look sharp. Clean the spit and the dripping-pan, make the fires, wind up the jack, and do all the scullery work nimbly, or…", and she would shake the ladle at him. Besides, she was so fond of basting, that when she had no meat to baste, she would baste poor Dick's head and shoulders with a broom, or anything else that happened to fall in her way. At last her ill-usage of him was told to Alice, Mr. Fitzwarren's daughter, who told the cook she should be turned away if she did not treat him kindlier.

The behaviour of the cook was now a little better, but besides this Dick had another hardship to get over. His bed stood in a garret, where there were so many holes in the floor and the walls that every night he was tormented with rats and mice. A gentleman had given Dick a penny for cleaning his shoes, and Dick thought he would buy a cat with it. The next day he saw a girl with a cat, and asked her, "Will you let me have that cat for a penny?"

The girl said, "Yes, that I will, master, though she is an excellent mouser."

Dick hid his cat in the garret, and always took care to carry a part of his dinner to her, and in a short time he had no more trouble with the rats and mice, but slept quite sound every night.

Soon after this, his master had a ship ready to sail, and as it was the custom that all his servants should have some chance for good fortune as well as himself, he called them all into the parlour and asked them what they would send out.

They all had something that they were willing to venture except poor Dick, who had neither money nor goods, and therefore could send nothing. For this reason he did not come into the parlour with the rest, but Miss Alice guessed what the matter was, and ordered him to be called in.

She then said, "I will lay down some money for him, from my own purse;" but her father told her: "This will not do, for it must be something of his own."

When poor Dick heard this, he said, "I have nothing but a cat which I bought for a penny some time since of a little girl."

"Fetch your cat then, my lad," said Mr. Fitzwarren, "and let her go."

Dick went upstairs and brought down poor puss, with tears in his eyes, and gave her to the captain, "For," he said, "I shall now be kept awake all night by the rats and mice."

All the company laughed at Dick's odd venture, and Miss Alice, who felt pity for him, gave him some money to buy another cat.

This, and many other marks of kindness shown him by Miss Alice, made the ill-tempered cook jealous of poor Dick, and she began to use him more cruelly than ever, and always made game of him for sending his cat to sea. She asked him, "Do you think your cat will sell for as much money as would buy a stick to beat you?"

At last poor Dick could not bear this usage any longer, and he thought he would run away from his place; so he packed up his few things, and started very early in the morning, on All-hallows Day, the first of November. He walked as far as Holloway, and there sat down on a stone, which to this day is called "Whittington's Stone," and began to think to himself which road he should take.

While he was thinking what he should do, the Bells of Bow Church, which at that time were only six, began to ring, and their sound seemed to say to him:

"Turn again, Whittington, Thrice Lord Mayor of London."

"Lord Mayor of London!" said he to himself. "Why, to be sure, I would put up with almost anything now, to be Lord Mayor of London, and ride in a fine coach, when I grow to be a man! Well, I will go back, and think nothing of the cuffing and scolding of the old cook, if I am to be Lord Mayor of London at last."

Dick went back, and was lucky enough to get into the house, and set about his work, before the old cook came downstairs.

*

We must now follow Miss Puss to the coast of Africa. The ship with the cat on board, was a long time at sea, and was at last driven by the winds onto a part of the coast of Barbary, where the only people were the Moors, unknown to the English. The people came in great numbers to see the sailors, because they were of different colour to themselves, and treated them civilly; and, when they became better acquainted, were very eager to buy the fine things that the ship was loaded with.

When the captain saw this, he sent patterns of the best things he had to the king of the country, who was so much pleased with them, that he sent for the captain to come to the palace. Here they were placed, as it is the custom of the country, on rich carpets flowered with gold and silver. The king and queen were seated at the upper end of the room, and a number of dishes were brought in for dinner. They had not sat long, when a vast number of rats and mice rushed in, and devoured all the meat in an instant. The captain wondered at this, and asked if these vermin were not unpleasant.

"Oh yes," said they, "very offensive, and the king would give half his treasure to be freed of them, for they not only destroy his dinner, as you see, but they assault him in his chamber, and even in bed, and so that he is obliged to be watched while he is sleeping, for fear of them."

The captain jumped for joy. He remembered poor Whittington and his cat, and told the king he had a creature on board the ship that would despatch all these vermin immediately. The king jumped so high at the joy which the news gave him, that his turban dropped off his head. "Bring this creature to me," he said. "Vermin are dreadful in a court, and if she will perform what you say, I will load your ship with gold and jewels in exchange for her."

The captain, who knew his business, took this opportunity to set forth the merits of Miss Puss. He told his majesty, "It is not very convenient to part with her, as, when she is gone, the rats and mice may destroy the goods in the ship, but to oblige your majesty, I will fetch her."

"Run, run!" said the queen, "I am impatient to see the dear creature."

Away went the captain to the ship, while another dinner was got ready. He put Puss under his arm, and arrived at the place just in time to see the table full of rats. When the cat saw them, she did not wait for bidding, but jumped out of the captain's arms, and in a few minutes laid almost all the rats and mice dead at her feet. The rest of them in their fright scampered away to their holes.

The king was quite charmed to get rid so easily of such plagues, and the queen desired that the creature who had done them so great a kindness might be brought to her, that she might look at her.

The captain called, "Pussy, pussy, pussy!", and she came to him. He then presented her to the queen, who started back, and was afraid to touch a creature who had made such a havoc among the rats and mice. However, when the captain stroked the cat and said, "Pussy, pussy," the queen also touched her and cried, "Putty, putty," for she had not learned English. He then put the cat down on the queen's lap, where she purred and played with her majesty's hand, and then purred herself to sleep.

The king, having seen the exploits of Mrs. Puss, and being informed that her kittens would stock the whole country, and keep it free from rats, bargained with the captain for the whole ship's cargo, and then gave him ten times as much for the cat as all the rest amounted to.

The captain then took leave of the royal party, and set sail with a fair wind for England, and after a happy voyage arrived safe in London.

One morning, early, Mr. Fitzwarren had just come to his counting-house and seated himself at the desk, to count over the cash, and settle the business for the day, when somebody came tap, tap, at the door. "Who's there?" said Mr. Fitzwarren.

"A friend," answered the other, "I come to bring you good news of your ship Unicorn."

The merchant, bustling up in such a hurry that he forgot his gout, opened the door, and who should he see waiting but the captain and factor, with a cabinet of jewels, and a bill of lading. When he looked at this the merchant lifted up his eyes and thanked Heaven for sending him such a prosperous voyage.

They then told the story of the cat, and showed the rich present that the king and queen had sent for her to poor Dick. As soon as the merchant heard this, he called out to his servants, "Go send him in, and tell him of his fame. Pray call him Mr. Whittington by name."

Mr. Fitzwarren now showed himself to be a good man, for when some of his servants said so great a treasure was too much for such a boy, he answered: "God forbid I should deprive him of the value of a single penny, it is his own, and he shall have it to a farthing."

He then sent for Dick, who at that time was scouring pots for the cook, and was quite dirty. He would have excused himself from coming into the counting-house, saying, "The room is swept, and my shoes are dirty and full of hob-nails," but the merchant ordered him to come in.

Mr. Fitzwarren ordered a chair to be set for him, and so he began to think they were making game of him. At the same time Dick said to them, "Do not play tricks with a poor simple boy, but let me go down again, if you please, to my work."

"Indeed, Mr. Whittington," said the merchant, "we are all quite in earnest with you, and I most heartily rejoice in the news that these gentlemen have brought you, for the captain has sold your cat to the King of Barbary, and brought you in return for her more riches than I possess in the whole world, and I wish you may long enjoy them!"

Mr. Fitzwarren then told the men to open the great treasure they had brought with them, and said, "Mr. Whittington has nothing to do but to put it in some place of safety."

Poor Dick hardly knew how to behave himself for joy. He begged his master to take what part of it he pleased, since he owed it all to his kindness.

"No, no," answered Mr. Fitzwarren, "this is all your own, and I have no doubt that you will use it well."

Dick next asked his mistress, and then Miss Alice, to accept a part of his good fortune, but they would not, and at the same time told him they felt great joy at his good success. But this poor fellow was too kind-hearted to keep it all to himself, so he made a present to the captain, the mate, and the rest of Mr. Fitzwarren's servants, and even to the ill-natured old cook.

After this Mr. Fitzwarren advised him to send for a proper tailor and get himself dressed like a gentleman, and told him he was welcome to live in his house till he could provide himself with a better.

When Whittington's face was washed, his hair curled, his hat cocked, and he was dressed in a nice suit of clothes he was as handsome and genteel as any young man who visited at Mr. Fitzwarren's. Miss Alice, who had once been so kind to him, and thought of him with pity, now looked upon him as fit to be her sweetheart, and the more so, no doubt, because Whittington was now always thinking what he could do to oblige her, and making her the prettiest presents that could be.

Mr. Fitzwarren soon saw their love for each other, and proposed to join them in marriage, and to this they both readily agreed. A day for the wedding was soon fixed, and they were attended to church by the Lord Mayor, the court of aldermen, the sheriffs, and a great number of the richest merchants in London, whom they afterwards treated with a very rich feast.

History tells us that Mr. Whittington and his lady lived in great splendour, and were very happy. They had several children. He was Sheriff of London, three times Lord Mayor, and received the honour of knighthood by Henry V.

He entertained this king and his queen at dinner after his conquest of France so grandly, that the king said, "Never had prince such a subject!"

When Sir Richard heard this, he said, "Never had subject such a prince."

The figure of Sir Richard Whittington with his cat in his arms, carved in stone, was to be seen till the year 1780 over the archway of the old prison of Newgate, which he built for criminals.

Why Does A Cat Sit On The Doorstep In The Sun?

This is a Romanian tale

This tale has been adapted from Rumanian Bird and Beast Stories translated by Moses Gaster. The book was published in 1915 by Sidgwick & Jackson, Ltd., London. The book features a variety of folk tales from Romania that centre around birds and beasts, including both domestic and wild animals. These stories often anthropomorphize animals, imbuing them with human-like qualities, emotions, and behaviours. The tales explore themes such as friendship, loyalty, cunning, and bravery, offering readers insight into Romanian folklore and cultural values.

When Noah had built the ark, he kept the door wide open for the animals to enter. After they had all gone in, his own family came, and last of all his wife.

Noah said to her "Come in."

She obstinately said "No."

Noah again said "Come in."

She again said "No."

Noah, getting angry, said "Oh, you devil, come in."

That was just what the devil was waiting for. He knew that Noah would not allow him to come in otherwise, and so he waited for an invitation, of which he promptly availed himself. Getting into the ark the devil changed himself into a mouse.

When the devil has nothing to do he weighs his tail. But here he found plenty to do, for, he thought, now is an opportunity of putting an end to the whole of God's creatures. So he started gnawing on one of the planks, trying to make a hole in it. When Noah surprised him at this devilish work he threw his fur glove at him. It turned into a cat, and, in the twinkling of an eye, the mouse was in the mouth of the cat.

But Noah could not allow the peace of the ark to be broken, the animals had to live in peace with one another. So he seized the cat, with the mouse in her mouth, and flung her out of the ark into the water.

The cat swam to the ark and, getting hold of the doorstep, climbed on to the sill and lay down there to bask in the sun.

There she remained until the water had subsided, and ever since then, the cat likes to lie on the doorstep of the house and bask in the sun.

The Cat, The Cock, And The Fox

This is a Russian tale

This tale has been adapted from Cossack Fairy Tales and Folk Tales by R. Nisbet Bain. The book was published in 1916 by George G. Harrap & Company, London. The Cossacks are a group of predominantly East Slavic-speaking people who historically inhabited the Pontic-Caspian steppe, known for their distinctive culture, traditions, and folklore. The book contains a selection of traditional tales and legends passed down orally among the Cossack communities. These stories offer insights into the worldview, values, and cultural practices of the Cossack people, reflecting their historical experiences, beliefs, and imagination.

There was once upon a time a cat and a cock, who agreed to live together, so they built a hut on an ash-heap, and the cock kept house while the cat went foraging for sausages.

One day the fox came running up, saying, "Open the door, little cock!"

"Pussy told me not to, little fox!" said the cock.

"Open the door, little cock!" repeated the fox.

"I tell you, pussy told me not to, little fox!"

At last, however, the cock grew tired of always saying "No!" so he opened the door, and in the fox rushed, seized him in her jaws, and ran off with him. Then the cock cried:

"Help! Pussy-pussy!

That foxy hussy

Has got me tight

With all her might.

Across her tail

My legs do trail

Along the bridge so stony!"

The cat heard it, gave chase to the fox, rescued the cock, brought him home, scolded him well, and said, "Now keep out of her jaws in the future, if you don't want to be killed altogether!"

Then the cat went out foraging for wheat, so that the cock might have something to eat. He had scarcely gone when the sly she-fox again came creeping up. "Dear little cock!" said she, "pray open the door!"

"No, little fox! Pussy said I wasn't to."

But the fox went on asking and asking till at last the cock let him in. Then the fox rushed at him, seized him by the neck, and ran off with him. Then the cock cried out:

"Help! Pussy-pussy!
That foxy hussy
Has got me tight
With all her might.
Across her tail
My legs do trail
Along the bridge so stony!"

The cat heard it, and again he ran after the fox and rescued the cock, and gave the fox a sound drubbing. Then he said to the cock, "Now, mind you never let her come in again, or she'll eat you."

But the next time the cat went out, the she-fox came again, and said, "Dear little cock, open the door!"

"No, little fox! Pussy said I wasn't to."

But the fox begged and begged so piteously that, at last, the cock was quite touched, and opened the door. Then the fox caught him by the throat again, and ran away with him, and the cock cried:

"Help! Pussy-pussy!
That foxy hussy
Has got me tight
With all her might.
Across her tail
My legs do trail
Along the bridge so stony!"

The cat heard it, and gave chase again. He ran and ran, but this time he couldn't catch the fox up, so he returned home and wept bitterly, because he was now all alone. At last, however, he dried his tears and got a little fiddle, a little fiddle-bow, and a big sack, and went to the fox's hole and began to play:

"Fiddle-de-dee!
The foxy so wee
Had daughters twice two,
And a little son too,
Called Phil.--Fiddle-dee!
Come, foxy, and see
My sweet minstrelsy!"

Then the fox's daughter said, "Mummy, I'll go out and see who it is that is playing so nicely!"

So out she skipped, but no sooner did pussy see her than he caught hold of her and popped her into his sack. Then he played again:

"Fiddle-de-dee!

The foxy so wee

Had daughters twice two,

And a little son too,

Called Phil.--Fiddle-dee!

Come, foxy, and see

My sweet minstrelsy!"

Then the second daughter skipped out, and pussy caught her by the forehead, and popped her into his sack, and went on playing and singing till he had got all four daughters into his sack, and the little son also.

Then the old fox was left all alone, and she waited and waited, but not one of them came back. At last she said to herself, "I'll go out and call them home, for the cock is roasting, and the milk pottage is simmering, and 'tis high time we had something to eat."

So out she popped, and the cat pounced upon her, and killed her too. Then he went and drank up all the soup, and gobbled up all the pottage, and then he saw the cock lying on a plate.

"Come, shake yourself, cock!" said puss.

So the cock shook himself, and got up, and the cat took the cock home, and the dead foxes too. And when they got home they skinned them to make nice beds to lie upon, and lived happily together in peace and plenty. And as they laughed over the joke as a good joke, we may laugh over it too!

Cat Tails – Feline Fairy Tales, Myths And Legends

A 'Rastle With A Wildcat

This is a New England tale

This tale has been adapted from The Enchanted Burro by Charles Fletcher Lummis. The book was published in 1912 by A. C. McClurg And Co., Chicago. Charles Fletcher Lummis (1859–1928) was an American journalist, author, ethnographer, archaeologist, and activist for Native American rights. He is notable for his contributions to preserving and promoting the cultural heritage of the American Southwest.

One of my very first experiences in the West was a midnight tussle with a fifty-four pound wildcat in a lonely cabin in the Greenhorn Mountains of Colorado. I shall never forget my horror at the sight of that huge puss on a beam over my head, for I had had a serious experience with the wildcat of the Northeast, and supposed that this fellow, who was twice as big, was likewise twice as much to be dreaded.

I did not know that the Rocky Mountain wildcat is not nearly so fierce, and that he never attacks man as does sometimes his cousin of the Maine and New Hampshire forests, and I had very slight hopes for the outcome of a struggle twice as severe as that which a furry freebooter in the Pemigewassett wilderness gave me a good many years ago. I need not have worried. The Colorado Cat was easy game, and when the last charge in my six-shooter had brought him to the floor, his life was soon ended.

That first encounter, in New Hampshire, was more than thirty years ago—years filled with roving adventure and many other things which are apt to crowd the past back into forgetfulness. But I remember it as though it had been yesterday. Small, white "exclamation-points" on my chest, with several other scars, occasionally call it to mind.

I had grown from a consumptive boy to a small but thoroughly athletic young man. Wrestling, boxing, canoeing, hunting and fishing had brought me into good condition, and every muscle was hard as wire. But for that fact, I should not be writing this, for the fight took my utmost ounce of strength. Had it come a year earlier, my grave would be in the wilderness today.

Of the yearly thousands who visit the great summer hotels of the White and Franconia Mountains, extremely few ever penetrate the Pemigewassett wilderness. The wild ranges wall its sides, and between them is a huge and virgin forest, full of game, dotted and seamed by lakes and brooks that swarm with trout. In this almost untrodden wild rises the east branch of the Pemigewassett, the beautiful little river which later becomes the Merrimac.

I was hunting and fishing that spring on the head waters of the east branch. My canoe swam a lovely but nameless lakelet, and my camp, roofed with birch-bark, was near the shore. There were three brooks running into the lake noisily, and at the south end the clear young river slipped silently out through the dark trees.

It was the last day of May, and still cold in that mountain bowl. I had a fat deer hung high beside my shelter; so there was meat for some time. In a little while the fishing would be very tame, for there the trout have not fully learned what a deceiver man is, and there is little sport in standing almost astride a rill, and with a five-foot willow pulling a dozen or twenty fish out of one pool. But now I knew the big fish were around, and I determined to spend the day with my rod.

By ten o'clock I was well over toward Mount Lafayette, on the largest of the brooks which came into my lake from the west; and, descending the steep banks to the bed of the stream, prepared to fish down toward camp.

The brook fell very rapidly here, in a series of short falls, at the bottom of each of which was a deep, lovely pool of water, so clear that it seemed only air with a light tinge of green. I could see pebbles ten feet below the surface, and the brown flashes of the sportive trout.

In five minutes I was landing my first fish, a game half-pounder, and others bit as fast as I could attend to them.

There was no need of covering much ground. I could have caught in fifty yards all I could eat in a week. But I kept moving homeward, taking only one or two of the largest fish from a pool and throwing back any accidental small ones.

In this way I had gone down, perhaps, half a mile, when I came to the largest pool I had found on that brook. Here it seemed likely that there might be some particularly large trout. In fact, the first one I struck seemed to be much larger than any on my string, but he snapped the hook and was gone with a splash.

I had drawn an extra hook from my box and was "ganging" it upon the line, when some impulse caused me to look up. As I did so, the tin box fell clattering upon the rocks and my rod at my feet.

The brook here had cut a narrow gorge through a ridge, and the pool at whose head I stood touched on each side the very foot of a rocky wall nearly forty feet high. I was standing on a ledge where the brook dropped, perhaps, ten feet into the pool, and the banks were not nearly so high there. Still, I presume the tops were fifteen feet above my head.

A giant pine had fallen across the gorge from bank to bank, making a knotty bridge, which was almost over me, but a little in front, and upon that great log was the Something which had brought my heart up into my mouth with such a bump.

On the dark side of the tree, behind the stump of a huge limb, flat and motionless as you could press your hand upon the table, lay almost the last thing in the world that I desired to see there—a wildcat.

Whether it was crouching there when I came, or, as is more likely, had crawled out from the bank to surprise me, I never knew, but there it was confronting me.

I could just see the fierce glints in its eyes, and when its gaze met mine, the tip of the ears, outlined on a patch of sky, seemed to flatten. My rifle was in camp, for it was too long a walk to bring it when I wished to fish. I had not even a revolver—nothing but a keen-edged, clip-point hunting-knife, which hung in its sheath on my left hip.

I hardly dared move, but that knife I must have. Slipping my right hand cautiously behind my back, I reached far around, till at last it touched the welcome hilt, and I began to slip the sheath slowly around my belt to the right side, where the knife could be drawn less ostentatiously.

All this time I had never taken my eyes from those of the unwelcome intruder, and I kept scowling at him with a savage expression which was meant to alarm him, but which sadly flattered my real feelings.

How long we stood eyeing each other thus, I do not know. It seemed an age and must have been several minutes. Neither of us moved. He lay crouched and menacing; I stood outwardly defiant, with my hand on that precious buckhorn handle. And then my wet feet, chilled with the icy water of the brook, betrayed me. I felt a sneeze working toward the surface.

Now, when I sneeze, it is no gentle tschoo, but half a dozen or more wild and uncontrollable explosions, which never fail to bring tears to my own eyes, if they are lucky enough not to scare some unsuspecting stranger.

I struggled to choke that sneeze, to hold it back, but I might as well have tried to hold the foaming brook.

Ker-cheooo! Ker-cheooo! Ker-cheooo-oo! With each eruption my head flew down and my body shook, and as I straightened up after the fifth burst, I saw, through the mist that filled my eyes, something dark descending upon me like a great, hazy bird.

I had not once changed my position since first seeing the wildcat. He was a trifle to my left, and my left foot and shoulder were pointed up-stream. Our lives hang on such trifles as that! Now, with the trained instinct of the boxer—who has first to learn to act without stopping to think how to act—I threw my left hand up and out! Half-way to arms-length it met that furry avalanche, and broke its force. The cat landed full against my side.

Its sharp hind claws sank into my thigh, and the sharper fore claws clutched me in the pectoral muscles in front and between the shoulder-blades behind. The pain was cruel, but I had no time even to cry out. At the instant I expected to feel those merciless jaws on my neck, and that would be the last.

The wildcat knows where the jugular vein is as well as the best surgeon of them all, and it is for that that he invariably jumps. Animals killed by these cruel ambuscaders are sometimes left whole and unmangled, save for that wicked little gap at the side of the throat.

But my boxing lessons had saved me. As my left hand went out in that "straight counter," it struck full in the throat of the cat, and with the swift inspiration of desperate men, I clutched the folds of fur there with all my might.

The cat strained hard to pull-in to me—and that was a cruel leverage it had in my own flesh. But my arm, never a weak one, was doubly strong now; and, though I could not force him from his hold, I kept his head well away from mine, which I "ducked" to increase the still unsatisfactory distance.

Then, drawing the keen six-inch blade, I drove it against his side. His left side was, of course, the one exposed to me, but we were so "mixed up" that I could take no accurate aim at his heart, and just thrust blindly and madly at that stretch of mottled fur.

Nothing will ever dim my recollection of that desperate struggle, and yet I seemed in a sort of trance. You have had nightmares, wherein some savage beast pursued you, and you slammed vain doors on him which he brushed open, and fired ineffective rifles at him whose diminished pop did not affect him in the least; and, do what you would, nothing availed against that implacable danger. So it was with me. I seemed under a spell.

Those awful claws were tearing me everywhere; that fatal head was struggling to break down my tiring arm, and the desperate thrusts of the knife with all the force of my right arm seemed not even to penetrate the tough hide. They went deep enough, as I found later, but at the moment I was sure they hardly scratched him.

Since that day I have been through a great many of the things of whose suspense we say, "They seemed eternities," but never one, I think, that seemed so endless as that. And yet it could hardly have lasted a minute. I was growing very weak. Blood was running down in my boots, and my weary left arm was no longer rigid. My right was no longer fully under control, and once, when the knife glanced a rib, it nearly flew from my hand.

Once, too, I struck high, and the cat caught my right wrist between his savage teeth and tore out a piece. Was he invulnerable? I began actually to believe so—to fancy that, after all, it must be a hideous dream.

You may imagine from that into what a state my mind had come. But still I plied the knife, and still with cramped and trembling arm held off the creature's jaws.

And then, on a sudden, a great wave of joy swept over me, and I yelled madly. The curving claws, set deep in my back and breast, relaxed. It was only the least bit in the world, but I could feel the exquisite pain of that slight withdrawal, and in another instant they came out altogether, and my foe fell limp upon the rocks beside me, where he never moved again.

I looked at him once; my eyes grew dim, and I fell across him.

When I recovered consciousness, we were lying in a heap, wet with our common blood. I crawled a couple of feet to the brook, and the icy water revived me, so that I could rise and limp about the field of our strange battle.

The cat was a mass of wounds, and as I counted the eleven fatal thrusts, I marvelled at his vitality and pluck—and very heartily respected them, too. Any one of ten of them would have finally killed him, but he had kept his hold to the very last, which had sunk deep into his heart.

And such a small beast to attack the lord of creation! I do not think he weighed over thirty pounds, but what a model of compact strength and agility! His skin was so slashed as to be absolutely unsavable, but I kept his scalp a long time, till the moths destroyed it.

As for myself, I was in little more attractive shape than he. Of my stout duck coat and trousers only the right half remained. My duck vest and heavy flannel shirt boasted little but a few shreds two-thirds of the way around my body. I was half-naked, and my breast, back, left side and left thigh were laced with deep, bleeding gashes.

There is only one thing about that day which I do not remember, and that is, how I got back that ten miles to camp. But somehow I got there, for when I awoke next morning, very weak and stiff—for of all wounds I know of none so painful as those inflicted by a cat—I was under my roof of birch bark, and a spotted scalp lay on the sand beside me.

Cat Tails – Feline Fairy Tales, Myths And Legends

Bobcat And Birch Tree

This is a Blackfoot tale

This tale has been adapted from Blackfeet Indian Stories by George Bird Grinnell, published by Charles Scribner's Sons, London & New York in 1913. George Bird Grinnell (1849–1938) was a prominent American anthropologist, historian, naturalist, and writer, best known for his work with First Nations tribes and his advocacy for conservation.

Once Old Man was travelling over the prairie, when he saw far off a fire burning, and as he drew near it he saw many prairie-dogs sitting in a circle around the fire. There were so many of them that there was no place for anyone to sit down. Old Man stood there behind the circle, and presently he began to cry, and then he said to the prairie-dogs, "Let me, too, sit by that fire."

The prairie-dogs said, "All right, Old Man, don't cry. Come and sit by the fire." They moved aside so as to make a place for him, and Old Man sat down and looked on at what they were doing.

He saw that they were playing a game, and this was the way they did it: they put one prairie-dog in the fire and covered him up with hot ashes, and then, after he had been there a little while, he would say, "Tsk! Tsk!" And then they pushed the ashes off him and pulled him out.

Old Man said, "Little brothers, teach me how to do that."

The prairie-dogs told him what to do, and put him in the fire and covered him up with the ashes, and after a little time he said, "Tsk! Tsk!" like a prairie-dog, and they pulled him out again. Then he did it to the prairie-dogs.

At first he put them in one at a time, but there were many of them, and soon he got tired and said, "I will put you all in at once."

They said, "Very well, Old Man," and all got in the ashes, but just as Old Man was about to cover them up one of them, a female, said, "Do not cover me up, for I fear the heat will hurt me."

Old Man said, "Very well. If you do not wish to be covered up, you may sit over by the fire and watch the rest." Then he covered over all the others.

At length the prairie-dogs said, "Tsk! Tsk!" but Old Man did not sweep off the ashes and pull them out of the fire. He let them stay there and die. The she one that was looking on ran to a hole, and as she went down in it, said, "Tsk!, Tsk!". Old Man chased her, but he got to the hole too late to catch her.

"Oh, well, you can go," he said, "there will be more prairie-dogs by and by."

When the prairie-dogs were roasted, Old Man cut some red willow twigs to place them on, and then sat down and began to eat. He ate until he was full, and then felt sleepy. He said to his nose, "I am going to sleep now, so; watch out, and in case any bad thing comes about, wake me up." Then Old Man slept.

Pretty soon his nose snored, and Old Man woke up and said, "What is it?"

The nose said, "A raven is flying by, over there."

Old Man said, "That is nothing," and went to sleep again.

Soon his nose snored again, and Old Man said, "What is it now?"

The nose said, "There is a coyote over there, coming this way."

Old Man said, "A coyote is nothing," and again went to sleep.

Presently his nose snored again, but Old Man did not wake up. Again it snored, and called out, "Wake up, a bobcat is coming." Old Man paid no attention; he slept on.

The bobcat crept up to the fire and ate all the roasted prairie-dogs, and then went off and lay down on a flat rock and went to sleep. All this time the nose kept trying to awaken Old Man, and at last he awoke, and the nose said, "A bobcat is over there on that flat rock. He has eaten all your food."

Then Old Man was so angry that he called out loud.

The tracks of the bobcat were all greasy from the food it had been eating, and Old Man followed these tracks. He went softly over to where the bobcat was sleeping, and seized it before it could wake up to bite or scratch him. The bobcat cried out, "Wait, let me speak a word or two," but Old Man would not listen.

"I will teach you to steal my food," he said. He pulled off the lynx's tail, pounded his head against the rock so as to make his face flat, pulled him out long so as to make him small-bellied, and then threw him into the brush. As he went sneaking away, Old Man said, "There, that is the way you bobcats shall always be." It is for this reason that the lynxes today look like that.

Old Man went to the fire, and looked at the red willow sticks where the roasted prairie-dogs had been, and when he saw them, and thought how his food was all gone, it made him angry at his nose. He said, "You fool, why did you not wake me?"

He took the willow sticks and thrust them in the coals, and when they had caught fire he burnt his nose. This hurt, and he ran up on a hill and held his nose to the wind, and called to the wind to blow hard and cool him. A hard wind came, so hard that it blew him off the hill and away down to Birch Creek. As he was flying along he caught at the weeds and brush to stop himself, but nothing was strong enough to hold him. At last he grasped a birch tree. He held fast, and it did not give way. Although the wind whipped him about, this way and that, and tumbled him up and down, the tree held him. He kept calling to the wind to blow more softly, and at last it listened to him and went down.

Then he said, "This is a beautiful tree. It has saved me from being blown away and knocked all to pieces. I will make it pretty, and it shall always be like that."

So he gashed the bark across with his stone knife, as you see the marks today.

Cat And Dog

This is a Russian tale

This tale has been adapted from Louise Seymour Houghton's book, The Russian Grandmother's Wonder Tale, published by Charles Scribner's Sons, London & New York in 1906. Louise Seymour Houghton was an American author, editor, and philanthropist, notable for her work in social reform and her contributions to literature and history. Born on May 4, 1838, in New York City, she was the daughter of Thomas Worcester and Caroline (Child) Houghton.

A little boy was playing in the court with the moujik's dog that helped to guard the sheep. It was a clear, cold day, but the little boy was not cold, for he had on his warm quilted kaftan, his cap, which he called his chapka, on his head, and on his feet were sandals made of the tough bark of the linden-tree. He was not going to risk frozen toes another time!

The sheep-dog was old and rather cross, but he was always kind to the little boy. But when the house-cat followed the cow-herd woman out of the house, where she had gone to carry some milk, the dog bristled up and growled. The cat spat at him, and this was too much. He sprang at her, but kitty was too quick for him. She flew across the court and scrambled nimbly up to the shed roof by one of the supporting poles. The dog was too old and heavy to follow her, and he sat on his haunches in the court below, bristling and snarling, the cat spitting back at him and evidently enjoying the fun. The cow-herd woman and a moujik who was at work in the court were laughing heartily, and the little boy's brother, who was cutting wood in the shed, came out to see what it was all about. The little boy was highly excited, and he ran to call his grandmother to come and see.

But by the time the grandmother had risen slowly from her chair, for her rheumatism was bad that day, and had gone to the door, leaning on her stick, the fun was all over. The cat had gone around to another side of the shed, and lay basking in the sun, out of the dog's sight, while the moujik, the cow-herd woman, and the little boy's brother had gone back to their work. Only the dog remained, looking up at the deserted roof and growling at nothing.

The little boy went with his grandmother into the house. "Grandmamma," he asked, "why does the dog always quarrel with the cat?"

"My great-grandmother told me why," replied the grandmother. "I will tell you that story now, if you like."

"Oh, do, do!" cried the little boy.

"It is the story," said the grandmother, "of why the dog cannot endure the cat, nor the cat the mouse"

"In olden times, as my great-grandmother told me, dogs enjoyed great freedom, and among other privileges they had a right to all the meat that fell from the table. To guard this right for all time they drew up a manifesto, and copied it upon parchment. In this manifesto this right was expressly made known. For a long time the King of the Dogs had charge of this document, but finally he confided it to the care of his private secretary, the Tomcat. And the Tomcat carried the proclamation up into the garret and hid it behind a beam where no one could possibly find it.

"Now it happened that behind the beam dwelt a young Mouse, and on one of his walks he stumbled upon the roll. He tried to drag it from its hiding-place, but the stiff parchment stuck fast, and he could not pull it out. But it was quite within reach of his little teeth, and the Mouse was highly delighted with his lucky find, for now he had something to nibble upon. Day by day he paid a visit to the parchment and whetted his teeth upon it.

"Now it presently happened that one day a Dog picked up a piece of meat and was caught and his paw well rubbed with hot ashes. Weeping, he appeared before the King and told him the whole story.

"Then the King immediately summoned his private secretary, the Tomcat, and commanded him to show the proclamation. The Tomcat hastened to bring the parchment without delay, but, to his misfortune, what did he find? Only a few fragments!

"It was at once clear to him that this was the deed of some little Mouse. He told the story to all the other cats, who, to express their grief and sorrow, began to mew most piteously. When they had sufficiently expressed their feelings they declared war against all mice.

"After this the Tomcat made his report to the King of the Dogs, and the King immediately summoned the Dog-zemstvo. The dogs came together from all parts - sheep-dogs, wolf-dogs, boar-hounds, house-dogs, and to them all the King gave command that from thenceforth and forever they should treat the cat as the common enemy. Thus all cats would be made to rue that Tomcat's carelessness.

"And that is the end of the story."

"Now I understand all about it," said the little boy.

Cat Tails – Feline Fairy Tales, Myths And Legends

Cat And Mouse In Partnership

This is a German tale

This tale has been adapted from Jacob and Wilhelm Grimm's book, Grimms' Fairy Tales, published in Berlin in 1812 by Realschulbuchhandlung,.

A certain cat had made the acquaintance of a mouse, and had said so much to her about the great love and friendship she felt for her, that at length the mouse agreed that they should live and keep house together.

"But we must make a provision for winter, or else we shall suffer from hunger," said the cat, "and you, little mouse, cannot venture everywhere, or you will be caught in a trap someday."

The good advice was followed, and a pot of fat was bought, but they did not know where to put it. At length, after much consideration, the cat said, "I know no place where it will be better stored up than in the church, for no one dares take anything away from there. We will set it beneath the altar, and not touch it until we are really in need of it."

So the pot was placed in safety, but it was not long before the cat had a great yearning for it, and said to the mouse, "I want to tell you something, little mouse; my cousin has brought a little son into the world, and has asked me to be godmother. He is white with brown spots, and I am to hold him over the font at the christening. Let me go out today, and you look after the house by yourself."

"Yes, yes,' answered the mouse, 'by all means go, and if you get anything very good to eat, think of me. I should like a drop of sweet red christening wine myself."

All this, however, was untrue. The cat had no cousin, and had not been asked to be godmother. She went straight to the church, stole to the pot of fat, began to lick at it, and licked the top of the fat right off. Then she took a walk upon the roofs of the town, looked out for opportunities, and then stretched herself in the sun, and licked her lips whenever she thought of the pot of fat, and not until it was evening did she return home.

"Well, here you are again," said the mouse, "no doubt you have had a merry day."

"All went off well," answered the cat.

"What name did they give the child?"

"Top off!" said the cat quite coolly.

"Top off!" cried the mouse, "that is a very odd and uncommon name, is it a usual one in your family?"

"What does that matter," said the cat. "It is no worse than Crumb-stealer, as your godchildren are called."

Before long the cat was seized by another fit of yearning. She said to the mouse, "You must do me a favour, and once more manage the house for a day alone. I am again asked to be godmother, and, as the child has a white ring round its neck, I cannot refuse."

The good mouse consented, but the cat crept behind the town walls to the church, and devoured half the pot of fat. "Nothing ever seems so good as what one keeps to oneself," said she, and was quite satisfied with her day's work.

When she went home the mouse inquired, "And what was the child christened?"

"Half-done," answered the cat.

"Half-done! What are you saying? I never heard the name in my life, I'll wager anything it is not in the calendar!"

The cat's mouth soon began to water for some more licking. "All good things go in threes," said she, "' am asked to stand godmother again. The child is quite black, only it has white paws, but with that exception, it has not a single white hair on its whole body. This only happens once every few years, you will let me go, won't you?"

"Top-off! Half-done!" answered the mouse, "they are such odd names, they make me very thoughtful."

"You sit at home," said the cat, "in your dark-grey fur coat and long tail, and are filled with fancies, that's because you do not go out in the daytime."

During the cat's absence the mouse cleaned the house, and put it in order, but the greedy cat entirely emptied the pot of fat. "When everything is eaten up one has some peace," said she to herself, and well filled and fat she did not return home till night.

The mouse at once asked what name had been given to the third child. "It will not please you more than the others," said the cat. "He is called All-gone."

"All-gone," cried the mouse "that is the most suspicious name of all! I have never seen it in print. All-gone - what can that mean?" and she shook her head, curled herself up, and lay down to sleep.

From this time forth no one invited the cat to be godmother, but when the winter had come and there was no longer anything to be found outside, the mouse thought of their provision, and said, "Come, cat, we will go to our pot of fat which we have stored up for ourselves, and we shall enjoy that."

"Yes," answered the cat, "you will enjoy it as much as you would enjoy sticking that dainty tongue of yours out of the window."

They set out on their way, but when they arrived, the pot of fat certainly was still in its place, but it was empty. "Alas!" said the mouse. "Now I see what has happened, now it comes to light! You are a true friend! You have devoured all when you were standing godmother. First top off, then half-done, then…"

"Will you hold your tongue," cried the cat, "one word more, and I will eat you too."

"All-gone" was already on the poor mouse's lips, and scarcely had she spoken it before the cat sprang on her, seized her, and swallowed her down. Truely, that is the way of the world.

Cat-Skin

This is a German tale

This tale has been adapted from Jacob and Wilhelm Grimm's book, Grimms' Fairy Tales, published in Berlin in 1812, by Realschulbuchhandlung. Although there are some clear parallels with the Cinderella stories, the outcome is a little different…

There was once a king, whose queen had hair of the purest gold, and was so beautiful that her match was not to be met with on the whole face of the earth. But this beautiful queen fell ill, and when she felt that her end drew near she called the king to her and said, "Promise me that you will never marry again, unless you meet with a wife who is as beautiful as I am, and who has golden hair like mine."

Then when the king in his grief promised all she asked, she shut her eyes and died. But the king was not to be comforted, and for a long time never thought of taking another wife. At last, however, his wise men said, "this will not do. The king must marry again, that we may have a queen."

So messengers were sent far and wide, to seek for a bride as beautiful as the late queen. But there was no princess in the world so beautiful, and if there had been, still there was not one to be found who had golden hair. So the messengers came home, and had had all their trouble for nothing.

Now the king had a daughter, who was just as beautiful as her mother, and had the same golden hair. And when she was grown up, the king looked at her and saw that she was just like this late queen. Then he said to his courtiers, "May I not marry my daughter? She is the very image of my dead wife. Unless I have her, I shall not find any bride upon the whole earth, and you say there must be a queen."

When the courtiers heard this they were shocked, and said, "Heaven forbid that a father should marry his daughter! Out of so great a sin no good can come."

And his daughter was also shocked, but hoped the king would soon give up such thoughts, so she said to him, "Before I marry anyone I must have three dresses. One must be of gold, like the sun. Another must be of shining silver, like the moon, and a third must be as dazzling as the stars. Besides this, I want a mantle of a thousand different kinds of fur put together, to which every beast in the kingdom must give a part of his skin." And so she thought he would think of the matter no more.

But the king made the most skilful workmen in his kingdom weave the three dresses, one golden, like the sun, another silvery, like the moon, and a third sparkling, like the stars.

His hunters were told to hunt out all the beasts in his kingdom, and to take the finest fur out of their skins, and so a mantle of a thousand furs was made.

When all were ready, the king sent them to her, but she got up in the night when all were asleep, and took three of her trinkets, a golden ring, a golden necklace, and a golden brooch, and packed the three dresses, one of the sun, one of the moon, and one of the stars, up in a nutshell, and wrapped herself up in the mantle made of all sorts of fur, and smeared her face and hands with soot. Then she threw herself upon Heaven for help in her need, and went away, and journeyed on the whole night, till at last she down in the hollow of a tree and soon fell asleep: and there she slept on till it was midday.

Now as the king to whom the wood belonged was hunting in it, his dogs came to the tree, and began to snuff about, and run round and round, and bark. "Look sharp!" said the king to the huntsmen, "and see what sort of game lies there."

And the huntsmen went up to the tree, and when they came back again said, "In the hollow tree there lies a most wonderful beast, such as we never saw before. Its skin seems to be of a thousand kinds of fur, but there it lies fast asleep."

"See," said the king, "if you can catch it alive, and we will take it with us."

So the huntsmen took it up, and the maiden awoke and was greatly frightened, and said, "I am a poor child that has neither father nor mother left. Have pity on me and take me with you."

Then they said, "Yes, Miss Cat-skin, you will do for the kitchen. You can sweep up the ashes, and do things of that sort."

So they put her into the coach, and took her home to the king's palace. Then they showed her a little corner under the staircase, where no light of day ever peeped in, and said, "Cat-skin, you may lie and sleep there." And she was sent into the kitchen, and made to fetch wood and water, to blow the fire, pluck the poultry, pick the herbs, sift the ashes, and do all the dirty work.

Thus Cat-skin lived for a long time very sorrowfully. "Ah, pretty princess!" she thought, 'What will now become of you?"

But it happened one day that a feast was to be held in the king's castle, so she said to the cook, "May I go up a little while and see what is going on? I will take care and stand behind the door."

And the cook said, "Yes, you may go, but be back again in half an hour's time, to rake out the ashes."

Then she took her little lamp, and went into her cabin, and took off the fur skin, and washed the soot from off her face and hands, so that her beauty shone forth like the sun from behind the clouds. She next opened her nutshell, and brought out of it the dress that shone like the sun, and so went to the feast. Everyone made way for her, for nobody knew her, and they thought she could be no less than a king's daughter. But the king came up to her, and held out his hand and danced with her, and he thought in his heart, "I never saw any one half so beautiful."

When the dance was at an end she curtsied, and when the king looked round for her, she was gone, no one knew where. The guards that stood at the castle gate were called in: but they had seen no one. The truth was, that she had run into her little cabin, pulled off her dress, blackened her face and hands, put on the fur-skin cloak, and was Cat-skin again. When she went into the kitchen to her work, and began to rake the ashes, the cook said, "Let that alone till the morning, and heat the king's soup. I should like to run up now and give a peep, but take care you don't let a hair fall into the soup, or you will run a chance of never eating again."

As soon as the cook went away, Cat-skin heated the king's soup, and toasted a slice of bread first, as nicely as ever she could, and when it was ready, she went and looked in the cabin for her little golden ring, and put it into the dish in which the soup was. When the dance was over, the king ordered his soup to be brought in, and it pleased him so well, that he thought he had never tasted any so good before. At the bottom he saw a gold ring lying, and as he could not make out how it had got there, he ordered the cook to be sent for.

The cook was frightened when he heard the order, and said to Cat-skin, "You must have let a hair fall into the soup. If it be so, you will have a good beating."

Then he went before the king, and he asked him who had cooked the soup. "I did," answered the cook.

But the king said, "That is not true. It was better done than you could do it."

Then the cook answered, "To tell the truth I did not cook it, but Cat-skin did."

"Then let Cat-skin come up," said the king, and when she came he said to her, "Who are you?"

"I am a poor child," she said, "that has lost both father and mother."

"How have you come to be my palace?' the king asked.

"I am good for nothing," said she, "but to be scullion-girl, and to have boots and shoes thrown at my head."

"But how did you get the ring that was in the soup?" asked the king.

Then she would not admit that she knew anything about the ring, and so the king sent her away again about her business.

After a time there was another feast, and Cat-skin asked the cook to let her go up and see it as before. "Yes," said he, "but come again in half an hour, and cook the king the soup that he likes so much."

Then she ran to her little cabin, washed herself quickly, and took her dress out which was silvery as the moon, and put it on, and when she went in, looking like a king's daughter, the king went up to her, and rejoiced at seeing her again, and when the dance began he danced with her.

After the dance was at an end she managed to slip out, so slyly that the king did not see where she was gone, but she sprang into her little cabin, and made herself into Cat-skin again, and went into the kitchen to cook the soup. Whilst the cook was above stairs, she got the golden necklace and dropped it into the soup, then it was brought to the king, who ate it, and it pleased him as well as before, so he sent for the cook, who was again forced to tell him that Cat-skin had cooked it. Cat-skin was brought again before the king, but she still told him that she was only fit to have boots and shoes thrown at her head.

But when the king had ordered a feast to be got ready for the third time, it happened just the same as before. "You must be a witch, Cat-skin," said the cook, "for you always put something into your soup, so that it pleases the king better than mine."

However, he let her go up as before. Then she put on her dress which sparkled like the stars, and went into the ball-room, and the king danced with her again, and thought she had never looked so beautiful as she did then. So whilst he was dancing with her, he put a gold ring on her finger without her seeing it, and ordered that the dance should be kept up a long time. When it was at an end, he would have held her fast by the hand, but she slipped away, and sprang so quickly through the crowd that he lost sight of her, and she ran as fast as she could into her little cabin under the stairs. But this time she kept away too long, and stayed beyond the half-hour, so she had no time to take off her fine dress, and simply threw her fur mantle over it, and in her haste did not blacken herself all over with soot, but left one of her fingers white.

Then she ran into the kitchen, and cooked the king's soup, and as soon as the cook was gone, she put the golden brooch into the dish. When the king got to the bottom, he ordered Cat-skin to be called once more, and soon saw the white finger, and the ring that he had put on it whilst they were dancing, so he seized her hand, and kept fast hold of it, and when she wanted to loose herself and spring away, the fur cloak fell off a little on one side, and the starry dress sparkled underneath it.

Then he got hold of the fur and tore it off, and her golden hair and beautiful form were seen, and she could no longer hide herself. She washed the soot and ashes from her face, and showed herself to be the most beautiful princess upon the face of the earth. But the king said, "You are my beloved bride, and we will never more be parted from each other." And the wedding feast was held, and a merry day it was, as ever was heard of or seen in that country, or indeed in any other.

The Old Woman's Cat

This is a tale from India

This tale has been adapted from Kate Douglas Wiggin's and Nora Archibald Smith's book, The Talking Beasts, published by Houghton Mifflin Company, New York & Boston in 1911. "The Talking Beasts" remains a valuable collection of fables that continues to educate and entertain, reflecting her commitment to literature and moral education.

Once upon a time, there was an old woman living in extreme frailty. She had a tiny, dark cottage and a cat as her companion. This cat had never seen a loaf of bread nor heard of meat. It was content just to smell the scent of a mouse or see its footprints on a board. On the rare occasion it caught a mouse, it would survive on that meal for a week.

Because the old woman's home was a place of perpetual scarcity for the cat, it was always miserable and thin, looking more like a shadow than a real creature. One day, with great difficulty due to its weakness, it climbed to the roof and saw a neighboring cat strutting proudly along the wall of a nearby house. This cat moved slowly because of its excessive fatness.

The old woman's cat, astonished, called out, "You, who live so comfortably, where do you come from? You look like you feast in the banquet hall of a king. How did you become so sleek and strong?"

The neighboring cat replied, "I eat the crumbs from the Sultan's tray. Every morning, I go to the king's court, and when the feast is spread, I boldly snatch morsels of fat meat and fine bread. This keeps me happy and satisfied until the next day."

The old woman's cat asked, "What is fat meat like? And what does fine bread taste like? I have only ever had the old woman's broths and the occasional mouse."

The neighboring cat laughed and said, "No wonder you look like a spider! If you saw the Sultan's court and smelled those delicious dishes, you would transform."

The old woman's cat pleaded, "Brother, as a neighbour and kin, take me with you next time. Maybe, with your help, I can find some food."

The neighbouring cat, moved by the old woman's cat's plight, agreed not to go to the feast without him. Excited, the old woman's cat told his mistress the plan. She advised, "Dear companion, don't be misled by worldly desires. Don't leave your humble home, for greed leads to the grave."

But the cat, longing for the Sultan's delicacies, ignored her advice. The next day, with wobbly steps, it followed the neighbouring cat to the court. Unfortunately, ill-fortune awaited. The previous day, the cats had caused such a ruckus at the table that the Sultan ordered archers to stand guard. Any cat that dared approach would be shot.

Unaware of this, the old woman's cat eagerly approached the feast. Before it could take more than a few bites, a heart-piercing arrow struck it down.

And so, dear friend, remember: the sweetness of honey isn't worth the pain of a sting. It's better to be content with simpler pleasures.

Cat Tails – Feline Fairy Tales, Myths And Legends

About The Editor

Born in 1962 into a household that lived and breathed sports, the editor's dad was a seasoned senior amateur and lower league professional footballer. Not just that, he managed his own businesses in cahoots with Clive's mum, who was no slouch either – she was a skilled and award-winning dancer.

After snagging a degree in History from Leeds University, our storyteller took a rather serendipitous stroll into the burgeoning world of information technology in the late '80s. Like father, like son, they say. Alongside a flourishing tech career, Clive dabbled in various writing and acting pursuits, from freelancing as a journalist and book reviewer (with a coveted by-line in The Sunday People) to gracing stages in village halls and even professional theatres all across the south of the UK for a good decade.

In a nod to the family's sporting legacy, Clive - long after hanging up his own boots - delved into the world of live TV broadcasts. Armed with a wealth of rugby knowledge, he became one of the go-to 'statos' for the BBC, ITV, TVNZ, and EuroSport, covering everything from Heineken Cups to Six Nations, World Sevens, and World Cups in the late '90s.

For a deeper dive into this fascinating journey, head over to clivegilson.com, where there's a whole trove of tales waiting to be uncovered!

Cat Tails – Feline Fairy Tales, Myths And Legends

ORIGINAL FICTION BY CLIVE GILSON

- *Songs of Bliss*
- *Out of the Walled Garden*
- *The Mechanic's Curse*
- *The Insomniac Booth*
- *A Solitude of Stars*

AS EDITOR – *FIRESIDE TALES*

- **Wales** - *Tales From the Land of Dragons*
- **Scotland** - *Tales From the Land of The Brave*
- **Ireland** - *Tales From the Land of Saints And Scholars*
- **England** - *Tales From the Land of Hope And Glory*
- **France** - *Tales from Gallia*
- **Germany** - *Tales from Germania*
- **Scandinavia** - *Tales From Lands of Snow and Ice*
- **Scandinavia** - *Tales From the Viking Isles*
- **Finland** - *Tales From the Forest Lands*
- **Scandinavia** - *Tales From the Old Norse*
- **Spain & Portugal** - *Tales From the Land of Rabbits*
- **Italy** - *Tales Told by Bulls and Wolves*
- **Greece** - *Tales of Fire and Bronze*
- **The Balkans** - *Tales From the Samodivi*
- **Romania** - *Tales From the Land of the Strigoi*
- **Hungary** - *Tales Told by the Wind Mother*
- **First Nations** - *Okaraxta - Tales from The Great Plains*
- **First Nations** - *Tibik-Kìzis – Tales from The Great Lakes & Canada*
- **First Nations** - *Jóhonaa'éí –Tales from America's Southwest*
- **First Nations** - *Qugaaĝix̂ - Tales from Alaska & The Arctic*
- **First Nations** - *Karahkwa - Tales from America's Eastern States*